UNDERSTANDING RELIGIOUS VIOLENCE

I've given you all the little, that I've to give,
You've given me all, that for me is all there is;
So now I just give back what you have given –
If there is anything to give in this.

– Leonard Wolf, *Village in the Jungle*

Understanding Religious Violence

Thinking Outside the Box on Terrorism

J.P. LARSSON

ASHGATE

Published by
Ashgate Publishing Limited
Gower House
Croft Road
Aldershot
Hants GU11 3HR
England

Ashgate Publishing Company
Suite 420
101 Cherry Street
Burlington, VT 05401-4405
USA

Ashgate website: http://www.ashgate.com

British Library Cataloguing in Publication Data
Larsson, J. P.
Understanding religious violence : thinking outside the box on terrorism
1. Violence - Religious aspects 2. Terrorism - Religious aspects 3. War - Religious aspects
I. Title
291.5'697

Library of Congress Cataloging-in-Publication Data
Larsson, J. P., 1977-
Understanding religious violence : thinking outside the box on terrorism / J.P. Larsson.
p. cm.
Includes bibliographical references and index.
ISBN 0-7546-3908-8
1. Violence--Religious aspects. I. Title.

BL65.V55L37 2004
201'.7273--dc22 2003054486

ISBN 0 7546 3908 8

Printed and bound in Great Britain by MPG Books Ltd, Bodmin, Cornwall

Contents

Preface

In the Roman era, his temple was closed during peace and open in times of war. Today, when the doors of the Temple of Janus seem permanently wedged open, it is easy to become despairing of the present and disillusioned about the future. On an almost daily basis, the mass media are inundated with accounts of violence, terrorism, armed conflict and war. In most of these, religion seems to be a prevailing factor. The main reason for the amount and intensity of religious violence on the international arena is arguably because it is not properly understood, and is thus perpetuated. By taking my cue from British strategist Basil Henry Liddell-Hart, therefore, I argue in this book that in order to achieve peace it is necessary to understand war. By making this my explicit starting-point, I do not agree with such scholars who insist that when it comes to trying to understand war, only a fool – or worse – thinks he can find the truth.

It does not take an in-depth study to see that the contemporary world is plagued by violence, terrorism and armed conflict. More often than not, and for a variety of motives, religion is implicated in violent events, ranging from terrorism to territorial disputes. In order to make the world a less violent place, however, an in-depth analysis *is* necessary for dispelling the misperceptions underlying much of the religious violence of the world. This is not to say that all violence or terrorism has religious elements, or that religion should be removed from international politics (in fact, I refute both positions). Today, most attempts at explaining and describing the world suffer from one major defect, namely the lack of genuine understanding of the relationship between religion and violence. Therefore, this is a book about religious armed conflict.

It is the ultimate aim of this study to investigate the ontological roots of this defect, and to offer a useful framework for conflict transformation. This is done by progressively moving from the conventional view of religion and armed conflict (explanation) to a sound basis for understanding the logic and rationality of such conflict. It thus aims to show that not only is global religious violence a deeply rational and logical phenomenon, but also one which has previously not been thoroughly (or satisfactorily) investigated. A journey is therefore undertaken from explanation to understanding.

This journey would not have been possible without the research of other scholars of religious violence around the world. In particular I am grateful for the pioneering research and insights of Mark Juergensmeyer in the comparative study of religious violence in an era of globalisation. I am also grateful for his earlier work on Gandhian conflict resolution which I have utilized in my thinking about alternatives to religious violence. Too many scholars have influenced my own thinking to be individually acknowledged here, but I hope I have clearly attributed wherever and whenever I am in their debt, as this work uses such existing research that I hope will illuminate the logic of religious violence, relate it to contemporary thinking in the social sciences, and help to alleviate the causes of religious violence wherever it occurs.

With a bit of ingenuity, inventive thinking and certainly patience, I believe that we can overcome the forces of terrorism and religious violence that today plague the world. Any conflict can be overcome, no matter how intractable and inevitable it at first seems. It may involve making concessions we thought we were not willing to make, or it may merely involve altering our own perceptions through deeper knowledge. At times, what we thought we knew as fact may not be so, and new research and thinking may completely alter the face of the world. For example, rather than a 'roadmap to peace', which seems to imply that peace is a static 'goal' that can be reached rather than a continuous *relationship* or state of being, an alternative angle – like Ernest Martin's research into the site of the temples at Jerusalem – may be more beneficial, in line with the quest for understanding I advocate in this book.

Definitions, confessions and apologies

This book started its life as a PhD thesis, and in their present form, many of the arguments have thus been somewhat simplified from their original rigour. The same is true of the elaborate citations and research, much of which has been docked or severely modified. The research deals with several concepts and phenomena that are either not in popular usage or applied in a somewhat specific manner throughout this book. The reader's tacit understanding of various concepts (such as 'religion') will be sufficient at the outset, and I will highlight particular usage along the way.

In line with the welcomed recent trend by some scholars to identify their personal position, it should be made clear that the roots of this book stem primarily from the Western philosophical tradition. It is the work of a 'reformed political scientist' and an atheistic pacifist. As such, this book cannot be seen as condoning violence in any way, or endorsing any particular religious tradition. However, being a 'reformed political scientist' also means that neither secularism nor religious politics are advocated. Like a bullet which has no *sui generis* alignment or cause, however, it can be used as a tool for killers, a weapon to be used by whoever wants to create damage. For this there is nothing but a pre-emptive apology, and an insistence that the understandings advocated herein are taken to heart.

It would be impossible to undertake a task of this magnitude alone, and a number of people – friends, relatives, colleagues, acquaintances and scholars – from all over the world have indeed made this journey possible. To thank all would be impossible, and it is hoped that those concerned know the gratitude felt. A special mention does, however, go out to a number of people without whom this book would never have been completed. The eclectic mix of people at the University of Wales Lampeter, made the PhD possible, and the staff at Ashgate made the book a reality. Family and friends know I value their support, their comments and criticisms, though I am often inept at showing this. Last, but certainly not least, for meticulous proofreading and editing and for putting up with even the foulest of moods, a very special *thank you!* goes to the very best friend I have ever had, Lisa.

In order to discover new lands, one must be willing to
lose sight of the shore for a very long time.

– *Anon.*

Foreword

Mark Juergensmeyer

In a disturbing way, religion seems to have lost its innocence in the modern world. No one could view religion solely as an agent for peace after seeing the televised images of the tragic attack on the twin towers of the World Trade Center on September 11, 2001, or listening to the religious rhetoric of angry politicians in response, as they waged their own war on terrorism.

Increasingly religion plays a public role in world affairs, and it is often a violent one. Religious ideas and images are utilized as a source of support for both sides of a global war. As members of the media and the general public turn to scholars of religion to ask why this is increasingly the case, the answers are not always been assuring, nor clear. Scholars have correctly pointed out that bellicose saber-rattling is not characteristic of Christianity or Islam, or any other religion. Yet the scholarly world has also presented us with the fact that religious images have been associated with violence and warfare throughout human history.

This presents scholars with an interesting problem: how can they show the different sides of religion in ways that do not make it appear that religion is either totally innocent or totally bad? They correctly want to avoid the kind of simplification that is sometimes found in the news media when religion is characterized either in two extremes. On the one hand, there is the image of an innocent religion that is exploited by nasty politicians. This is usually what is meant when religion is described as being "used" for political purposes. On the other hand, there is the notion that religion itself can be bad—as if the whole of Islam, for instance, supported acts of terrorism. The frequent use of the term "Islamic terrorism" falls into this pattern of thinking, as does the exaggeration of the importance of *jihad*—as if all Muslims agreed with the militarized usage of the term by unauthorized extremist groups. The term "fundamentalism"—applied not just to Christianity but to a whole host of religious traditions—is another way of excusing "normal" religion and isolating religion's problems to a deviant form of the species. It is used sometimes to suggest an almost viral spread of an odd and dangerous mutation of religion that if left on its own naturally leads to violence, autocracy, and things too horrible to mention. Fortunately, so this line of thinking goes, normal religion is exempt from such extremes.

In this book, JP Larsson rejects these easy explanations and makes clear that the quick attempt to explain cannot replace the hard task of understanding. The involvement of religion in contemporary public life is more complicated than simply a matter of peculiar religion gone bad or good religion being used by bad people. Through a sensitive survey of the literature on religious violence he shows that violence is deeply a part of religious traditions, but is employed in real-world political conflicts only in certain times and circumstances. Utilizing his own background in the Western philosophical tradition, he shows that religious violence is part of the language of cultural understanding, and he rightly points to the concept of sacred war as seminal to the social use of violent religious images and ideas.

Ultimately Larsson's objective is not to belittle religion but to show its enduring role in human endeavors, nonviolent as well as violent. Turning to Gandhi among other nonviolent religious leaders, he shows how religion can provide a moral dimension in political encounters that leads in a positive direction as well as in a destructive one. Religion is, after all, a multifaced thing. There are strata of religious imagination that deal with all sides and moods of human existence, the terror and the tranquility, the perversity and the peace.

Mark Juergensmeyer
- author of *Terror in the Mind of God: The Global Rise of Religious Violence*

Chapter 1
Introduction

It is not only leaders like Usama bin Laden or George W. Bush who wage wars against the infidel and against the Axis of Evil respectively. Throughout history, and in every tradition, similar claims have been made and similar wars fought. More often than not, these claims are founded upon some religious ideal or code. Indeed, we live in a world that seems plagued by religious violence. It is easy to be disconcerted about the state of the current international arena: the Middle East is simmering, extremist and fundamentalist groups are emerging on an almost daily basis in every continent and more than 100 armed conflicts of various intensity rage around the world. We live in a world where an AK-47 can be bought in almost every major city, where a vial of anthrax can be relatively easily obtained and a passenger jet can be used as a weapon with the aid of box-cutters. In this world neighbour seems pitted against neighbour in intractable conflict, statutory rape is more than common and 'honour killings' seemingly the norm. Most terrorism and (political) violence today seem to have religious undertones, either implicitly or explicitly. To most political scientists, politicians, decision-makers, media professionals and the general public such violence appears inherently irrational and illogical. As it is my belief that it is not, my aim here is to try to highlight on what I base this belief and how we can attempt to understand religious violence with a view of overcoming it.

With more than 9,000 distinct religions in the world today, existing in just over 200 recognised nation-states, conflict is inevitable. Indeed, there is little doubt that religion has had a somewhat ambivalent, or even paradoxical, role in international affairs throughout history, as bearer of both olive branch and sword. Most wars in the modern international system (350 years) have been fought for religion (religious causes), framed and contextualised by religious language or fought with the belief that god was on the side of good and the right cause. Due to the central part religion has played in individual human lives, and thus in individuals' interaction and consequently in social affairs, much has been written on the role of religion in armed conflict and violence. However, much of what has been written is necessarily tainted by the authors' own belief-systems, values, presuppositions, assumptions and – for whatever reason – blatant bias. When faced with new situations, Christian theologians, for example, must defend the faith and have thus invested a great deal of effort searching for, and often finding, justifications for the use of violence. Alternatively, if not completely legitimising violence, they have at least tried to make it more bearable with various just war doctrines and by offering guidance and assistance to those affected by conflict and violence. Similarly, Islamic jurists have found themselves required to justify to the believers how violence and peaceful submission to Allah are entirely compatible. More recently, of course, their explanations have been sought by outsiders (Western politicians, media, and public) as to why their ultimately peaceful faith is able to prescribe violence. As religion is at the centre of human civilisation, religious leaders and religious scholars of all traditions often find it necessary to attempt to offer such understanding. However, the relationship between religion and armed conflict is not merely a religious issue.

Social scientists, politicians, political analysts, academics (of all denominations, and of most disciplines) and laymen without any religious training often feel that the role of religion in armed conflict, or – indeed – the relationship between religion and violence is too serious to avoid. Here, however, the conclusions are widely different from the religious attempts at understanding. Often, social scientists feel compelled to *explain* in some way this relationship, rather than to understand it, which is more likely for a believer. Explanations range from the facile 'religion is the cause of all violence' to the possibly even more simplistic 'religion is the only road to peace'. Indeed, even within the self-avowedly secular discipline of International Relations those academics that consciously avoid the issue, and will not mention religion at all in their analyses of armed conflict, are in fact making the most popular statement in that particular discipline, that religion should not even be an issue worth contemplating. Politicians tend to be ambiguous, and necessarily so when it comes to religion's relationship to foreign policy, armed conflict and peace. Without losing valuable support in the electorate, they feel the need to relegate religion out of the 'public sphere' and into the 'private sphere' in the multi-religious and (with globalisation) increasingly shrinking world of today. In a world where global communication is becoming as much an advantage as it is proving to be a problem, media are playing a large part, and as such, are becoming a focus of some debate. This debate is still young, and has yet to be turned inwards onto itself. The language used in media concerning the relationship between religion and violence is often more perforated by presuppositions and inherent value-statements than are commonly recognised, as will be explored at some length in chapter four. Media have to a great extent perpetuated religious antagonisms, solidified erroneous stereotypes about 'the other' and prolonged armed conflicts. Sometimes this is done unwittingly, but what is worse is that it is often done with the most cunning of intentions.

There are, as such, no 'origins' of any war, for example, apart from the stories that are told about them.[1] As has been shown throughout history, due to its dynamics war is paramount to any society. This is where historians, and others, come to play vital parts in the identity building of a society, providing the myths and *lieux de mémoire* that are necessary for a communal identity, which to a large extent, therefore, is an 'imagined community'.[2] The trick for the scholar, apart from realising that all stories are told for a purpose, would be to investigate what the causes of the stories are, rather than the causes of the events. The narrativist would further be interested in *how* the stories are told, and perhaps in drawing parallels to ancient Greek dramas, as some scholars have indeed done. That is, exploring whether the narrative of a particular event is a comedy, tragedy, romance, epic or satire may point to some interesting conclusions. These conclusions would be of great importance in any analysis of an individual's or group's historical consciousness. The all-important role of the historian, within any society, is to '*re*-member' the past asserting that the narrative is true and that 'what is alleged to have happened did happen'.[3] Whilst this is neither the place nor time for a complete survey of the Narrativist tradition of International Relations Theory, or even an overview of the main scholars within the field, it is important to see that Narrativism is largely a philosophical and linguistic instrument for understanding historical interpretation, which is the application I use in this book.

This study is neither a presentation of Narrativism, nor is it using its methodology or terminology. However, I will continuously draw upon the Narrativist basis that no story is value-free, and that all narratives exist for some purpose or another. Indeed, although these reasons are often legitimate, the limitation on a particular aspect of armed conflict (namely religion) and of religion (namely violence) does raise certain new issues and considerations that I will highlight in chapter 4. In the present post-modern academic era, any analysis will inevitably shape the discourse it aspires to investigate, and thus it will change the phenomena it is describing.

In order to come to an understanding of religious violence, 'terrorism' and armed conflict I propose that we embark on a journey. This journey will take us from explanations of these phenomena, as espoused and advocated by secular political scientists, and end by looking at how the problems that will be highlighted in the earlier part of our 'journey' can be overcome by understanding. I call this a framework for conflict transformation. As with any journey, physical or academic, I believe that it is as important to have a smooth ride as it is not to miss any vital sights (or insights) along the way. I have therefore structured this journey in five stages, each interlinking with the other.

First, therefore, I offer a number of '*questions/problems*' of religion in relation to armed conflict. Rather than exploring tacit questions, I look at the explicit 'answers' often given by scholars. It is termed 'questions/problems' as it highlights the contemporary – and often problematic – perspectives from the traditionally 'realist' or 'positivist' perspectives that exist within international relations in academia and practice with regard to the general issue of religion and armed conflict. Although these perspectives are portrayed as answers, I would argue that they are nonetheless part of the questions and problems, rather than helpful for understanding. I have adopted a mainly social scientific perspective and most of the arguments of the chapter will in fact be refuted as we proceed on the journey. In many respects, this first main chapter is the building upon which present International Relations rests, which – in terms of this book – explains the role of religion. This 'building' will be dismantled and in its place the framework for understanding will be erected as another and potentially more functional, structure.

Continuing this metaphor for a moment, in chapter 3 I aim to show how the building is used. In other words, this chapter is illustrative of how religion and armed conflict interact on the contemporary international arena, under what circumstances and when religious armed conflict becomes a fact. This is termed the '*correlates*' of the study, and is basically an empirical interlude in passing from explaining to understanding. In contrast to various 'Correlates of War' projects, I do not provide an analysis of the sorts of circumstances in which wars have occurred more frequently but rather when they occur today. I do not attempt to show any frequency of recurrence but rather a cross-section of religion and armed conflict on the contemporary international arena. This is achieved by highlighting a number of types of religious armed conflict, such as terrorism, inter- and intra-state war, millenarianism, apocalyptic violence and state-policy, and illustrating these with examples from the contemporary world. For balance of argument, religion's peacemaking and non-violent attributes are also briefly highlighted.

Chapter 4 will explore where the assumptions that make the discourse possible come from. This is termed the '*prerequisites*' for explanation, and – in other words – explores the philosophical prerequisites for contemporary perspectives. Here, rather than exploring the prerequisites for the actual events described in chapter 2 (and illustrated in chapter 3), that is, what conditions must be necessary for *events* to occur, I present a number of conditions that make the *discourse* possible. That is, it pertains to prerequisites for knowledge and for the paradigms. In order to do this, I investigate how definitions, assumptions and ontological bases make the questions/problems highlighted in chapter 3 possible for exploration.

Having explored the ways in which religion and armed conflict exist in practice, in chapter 5 I move on towards an understanding of why the perspectives highlighted in chapter 2 have come to light. That is, what made them possible at the most base level? This, in other words, refers to the historical '*causation*' of the contemporary perspectives. In this chapter I explore two ontological issues that make the discourses of chapter 2 possible. Firstly, this means an investigation of rationality and religion, and why it is commonly perceived within International Relations circles that religion is irrational and illogical and why this not only frames religion as a threat but also why it is an impediment to both scholarship and practice. This section pertains mainly to the Rational Actor Model (also known as Rational Choice Theory), which is the underlying ontology of most contemporary International Relations (IR). The second 'cause' of the perceptions of chapter 2 is the legacy of Westphalia and what this means both for IR as an academic discipline and practice and what it means for religion on the international arena. Here, I explore what the implications have been by explicitly taking religion out of international relations, as with the peace-treaties of 1648, and what this means for religion on the international arena today.

Finally, the last of the five stages on the journey refers to the religious '*origins*' of the contemporary perspectives; namely the logic of the violence of religion. This is not the same as the previous chapter as causation refers to what has caused the perspectives and discourse to develop into what they are, and origins pertains to what lies behind the actual phenomena. Chapter 6, therefore, concerns the underlying logic of religious violence, and what makes stereotypes, fears and ignorance rife. A number of religious phenomena pertaining to violence, such as when and how it may be legitimately used and against whom is given a serious and rational treatment with a view of getting to a position where the ultimate framework may be explored. Here, knowledge is the key and it is believed that religious violence can be understood logically and as a rational phenomenon.

Thus I end the journey by offering a 'solution' to the problems by providing a framework, as alluded to earlier. This is not necessarily the best framework, or even the only possible one, but one that I believe is useful to bear in mind for contemporary conflict transformation as it deals with many of the current problems of conflict resolution. In my concluding chapter (chapter 7), this framework is explicitly aired and tested using a variety of criteria. A number of recommendations to academics, practitioners and laymen pertaining to religion and armed conflict/violence are offered with a view to a more peaceful and unprejudiced world.

Although, as claimed above, the academic heritage of this study is grounded in narrativist theories of International Relations, there are – of course – other academic disciplines that have lent more than their names in passing to the research. Indeed, if by 'Theology' is meant the search for meaning, then it is very much a theological work. But since the term has come to take on subjectively Christian connotations, and also notions pertaining to the divine, I cannot align myself with such a view, although the discipline *is* changing. There is, however, some overlapping with 'Religious Studies' and 'Islamic Studies', the extent of which will be noticed by the reader. Similarly, any study of armed conflict would be lacking if it did not have a basis within traditional International Politics in general and 'Strategic Studies' in particular. Without doubt, chapter two is profoundly 'Strategic Studies' oriented in content and approach, whereas chapter four – for example – would be more from a 'Critical Security Studies' perspective. There is, however, something of an obsession with categorisation and labelling within the academy, and as such this is better left to the critics.

Although it must be acknowledged that my earliest academic roots stem from Buddhist 'Theory of Knowledge' (and the research is thus coloured by this tradition) this study aims in all aspects to be as neutral and 'non-confessional' as possible, if such neutrality is indeed possible. In accepting that there is no predetermined conclusion, however, a caveat must be that this book was written not only within a particular academic and societal context, but also in a particular language, and within that language's value-system. Here, it is important to note, as with Narrativism, that I see much mileage in the discipline of 'Critical Linguistics'. In this respect, 'Critical Linguistics', somewhat separate from the general academic discipline of Linguistics, pertains to the fact that language (popular, academic, media) cannot be neutral but contains certain inherent values. The academic roots of this study mentioned here, and others that will become apparent throughout, form an integral part of research that prides itself on its ability to have eidetic vision in a field notoriously either ignored or only approached from a very specific angle.

It should be clear, of course, that although references to particular groups like al-Qa'ida are rare and specific events, like 11 September 2001 are even rarer, the arguments made and conclusions drawn apply equally well to these as to any other. Events on the international arena – or in International Relations – have a peculiar tendency to become formalised concepts, with little or no conscious effort from the actors involved, observers or subsequent analysts. The Cuban Missile crisis of 1962, for example, is as little a mere incident as the fall of the Berlin Wall in 1989. We no longer remember the dates of 28 October and 9 November respectively. Both events have become concepts of International Relations. In the same way, the combined events of 11 September 2001 have also become a concept, rather than a 'mere' incident (although here the date of '9-11' is an integral part of the name of this concept). Whether we adopt the view that everything changed with this concept, or indeed the diametrically opposite line that nothing changed it does affirm that religion is seen as increasingly important on the international arena. This is clearly seen in the wake of those events. Laws that in the future may be considered to have been knee-jerk reactions, were quickly passed around the world following 11 September 2001. The UN Security Council were first off the mark, with resolution 1368 the day after the attacks. In the UK, the recently introduced Terrorism Act of 2000, was – in terms of the legal system – superseded at lightning speed by the Anti-Terrorism, Crime and Security Act of 2001. Already before this, however, and before the 'concept' of 9-11 entered the arena, the Act of 2000 had an interesting amendment, blatantly reflecting the mood of international relations as seen through the eyes of the British Government. In the 2000 Act, 14 groups were identified as being prohibited (or proscribed). Without exception, all these groups were connected with 'the Troubles' in Northern Ireland.[4] In March of 2001, a further 21 groups were added to the list of so-called proscribed organisations. Whilst none of the additions were related to the situation in Northern Ireland, as many (namely 14) were Islamic groups.[5] Out of the remaining 7 additions, half have affiliations to other religions. Since then, another handful of groups have been added to the list, all Islamic. Clearly, therefore, religion seems to matter very much to the policy makers, as most so-called terrorist-groups are related to religion in some way.

By becoming a concept, prolific writing and discussion on these issues are legitimised. What is usually forgotten in these is that the underlying world has changed very little, if at all. Other groups will emerge, and other events will become historicized into concepts. New – and old – experts will be called upon to again explain the occurrence and potential recurrence of such events.

In this book I argue that much of what happens in the world may not need to be explained on this case-by-case basis (that is ideographically), but that it may serve our purposes of a more peaceful and secure world better if we rather try to understand phenomena as wholes (that is, nomothetically). We can do this by looking at the narratives – stories – that are used to describe events and explain their occurrences. We can question the prerequisites for these narratives and their origins and causes. Ultimately, if the will is there we may be able to understand the relationship between religion and violence phenomenologically (that is, its essence). Once this is achieved, we may be closer to approaching a method for successfully dealing with these issues on the international arena. Until then, the 'threat of terrorism' will remain, and our only hope of overcoming this nemesis of modern society is to undermine its very *raison d'être*, namely to instil fear. The way to overcome fear – whether it be of the dark, spiders or terrorists – is, as always, through knowledge. With that in mind, join me on my journey to understand religious violence.

Notes

[1] H. Suganami (1997), p.402.
[2] B. Anderson (1991).
[3] E. Wyschogrod (1998), p.2; See also R. Bauman (1976), for whom conflict is not merely a domain in itself (eg. p.xi.).
[4] The Irish Republican Army, Cmann na mBann, Fianna na hEireann, the Red Hand Commando, Saor Eire, The Ulster Freedom Fighters, the Ulster Volunteer Force, the Irish National Liberation Army, the Irish People's Liberation Organisation, the Ulster Defence Association, the Loyalist Volunteer Force, the Continuity Army Council, the Orange Volunteers, and the Red Hand Defenders.
[5] These are Al-Qa'ida, Egyptian Islamic Jihad, Al-Gama'at al-Islamiyya, Armed Islamic Group, Salafist Group for Call and Combat, Harakat al-Mujahideen, Jaish e Mohammed, Lashkar e Tayyaba, Hizballah External Security Organisation, Hamas-Izz al-Din al-Qassem Brigades, Palestinian Islamic Jihad – Shaqaqi, Abu Nidal Organisation, Islamic Army of Aden, Mujaheddin e Khalq. As of April 2003, Abu Sayyaf Group and Asbat al-Ansal had also been added, along with a couple of non-Islamic religious groups.

Chapter 2

Questions/Problems: Contemporary Perspectives

Although history shows that 'the worst things ever done in the world on a large scale by decent people have been done in the name of religion',[1] it has sometimes been observed that the study of religious phenomena is not of importance to secular man, or the contemporary student. Although religion should never be a source of conflict, it is today clear that many – if not all – armed conflicts have religious undertones, and it is widely recognised as 'the major source of domestic and international conflict in the post-Cold War world'.[2] This poses grave difficulties for policy-makers and practitioners of international relations, which is a practice that is fundamentally inept at coping with conflicts of this nature. I believe that there are a number of 'unique' strategic dangers associated with conflicts of this sort, a number of which will be explored in this chapter and three notions of religion and armed conflict extracted, and investigated.

The first of these notions that I will highlight is that which refers to the contemporary buzzword of 'resurgence' of religion on the international arena. It is generally believed that since the Islamic Revolution in Iran in 1979 there has been an increased salience of religiously motivated actors on the international arena. This resurgence has more often than not been violent, or at least has been perceived that way. It must be remembered (here, and throughout the book) that if the focus of research is on the relationship between religion and violence, rather than religion and peace, then the divisive character of religion will of course not only be emphasised but will also form the basis of any subsequent conclusion.

The second concept is that of religion as a 'threat to international peace and security' on the contemporary international scene. By far the most common perception amongst social scientists and political scientists is the perspective that the resurgence and salience of religion on the international arena is dangerous. The threat is two-fold, as will be explained. One aspect concerns strategic threats, such as those which will be highlighted next, and the other – that is of a more fundamental character – is the perceived threat to the actual state *system*. The search for a 'new world order' that may not be as purportedly secular as the Westphalian state-system of the moment, makes academics and practitioners within the field of international relations recoil in horror. The thought of a 'clash of civilizations', a 'revolt against the West' or another Islamic revolution is sufficient for most 'secular' (Western) analysts to relegate religion completely from all research and enquiry.

Lastly, the three most prevalent methodologies of analysing religion and conflict are investigated. Without elaboration here, these are primordialism, instrumentalism and constructivism. Whilst adherents of these suggest that the three perspectives are diametrically opposite, it is my belief that since they are part of the same ontological foundation they are therefore merely different aspects of the same basic methodology, that of explanation.

Religion is a contentious issue on the international arena, and the research of it is often sadly lacking on several counts. This chapter, which deals with the 'current state of affairs' of religion and armed conflict, aims to highlight why the relationship between religion and international relations is at present an issue fraught with difficulty and danger for scholars and practitioners alike, and why it – in fact – is preferably ignored rather than investigated. This chapter thus takes the side of international relations for the purposes of argument and highlights several notions that are of importance here. These could be seen as the *questions/problems* pertaining to religion and armed conflict within contemporary international relations and its academic counterpart.

As will become clear, the inherent conceptual problems do not disappear merely because the subject of study concerns 'real-world' issues. However, it is by conscious decision that at this stage I do not offer any definitions of concepts nor does it explicitly air the underlying assumptions and presuppositions. These conceptual problems, that are at the heart of this study, will be explored in detail later. In order to facilitate a clear line of argument, the present chapter works with implicit definitions.

To set the scene for the subsequent chapters, it is possible to agree with John Esposito that today 'the world is a battleground on which believers and unbelievers, the friends of God and the enemies of God or followers of Satan wage war'.[3] Without further elaborating on the actual role of religion in this war just yet, as this will be pursued later, it is possible to see that religious concepts and ideals have been used, misused, abused or – indeed – genuinely believed to 'fight the battles of an earlier age',[4] though with more awesome weapons and graver consequences than when sword met sword on the fields of, say, the Byzantine empire 900 years ago.

'Strategic Appraisal' of Religion in International Armed Conflicts

The academic study of war and armed conflict is self-professedly stuck in a time warp. This means that it does little to aid understanding, a factor that is both unfortunate and dangerous. Indeed, in an age of readily available CBRN (chemical/biological/radiological/nuclear) weapons of mass destruction (WMD) the lack of understanding may be dangerous in the extreme. It is true that the work of Prussian military-strategist and thinker Carl von Clausewitz, to whom almost every strategist and military thinker 200 years later still pledges allegiance, still has some relevance in strategic analyses today. Unfortunately, many strategists and military-commanders today fail to realise that Clausewitz was very much a man of his time, and what he refers to as irregular warfare, which is the main 'type' of warfare under investigation in this book, was not yet very common in his day, as he himself admits. Today, the opposite is true. There are more occurrences of intra-state wars than there are of inter-state wars.

This chapter will attempt to offer an overview of how religion is perceived on the contemporary international arena. This may be called a strategic appraisal, as the type of International Relations under ultimate investigation is the strategic side, that which is concerned with armed conflict. Some contemporary issues concerning religion – such as threats, dangers, problems and possibilities – are explored by way of laying the foundations for the subsequent investigation. In other words, the role of religion in armed conflict is explained in the best way known to political scientists. The appraisal shows in what ways a conflict with a religious element differs from conflicts that have no, or very little, religious significance. In many ways, this strategic appraisal is similar to the next chapter, which deals with the same issues, issues of the actual role of religion in armed conflict. The present section deals with the perceived reality, whereas chapter three aims to deal with factual reality.

It is today commonly believed that competition between religions is a source of hostility and hatred in the world. Often, religion is a fuel that sustains violence and protracts conflicts and makes their resolution difficult to achieve, or in the words of the former Archbishop of Canterbury 'religion is a kind of diabolic yeast, fermenting and fomenting strife and discord'.[5] Indeed, since the end of the Cold War religion is often perceived as the 'new' dangerous force in the world, taking over the baton from Communism. Religion does, however, make a very different foe (or friend) from Communism and there are some strategic and tactical difficulties that are unique to ethno-religious conflicts.

Wars between sovereign states are becoming increasingly rare. Today, there are few conflicts that may be portrayed as conventional wars between states. The example of the territorial dispute between Pakistan and India may be one exception, and depending on one's political and communal allegiance so may others (for example the second Gulf War of 2003). According to these theories, the notion of the 'Clausewitzian war' (i.e. inter-state, land-based with two large and well organised armies opposing each other) is becoming increasingly obsolete and may – in fact – no longer be valid. This, however, is not an acceptable view, as part of the contemporary use of the Clausewitzian theory of war is that for Clausewitz war meant 'an act of force to compel the enemy to do our will'[6] and the often employed theorem that war is merely the continuation of politics by other means. These two fundamental statements regarding armed conflict could, of course, refer equally well to state-actors as to non-state actors, as revolutionaries and guerrillas have shown throughout the twentieth century.

The danger lies in the fact that there is a difference between 'old wars' (inter-state) and 'new wars' (intra-state), which is not adequately catered for by state-centric military strategies. State actors are poorly capable of dealing successfully with sub-state (or in any case non-state) actors. This is because the state must assume that its adversary acts within the same worldview as itself. That is, inter-state relations in both peace and war must be based on an intersubjective understanding and paradigm. Within international relations this is referred to as the Rational Actor Model (RAM). The state must assume that the opponent fits the RAM in order for its actions and counter-actions to be effective. Of course, in cases of religious conflict this is seldom the case. Not only does this inherent 'irrationality' make peace negotiations and anticipation of moves (and thus strategic and tactical planning) difficult, it also renders most state-based military strategy impossible. An illustration of this may be seen in the concept of deterrence, which was developed to apparent excellence during the Cold War where it reached its absurd extreme of MAD (Mutual Assured Destruction). The familiar logic of MAD pertains to the theory that although the first strike in a nuclear war may completely annihilate the enemy the retaliation of this enemy will none the less be of sufficient magnitude to annihilate in return. The doctrine of MAD, therefore guaranteed, or 'assured', that there would be no surviving victor of a nuclear war between the superpowers, and hence an attack was pointless. Deterrence 'perfected' like this is not viable today, as there is an inevitable question of who to deter and whether they will respond as a 'rational actor'. A United States Army report is poignant as it asks, 'who precisely do we need to deter?'[7] when confronted with a non-state faction armed with weapons of mass destruction. 'In some cases it might be an individual or two, in others a more collective leadership group'. Ultimately, the report is forced to admit that 'the relative predictability and familiarity … [present during the Cold War] is likely to be absent'. Deterrence, as with other acts of 'traditional' war, and strategy in general must necessarily be based on a 'Rational Actor Model' according to which the adversary's response can be anticipated, and counter-moves calculated. A practical illustration of this is readily provided by the actions of the US in the weeks immediately following the terrorist attacks of 11 September 2001. Who needed to be deterred or what their next actions would be could not be ascertained with complete accuracy, and the political/military response was thus 'measured'.

Religious actors are often not 'rational' in a further sense. This pertains to the philosophical foundations of ethno-religious conflict. As the justifications of the conflict usually have long histories and are often based in mythologies, metaphors, historical memories or mere rhetoric, irrationality is often inevitable, as these justifications play on individuals' emotions, and not to their rational minds. When the passions of the people are irritated, serious armed conflict often ensues as 'when men are angry they are easily persuaded to fight'.[8]

One phenomenon of religious conflicts is that they are invariably framed in terminology of being a 'cosmic war', of 'us' versus 'them' or of 'good' versus 'evil'. The religious basis of this will be investigated further in chapter six. From a strategic, or political, point of view, however, when a conflict takes on such characteristics the identities of the actors often become incompatible and everyone in the society must thus choose sides. It is impossible to be a bystander, innocent or 'neutral' in a cosmic war. This means that civilians – including women, children, and professionals of all kinds – must necessarily be combatants (apt illustrations of this may be Afghanistan and Palestine). The distinction between combatant and non-combatant is therefore very difficult or even impossible to discern. From a strategic point of view this is a great threat, as not only is it difficult to carry out successful surgical strikes, but counter-attacks are all the more likely and exceedingly difficult to predict. Further to this, as the exclusionary narratives inherent in religious conflicts often demonise or dehumanise the opponent, the danger of almost 'genocidal slaughter' is often imminent. This has grave implications for the validity and effectiveness of international law.

Whilst momentarily running the risk of implicitly claiming that religion is always violent, it is arguably true that although most religious systems have their own codes, rules or laws relating to the conduct of warfare, most do not adhere to what are commonly referred to as international laws of war. Part of this problem is that the international laws of war are based on the Judeo-Christian heritage out of which the concepts of *jus ad bellum* and *jus in bello* evolved. Another part of the problem, and something that is the cause of some concern, is that every party to the conflict must necessarily believe that they are fighting for the 'Right'. When that 'Right' is of a religious nature, purportedly secular laws of war are deemed to be inferior. It is striking to note that in virtually all of the nearly 500 major wars fought around the world since 1700 'each side has imagined itself to be exclusively on the side of God'[9] by whatever name. The breaking of international law, in the interests of abiding by the religious law, is not only condoned, but also actively pursued, and is an easy choice for most believers. This makes deceit, for example, 'legal' in most types of religious warfare, as is the killing of prisoners of war, as there are no 'innocents' and so forth.

A corollary of the problem of the ineffectiveness of international laws of war concerning religious armed conflict is the availability of weapons throughout the world. Due to proliferation, small arms, ranging from assault rifles (such as the Kalashnikov AK-47) to surface-to-air missiles (SAMs) are today readily available in most conflict zones around the world. However, the greater threat is that weapons of mass destruction, such as biological or chemical agents or even nuclear weapons, are today not very difficult for a religious group or regime to acquire, though the practical use of WMD is severely limited by a number of factors. As religious conflicts generate a high degree of tension, even when the conflict is latent or dormant (as is the case with most such conflicts at some point during their course), accidents, misjudgements or carelessness can have disastrous consequences.

The risk of tension suddenly erupting into violence poses further dangers. This is especially true in relation to inhabitants of a conflict-zone who may be caught in crossfire, indirectly or – indeed – directly targeted. This may easily incite other religious groups who until then had been passive actors to become actively involved in the conflict. The arguably greater danger, however, is the potential mass-movement of peoples; refugees. The humanitarian dangers of religious conflict are usually immense as when religious conflicts become wars of identity, the objective may very well be to completely obliterate or annihilate the enemy once and for all. In such a conflict, any means are allowed, as mentioned earlier. Often the military strategy of a religious group is more vicious than that employed by states due to the narratives that are used to explain and justify the conflict. Whilst the aim of a state-centric strategy is often to eliminate a clearly defined (state) enemy or threat, the military objective of religious groups is often the destabilisation of the entire society and 'what were side effects have become [the] central mode of fighting'. In such conflicts, deliberate military strategy thus includes 'conspicuous atrocity, systematic rape, hostage-taking, forced starvation and siege, destruction of religious and historic monuments, the use of shells and rockets against civilian targets, especially homes, hospitals or crowded places like markets or water sources'.[10]

There are, of course, many more dangers characteristic of religious conflict, regarding which the literature is now becoming impressive, and the catalogue of strategic dangers posed by religious conflict is thus immense. These include the fact that arguably there is no such thing as a *completely* intra-state conflict, as funding and support invariably come from abroad either directly or indirectly by training, affiliation or weapons-supply. This means that the existence of international 'terrorism', 'fundamentalism' and fanaticism today pose the gravest threat both to the system of states as a whole, and to groups and individuals within that system. Briefly, in any case, religion seems today to be a rather atavistic force on the international arena, although whether this is actually a threat to a meaningful international society or not will be left open to question at this point.

The notion of ultimate commitment is also very important from a strategic point of view, and this is made implicit in Machiavelli's advice to his Prince that one cannot escape death if one's attacker does not fear death himself.[11] This is where religion has ultimate hold over human interest for a large number of believers throughout the world and in virtually every religious tradition. The religion, or 'cause' is invariably thought to be more important than the individual, and personal death is therefore not always the last resort, but a conscious decision for the benefit of the religion.

Although the importance of religion on the international arena cannot be denied, with almost daily news-reports of yet another act of 'religious terrorism', a new Hollywood film about 'fundamentalists' or communal distress in religiously mixed cities, many analysts and researchers today implicitly or explicitly imply that a social belief in religion, or in any case a conviction of its importance in armed conflict, is ludicrous and a mere folly. As religion, however, seems to become increasingly important, the next section will explore the phenomenon of 'resurgence' of religion on the international arena during the last few decades, and how observers have perceived this phenomenon.

'Resurgence' of Religion on the International Arena

It has hardly escaped any writer, researcher or observer of international affairs that towards the end of the 20th century religion and religious movements have grown in importance throughout the world, and on many levels of society. As such a resurgence would weaken the purportedly secular basis of the state and state-system, it is often thought to be a cause of anarchy and detrimental to order in international society. The alleged threat posed by this religious resurgence will be further highlighted in the next section. Here, the actual phenomenon of 'resurgence' of religion on the international arena will be highlighted, and overly conventional thinking on the issue will be somewhat refuted.

The last 25 years of international relations/politics/studies in academia have been faced with an unexpected phenomenon. Unexpected not only because it was not predicted (many such phenomena have occurred in recent history), but also because it *could not* be predicted. Although a few skirmishes in the wake of decolonisation were related to religion, few events were seen as totally a threat to the secular system of states as the Islamic revolution in Iran in 1979. Since the Ayatollah Khomeini's return to Teheran, a vast body of literature has emerged dealing with this resurgence of religion, and academics and practitioners alike have highlighted a number of perspectives as to why this is dangerous.

As this 'new-found' importance of religion on the international arena has been realised, more and more individuals, movements and even governments have justified their actions and policies by religion, either explicitly or implicitly. A caveat that must be remembered here is that such policies have not only been *justified* by religion, but also *legitimised* by religion. The distinction may seem semantic, but it is not. Religious justification refers to politicised religion, which is often – albeit not always – 'used' for secular political ends, whereas religiously legitimate actions refer to a genuine belief or religious truth. Unfortunately, there are precious few observers who recognise that genuine belief does matter to believers throughout the world, even when empirical evidence to the contrary is in abundance. An illustrative example of this, in relation to the current issue of 'resurgence' is the salience of violent 'fundamentalists', religious fanatical terrorists and so forth. In addition, this is erroneously often thought to refer especially to Islamic groups.

Unfortunately, although religious fundamentalism is to a large extent the envy of the modern secular state, as it commands an all-encompassing view of life, it is also seen as the greatest threat to Western values, peace and security in the era after the Cold War. Curiously, the 'resurgence' of religious movements coincides well with the need for a new threat. Although religion is a form of denial of the material world, it is also the strongest power in that world, and it is generally believed that 'trouble seemed invariably to follow when God appeared to be interesting Himself in foreign policy'.[12] As with this statement by Joad's 'Reasonable Pacifist' (who was 'convinced but intelligent' in his belief) the society of states is avowedly 'atheist' in the sense that it has sought to remove religion from the public sphere. In the public sphere, religion is often seen more as a part of the problem than as part of the cure. Most contemporary analysts, therefore, agree that the resurgence of religion in international affairs is potentially a source of violent conflict. To advocate religion as an important factor on the international arena is thus seen as somewhat inappropriate in the modern, secular world. This is where fundamentalists most frequently clash with modernists (who invariably are secularists). Although there are other characteristics of the resurgence of religion, it is fundamentalism that has generally come to signify the phenomenon.

Fundamentalism, however, is not necessarily (or even mostly) violent or conflictual. For example, maybe it can even be argued that 'probably the majority of Muslims everywhere believe in fundamentalism',[13] but only very few act violently on these beliefs. This is not the generally accepted view of Western political scientists and public. For them, the resurgence of Islam is a serious problem, although – as alluded to above – it is nonetheless believed that the religion is in some way manipulated to accommodate colonialist, expansionist or racist secular claims. Of course, scholars of Islam, as scholars within every religious tradition, have spent much time and effort on the issues relating to the use of force in war, and this is the main reason for the somewhat skewed perspectives. It is wrong, nonetheless, to argue that religious belief does not matter in – say – European international affairs, or that religion today is not the cause of conflict between 'civilised' states. Often, this is merely academic anachronism, but sometimes it is more fundamentally important as it refers to the underlying ontology of the international system. This is where the essence of the alleged resurgence of religion comes into question.

Whereas there has been an increase in the awareness of the importance of religion on the international arena, it is not clear whether this is indeed a *resurgence* of religion or a *decline* of the secular international system. This has led to an unbalanced culture of research into the phenomena associated with the resurgence of religion. Whilst observers have noticed the revival of religious terrorism, for example, they have often failed to research the phenomenon successfully. It is unfortunate that within the academy, the phenomenon of religious resurgence is commonly accepted without question, rather than by an attempt to understand it. *Ad nauseam*, therefore, we are told that religion is an increasingly important factor in international relations, that its resurgence is a far-reaching phenomenon and that although this is a source of both violence and peace, the violent aspects are more salient and important. Unfortunately, such studies tell us little, if anything, of the underlying cause. In other words, they serve a purpose of explaining a particular conflict in terms of religious ideas but do not further any understanding as to why this happens. There are, of course, exceptions to this; for example, scholars who argue that religious resurgence is a reaction to globalisation, though this is not an argument investigated here.

Religion, according to Hobbes, may be the most potent of all sources of war. But this view is nothing new. Throughout history, the existence of religion has probably caused more warfare than it has prevented, whether serving as an otherworldly assurance of victory or as the glorification and justification of otherwise unjustifiable acts of war. Furthermore, genuine religious differences have also led to violence throughout the history of every religious tradition. Within the Judeo-Christian tradition, one has only to look at the first murder, committed with undeniable religious undertones. Religious violence has always existed although today it may take new shapes. There are two qualifications necessary here. First, it is not strange that religious conflict should change according to modern resources and practices as no religion is static (not even the fundamentally scriptural religions). Secondly, in many instances, religious terror has not changed noticeably at all. Descriptions of Ismaili Assassins, for example, although written almost 700 years ago, might equally well be applied to modern day religious terrorists or even contemporary mercenaries:

> They sell themselves, are thirsty for human blood, kill the innocent for a price, and care nothing for either life or salvation. Like the Devil, they transfigure themselves into angels of light, by imitating the gestures, garments, languages, customs and acts of various nations and peoples…[14]

The discrepancy between the age-old link between religious violence and conflict and the recently ‘discovered’ phenomena of ‘resurgence’, may be relatively easy to decipher as there is a certain risk associated with applying modern-day concepts like resurgence to ancient phenomena such as religion and similarly in using modern notions of religion to explain ancient events. This, however, is not frequently recognised in the world of International Politics where it is often thought impossible to acknowledge that religion and politics may be interrelated. By this standard, Jesus – for example – was a wholly religious person, and definitely not a political person, whereas this is arguably exactly what he was. Mohandas Gandhi, likewise, was not *either* a political *or* a religious person, he was both, and favoured saying that religion and politics were inseparable. Indeed, it has been claimed that it may be essential for anyone engaged in politics to avoid such separation, as this may jeopardise loyalties.

The qualification could thus be made that since religion has never disappeared as an element in violence and conflict it cannot now be in resurgence. However, this is not what is commonly meant by a resurgence of religion on the international arena. Indeed, although genuine and serious religious tension continues to create armed conflicts throughout the world, the salience of such violence is escalating. Religious fervour, in other words, seems to be increasingly important for people as a basic formulation of identity. The reason for this is that religion offers a fundamental type of security that is necessary in a world that is at best unstable and at worst manifestly hostile. This security is not merely on an individual level but also on a societal level. When threatened, therefore, the group mobilise along religious lines. This, then, means that 'no one in group A need be personally hostile to anyone in group B'[15] as Russell Hardin points out. Once this happens, the religion serves to excite the passions and emotions of the individuals in the groups and the conflict becomes cruel, heinous and intractable. The immediate obvious result is that religion is perceived as being a threat, as will be explored below.

Religion as a 'Threat to International Peace and Security'

A common progression from the idea of a resurgence of religiously motivated actors is the notion that this is a 'threat to international peace and security', which is the second main theme I pick up from the strategic appraisal. This is the most prevalent view of religion on the international arena today. Religion is often thought to be the main driving force behind modern political violence and terrorism and religious actors are usually the first ones to be pointed out as the 'usual suspects' after any incident of terrorism even before the true perpetrators are known, or any evidence gathered. Although later investigations may show that the perpetrators were different from those first suspected, the stereotypes live on and the same mistake is committed time and time again after every incident, which makes it easier for a new or 'copy-cat' cell to commit terrorist acts. This was seen both after the Oklahoma City bombing of 1995, for example, or in the wake of 11 September 2001.

Although recognising the difficulties with the term (and associated meanings) of 'terrorism' it is possible to agree with those scholars who argue that religiously motivated terrorism is on the increase. The underlying religious reasons behind this will be explored in more detail in chapter six. Here, however, it may be argued that most incidents of terrorism in recent years have been motivated (or justified) by religious beliefs. Bruce Hoffman and David Claridge write, when introducing statistics on this, that 'religion remained an important contributing factor to terrorism's rising lethality. Groups motivated wholly or in part by a salient religious or theological motivation committed ten out of the 13 "spectacular" [terrorist incidents]'.[16] These awesome statistics speak for themselves, and seem to accentuate the fact that religious beliefs are indeed a potent force often threatening the safety and security of the secular state-system.

Religious terrorism is often inextricably linked to what has pejoratively come to be known as religious fundamentalism. One of the greatest threats to 'our way of life' in the post-Cold War era is most keenly felt in the threat, or alleged threat, of 'fundamentalism'. It is, furthermore, the so-called *Islamic* 'fundamentalism' that is seen as the main threat facing the Western, 'secular' world spearheaded by the United States of America. Although there have been a number of notable cases in recent years of non-Islamic religious terrorism and 'fundamentalism', the 'West' has – like Nostradamus 500 years ago – settled for an Islamic 'other' in its search for a new enemy. The cause of much of this must be linked to modern mass media, which presents Islamic forces as evil and the West invariably as innocent victims, despite vociferous rhetoric to the contrary in recent years.

The belief is that religion and religious belief pose a great threat to international peace and security. Indeed, religion is often seen as the *greatest* threat to such peace and security in the post-Cold War era. Whether the threat is perceived as one of religiously motivated rogue states, religious terrorists, or proselytising, a number of threats can be identified as being influenced by religion.

It should be clear that the previous strategic appraisal is, in many ways, based on the Western secular perception of international politics, which means that the threat of secularisation – for example – is not a threat, but rather a promise and a possibility. The present section highlights this by *not* highlighting it. The underlying point is that the ultimately Western international politics is unable to deal with other types of 'international relations'.

In this, religion is seen as an inherently irrational phenomenon and thus a threat to a system that is believed to be ultimately rational. Although closely liked to irrationality, mindlessness is in this context rather different. A few observers do not refer to terrorism as 'mindless' as they recognise that in order to execute the carefully planned operations that are usually referred to as 'terrorism' it is arguably necessary to be particularly 'mindful'. However, most politicians and analysts do refer to them as being irrational, for example in their disregard for laws of war (attacking civilians, torture, killing prisoners, destroying monuments and buildings of cultural and religious significance, etc.) and as they are, as highlighted previously, impervious to 'traditional' means of deterrence and so forth. It follows from this that anything that is irrational is inherently – and by definition – dangerous and thus a threat. However, I tend to agree more with (the fictional) Dr. Joseph Workman who claims that religion does not 'induce insanity in a truly sound mind'.[17]

In relation to religious conflict, one aspect of threat-assessment that becomes vital, perhaps more than other aspects, was highlighted above, namely that threat-perception depends on the perspective of the analyst. A secular analyst will thus see the main threat as coming from a non-secular actor and vice versa. Likewise, an observer from a certain religious tradition will be more likely to see an actor from a rival tradition as being the foremost threat, especially if there is a history of antagonism and mistrust between the traditions in question. This, of course, has grave implications not only for the response to violence in times of conflict (who to retaliate against, and how), but also for the sometimes violent stereotyping taking place in 'peacetime'. This, in other words, is often a recipe for further violence in a spiral of violence. Whether this is a downwards, upwards or forwards spiral is open to some debate and is influenced by many elements, such as individual and group attitudes to violence (defensive and offensive), retaliation and ultimately one's morals and ethics. That many otherwise enlightening works fall short due to this sort of bias is understandable, though regrettable.

The threat of religion to international peace and security is usually explained as being one of low-level violence in respect of the number of casualties. Although religious groups may try to assert their influence – violently if necessary – on the international arena throughout the world, their financial and social support structure generally does not allow for a prolonged high-level conflict. The wide-spread proliferation of small arms throughout the world, the sharing of knowledge and skills between groups and generally available information on the internet has led to many terrorist groups today being able to continue functioning as independent cells even when the central power-structure may have been destroyed or disabled. However, although this entails an evident threat, it is usually small-scale and its largest number of casualties are usually the result of chance rather than planning. That is, a car bomb or even a suicide bomb still relies upon a number of factors usually outside the terrorists' influence, control or knowledge. With a world in transition, however, this is now changing, as terrorists are realising their potential and also the extent of their own incompetence.

This has led analysts to consider the possibility of terrorists acquiring some type of weapon of mass destruction (WMD). Today, it is believed that many groups have the capability to develop both biological and chemical agents, which may be used as weapons, as well as buying either complete nuclear weaponry or vital components (such as depleted Uranium) for use in either 'clean' or 'dirty' nuclear attacks. The former being a nuclear explosion, with the obvious immediate destruction, whereas the latter is a nuclear weapon without fission, that is 'merely' nuclear fall-out, with little structural damage but nonetheless detrimental to human beings, animals and plants. Despite the current political rhetoric of WMD, however, it must be remembered that very few – if any – non-state groups have the 'know-how' or resources to 'successfully' use such weapons.

The attacks on the World Trade Centre in New York and the Pentagon in Washington DC, in 2001, have highlighted a thereto scarcely researched form of weapon, namely mid-range terrorism. That is, not low-level (such as a car/truck bomb, 'normal' suicide attack or assassination) or WMD, but a previously rare type of mix between these. A terrorist attack resulting in a few thousand casualties cannot (legally) be considered mass destruction or labelled as low-level terrorism, but is nonetheless a threat. This particular event seems to solidify notions of religion as a threat to international peace and security. Such notions are prevalent and useful as explanations, but are scarce and worth little as bases for understanding.

As religion has been recognised as a powerful force, and perhaps *the* most powerful force on the international arena today, it is growing both in perception and in actual existence, as highlighted previously. Although scholars and other analysts disagree as to why, religion may, however, threaten international security since it pertains to individuals' most fundamental values and beliefs. Such fundamental beliefs, which are often combined under the general grouping of morals and ethics, include the importance of good as opposed to evil, right as opposed to wrong and survival (of both the group and the individual). When these are posited against other, often opposing, views and values it can be easy to mobilise support and justify almost any action. Religion is commonly believed to be the root of most – if not all – morals and ethics within most philosophical and societal systems. This means that when (rather than if) the conviction of what is right clashes with another conviction of right it is usually impossible to compromise. Compromise would in these circumstances involve concessions of fundamental moral significance, which would be inconceivable. Religious conflicts (whether real, imagined – or both) could thus not be resolved by negotiations.

This means that as most contemporary conflict resolution models build upon some sort of compromise by either or both parties and as a religion cannot concede on matters of right and wrong (as that would mean *it* would cease to exist), it is obviously a threat to 'international peace and security' if religious justification (and legitimation) is invoked, as any peace-process by negotiation and compromise is therefore likely to suffer or even cease completely.

It is a common perception today, and indeed has been throughout history, that nothing *could* (or should) be worth such suffering as is experienced following any religiously or otherwise motivated terrorist attack. Religion and religious belief, therefore, are usually seen as being used, abused and misused merely as a political tool on the international arena to reach secular goals albeit with the backing of faith. This is by far the most prevalent view amongst political scientists, academics and laymen throughout the Western world. The greatest failure of such a position is, however, that it cannot clarify *how* religion can be used in this way, unless there was indeed an underlying genuine belief that legitimised violent (armed) action. The conclusion is that religion, therefore, is seen both as a direct threat in that it is an extremely potent tool for mobilising support and rallying followers, and also as a further direct threat pertaining to genuine differences of belief. The violent aspects of religion, or in any case those that are permissive of violence, are investigated in chapter 7. Some scholars have argued that there is no necessary conflict between religions as they answer different questions, and thus can not be contradictory, but even a superficial scan of the historical and contemporary world would show that religion is deeply implicated in violence and war due to differences in belief. Indeed, it is not difficult to accept a proposition that the worst things ever done in the world have been done in the name of religion. The danger with the very phrase 'in the name of religion' is highlighted in the next section.

With the backdrop of current world politics, it may be argued as above that 'the world is a battleground on which believers and unbelievers, the friends of God and the enemies of God or followers of Satan, wage war'.[18] The reasoning behind such a statement is that there are around 100 armed conflicts of varying intensity around the world in any one year, and religion is frequently implicated in some way in these. From a social scientist perspective, as characterised by the academic study of International Relations, there are basically two ways in which religion has an impact on armed conflict, when the issue is given any thought. One of these is the notion of 'religious politics' and the other that superficially seems to be the same, namely 'political religion'.

The concept of 'religious politics' means that religion is nowadays used as a tool to mobilise forces and create unity on a political agenda or cause. Such (secular) agendas can include territory, resources, political power or wealth, and it seems as if there is no better method to rally support and provide legitimate justification than if the cause is supported by (a) god. Notions of a 'chosen people' or a land given by a god mobilise political forces to 'fight the battles of an earlier age'.[19] In other cases, the differences are purely political, but once a dispute starts and fighting breaks out between warring parties, then people are forced to choose sides, and discontent with the other side grows. If political agendas are tied to religious symbols, the outcome is religious war, despite political scientists claiming that notions of 'holy wars' and 'crusades' can be dismissed without further consideration, and despite the fact that it may have been purely secular motives that led to the original conflict.

Often, the intricate link between religion and war is explained by statements to the effect that 'the religious issue is often no more than an excuse for plunder'.[20] This may be so, since it is easier to bring about unity and gain support if the history of a certain cause is 're-membered'[21] as a religious issue, because these issues are often more tangible – or at least more justifiable – than purely political agendas from the believers' point of view. The present conflict in Sri Lanka, where the majority of the population is Buddhist, is an example of a conflict sustained by religious politics. To describe 'religious politics' in short, therefore, it can be argued that in order to reach a particular political goal, it is necessary to appeal to individual and collective emotions.

Religion is thus often a political pretext, but it must be remembered that this is not always the case, since in issues of armed conflict there are often certain genuine religious agendas as well. This has recently been admitted by the most avant-garde social scientists and conflict-researchers, but very little seems in reality to have changed, since this was exactly the point strategist Baron Antoine de Jomini argued almost two centuries ago,

> Sans doute, la religion fut quelquefois un prétexte politique ou un moyen, plutôt qu'une affair de dogmes. ... Lorsqu'il en est ainsi, le dogme n'est pas seulement le pretexte, c'est aussi quelquefois un puisant moyen, car il remplit le double but d'exciter l'ardeur des siens, et de se créer un parti. [see end-note for translation][22]

Such genuine belief is what is here referred to as 'political religion', which uses modern, political means for religious ends. In other words religious warfare for religious ends. Despite the West's and Christianity's historic record of being proselytising, through violent or imperialist means (or, indeed both), it is Islam in the contemporary world that has had to shoulder the burden of being seen as inherently violent, expansionist and war-prone, as highlighted above. Christian holy wars, so it is commonly argued, ended many hundred years ago, whilst Islamic *jihads* are thought to be the greatest threat against 'Western ideals' today. The continuing conflict in the Sudan (below), for example, may be used as an illustration of 'political religion', but there are other examples in abundance.

In contemporary international relations it must be realised that Islam is not unique – or even one of only a few religions – in its justification of violent conflict. With a number of negligible exceptions every human society throughout history has not only had some conception of religion, but also of violence. Often, gods and goddesses have mirrored all human emotions, virtues and vices. So too with war and violence. From Aipaloovik in the northwest to Kukalikimoku in the southeast, gods and goddesses personify the acts of violence and war, and also glorify them. In many cultures, gods/goddesses of war are also, for example, those of happiness (Bishamon), fertility (Indra) and sexuality (the Celtic goddess Medb). The large monotheistic religions are no exceptions to this fondness for imagery of war and violence. In fact, every religion necessarily has scope for violence and armed conflict, as I will investigate in chapter 6.

It is thus clear that religious actors may have influence on the international arena, but why is this a threat to international peace and security? Two remaining aspects of the relationship between religion and armed conflict will briefly serve to highlight this, the first is religion's attitude to the rule of law, and the second the phenomenon of nationalism, both of which have been alluded to earlier.

It is commonly accepted by believers around the world that the most true laws are not of human creation, but given by god. There are a number of ways to accommodate this belief. On a state-level, there are two main positions. Societies who pride themselves on some concept of secularity, like modern Western societies, for example, hide the fact that 'secular' law is often based on traditionally divine mandates. The other position may be illustrated by the case of Islamic societies, where the concept of *din wa dawla*, or the unity of religion and state, often means that the sovereignty of god is the source of governance, usually along the lines of *Sharia* (divine law). This means that *al-dawla islamiiyya* (Islamic state) takes precedence over *al-dawla qawmiyya* (the secular nation-state). These two positions are not exclusive, although most modern states occupy a place within either or both of these, by borrowing more or less from both. The ancient concept of the 'God-King' in Buddhism, which still serves a purpose (mainly) in South Asia, is a third position. Non-state positions usually tend to take more extreme forms, where it is indeed not only a moral right but also a duty to break the law if it contradicts the divine decree. Examples of this are in abundance, and necessarily exist within all religious systems. The threat associated with this is two-fold, the first part of which is obvious; if there is a right to break the law a community or society may descend into anarchy (which it is the goal of law to prevent). Furthermore, by logical progression, the right to violate a law that is not in accordance with the religion, will lead to the desire to further the right (of the religion) in preference to living with the wrong (of the opposing law).

The tangent pertaining to the justness of revolting against an unfair law must be omitted from the present discussion, and with it the associated topics of civil disobedience, moral consciousness and a right society/government. It must be remembered, however, that these ideals have indeed been both justified and actively pursued throughout history by all manner of people from democratic voters to conscientious objectors of Tolstoyan or Gandhian proportions. It is important, however, to bear in mind that the belief in the superiority of right over wrong often has implications for making or breaking the law.

On the international arena, where justness and fairness are firmly rooted within certain philosophical traditions, the threat of religious believers' relationship with law takes many shapes. It is not deemed to be a threat to international peace and security if a tyrannical or unjust government is overthrown, but a society may nonetheless descend into anarchy because certain elements believe the law to be fundamentally flawed. The result of a 'revolution' may indeed be a better society, but it may equally be a cause of violence and anarchy. Being based largely on market economies, the international system needs a large degree of stability in order to function. If that stability is lacking, many more societies may be forced into conflict and anarchy. This is an obvious, and not implausible, threat to international peace and security.

However, the threat more frequently referred to by those political scientists not too well versed in international political economies concerns the events once armed conflict is indeed a fact. This pertains to the effectiveness and perceived impartiality of international laws of war. An armed conflict where religion is invoked does not usually conform to international covenants on the laws of war, such as the Geneva Conventions of 1949 (which with some amendments are still the basic documents on the issue). This has led analysts to claim that there are no laws of war in a religious conflict, but this is only true with an important caveat; there are no *universal* laws of war. Although every religious tradition necessarily has violent elements (as will be explored in chapter six), every religious system also has rules as to their application. These rules or 'laws' of war are often very stringent and confine the believers to firm criteria of when and how to use violent force. Within the Judeo-Christian tradition this took the form of various 'just war' theories following the writings of Vitoria, Bellarmine and Suarez in the sixteenth century and earlier. From this, theories of *jus ad bellum* (laws towards war – when war is allowed) and *jus in bello* (laws in war – what is lawful during war) have developed and have become incorporated in international laws and ultimately in documents pertaining to human rights. Although alleging to be secular, their foundations are not only fundamentally religious, but are thus also firmly rooted within a *particular* religious tradition.

There is little doubt, outside the Western academy and policy centres, that such laws and rules are unacceptable in many communities and societies. It can be argued that there is no such thing as a 'universal' code of laws and rights, and a growing interest in the notion of the 'universality' of legal and moral concepts is now becoming apparent. As a threat to international peace and security, this has far-reaching implications on many levels. For example, a fundamentalist religious group may not feel obliged to offer any rights to outsiders of that group. This may range from violent treatment (or even the killing) of prisoners, to not distinguishing between combatant and non-combatant. As everyone is forced to choose sides, there are no innocents in a religious war and there are no victims, either, be they innocent or not. If a conventional military force is met by opposition from a religious military power, therefore, they are operating on completely different legal and moral bases and this is seen as one of the most potent threats to international peace and security.

The second main threat faced by religion on the international arena is connected with the issue of the legality of war and violence, and is often thought to be the main attribute of violent religion today. This is the concept of nationalism and although religious fundamentalism may not always be equal to nationalism, nationalism not only parallels religion but may also actually *be* a religion in itself. Nationalism frequently derives its structure and content from religion and also continuously draws on it. Religious feelings may today indeed be represented by such 'religions' as nationalism. Nationalism arguably mirrors religion on one of three levels; historical, quasi- and 'real'. Since the resurgence of religion has entitled scholars to look more closely at the relationship between religion and nationalism, a growing body of literature has emerged invariably arguing that religious nationalism is the 'new cold war' and a threat to international peace and security. It is undoubtedly true that religion is often politicised in nationalist conflicts, as explained previously, to mobilise support or justify a course of action. However, it must also be remembered that religion is often a vital aspect of the identity building of a community and it is in that context that political scientists concerned about religion as a 'threat to international peace and security' most keenly feel the fusion between religion and nationalism. Although not elaborating on it at the moment, it is important to realise that the 'threat' of nationalism is also a way of rationalising religion within a secular framework, without explicitly condoning the importance of religion in armed conflicts.

Tripartite Perspective of Analysis

Now, the theoretical methodologies for explaining the practical issues that have been raised so far will tie in with the themes of this predominantly social scientist chapter. These themes have been implicit throughout the strategic appraisal, the investigation of the alleged resurgence of religion on the international arena and in the previous section exploring notions of religion as a threat to international peace and security. However, they have not been explicitly assessed thus far. There are, in short, three predominant methodologies used in the process of analysing religion on the international arena. These have changed very little throughout history, and variants of them are still used in the majority of attempts at explaining the role of religion in armed conflict. Whilst the adherents of each are adamant that they are opposites, or tri-polar, I argue that they are, in fact, tripartite aspects of the same underlying epistemology. I will highlight why these three methodologies are used, and why they are unhelpful in trying successfully to understand religious armed conflict, after a brief discussion of each. The three perspectives are termed 'primordialism', 'instrumentalism' and 'constructivism'.[23]

The first perspective I will explore is 'primordialism', which pertains to the notion of 'ethnic hatreds' or a 'clash of civilisations'. According to the primordialist view, conflicts that in some way involve religion are unsolvable and bound to be an enduring feature of the world. Primordialists see religion as the main (or only) cause of war, and one that will always be a feature of conflict due to the incompatibility of religious traditions and truths. Russell Hardin claims that by using the term 'primordial' to explain how a concept of 'ancient hatreds' can possibly be carried from generation to generation, analysts actually explain nothing, but only label the phenomena. Hardin further makes the valid point that 'nothing that must be socially learned can be primordial' and even the most ardent religious believers agree that true religion must be taught.[24] Such an argument implies that religious identity, for example, cannot be primordial but is learnt in one's own lifetime.

It is no doubt true that primordialist analyses often constitute an 'easy way out' by explaining a certain conflict or actor as being driven by identities, desires and dreams outside of his or her immediate influence. However, that type of analysis fails to achieve any real change, as such a primordialist conflict, be it on a Yugoslavian field, a Central African plain or against a mountain hideout in Afghanistan, can never be resolved. By labelling it primordial it is already past salvage. With this in mind, there is another 'type' of primordialism that has not yet become the focus of much study, but which for the present research is paramount, that is primordialism as genuine belief. Understanding how differences of genuine belief may be a cause of conflict is vital for the transformation of conflicts. Without referring to ethnic hatreds, as such, but rather religious incompatibility, Julie Mertus (1999) for example, does not suggest that something that happened on a Kosovan battlefield in 1389 created the conflict of the 1990s but rather how different truths (and myths of truths) were posited against one another to create a brutal genocidal conflict. In defining primordialism as pertaining to genuine belief, it can be argued that primal distrust is still very much a part of contemporary world politics, and that it has an impact on all three forms of violence, namely direct, structural and cultural. By this reckoning, armed conflict and war are merely another form of ritual and sacrifice.

The second perspective to be highlighted is the newest, and it is increasingly employed by analysts. For simplicity of argument this is referred to as 'constructivism' although that term is somewhat problematic. Constructivist scholars recognise that purely religious wars are a relative rarity and that in any particular conflict there are a number of factors, such as raw materials, economic issues, political power struggles and any number of more or less important issues. Whatever the original cause of the conflict, religion serves as a fuel that sustains, prolongs and often worsens the intensity of the conflict. Indeed, the invocation of religion where other conflictual factors already exist may even make the war much more likely. Scholars generally agree that religious affiliations are often both a complicating and a negative factor in conflicts around the world, although they do not often agree as to why.

Constructivists agree with primordialists that religion is an important factor often adversely affecting peace and security on the international arena. However, constructivists believe that 'because [religious] motives can never be entirely 'pure', we find that material gain is mixed – indeed, perhaps even confused – with religious sentiments'.[25] The difficulty with such a statement is that it is easy to interpret all types of religious violence as necessarily being non-religious, which would be erroneous. Indeed, this would be to 'misunderstand religion and to underestimate its ability to underwrite deadly conflict on its own terms'.[26] It would, of course, be equally erroneous to perceive all the participants (combatants and others) as religiously motivated, as many combatants may be motivated by personal interests, by being forced into conscription or in some other way not agreeing with the aims of the warrior elite.

The constructivist methodology of analysing the role of religion in armed conflict, violence and terrorism takes religious beliefs seriously whilst not disregarding other factors, and – more importantly, perhaps – without overrating the impact of religion on the international arena. As such it is a very sensible position, and closely aligned to this book. However, as will be argued towards the end of this chapter, that is where the similarity stops, as constructivism together with the two other perspectives are essentially different aspects of the same general methodology, namely that of explaining. In addition, it is argued that this tripartite perspective of analysis actually shapes the discourse rather than successfully understanding it, and the reality it portrays. This refers to the commonly paraphrased notion of the 'policy informs discourse'-cycle that first emerged within Political Science in the early 1990s.

As seen above, whilst the primordialist perspective seriously compromises the possibilities of conflict transformation/resolution, the constructivist view is based in an aspiration for the peaceful resolution of conflicts by doing justice to religious views. However, the most prevalent view today, when it comes to the role of religion and conflict, also seriously compromises the likelihood of conflict resolution. This is because instrumentalism, which is the last of the three perspectives to be explored, does not recognise genuine religion as playing even a contributory role and never as a *sui generis* (in its own right) phenomenon, but that religion is always used as an instrument, hence its name.

'Instrumentalism', in other words, pertains to the notion that religion is always used merely as a tool in armed conflict, to mobilise support, justify a particular course of action or offer another dimension to political conflict. As mentioned above, this is by far the most common of perspectives in research and analyses into the role of religion on the international arena in general and in relation to armed conflict in particular, even within modern conflict resolution discourse. Political scientists cannot, by necessity, recognise the validity of religion on the international arena. For those who affiliate themselves with the instrumentalist view, genuine religious wars are a thing of the past, and today 'persons committed to peace as a goal and [who are] informed about the ambiguities of modern international relationship can no longer accept such a view of war. Even when they vigorously wage a particular war, they cannot regard it as a crusade'.[27] Despite this, President George W. Bush did declare a crusade on terrorism in the wake of the attacks on New York and Washington DC on 11 September 2001. Bush, on the other hand, was long previously referred to as a religious bigot, or in any case tolerant towards those who are,[28] although this is certainly a tangent here.

Throughout the history of politics, secular leaders have used religion for political ends. Earlier in this chapter this instrumentalist position was referred to as 'religious politics', although this is only true to an extent. The politics in question may not actually be religious in any discernable form apart from the rhetoric and language employed by policy-makers and observers, which thus makes it a social (and academic) reality. As highlighted in the previous section, since religion can pose a serious threat on the international arena it may thus be a very dangerous instrument. If religions are involved it is just a short step to a clash of civilizations, and ultimately the very survival of humanity is thought to be at stake.

However, as Machiavelli advised his Prince, wherever possible it *is* useful to employ religion for political purposes, or cover a secular agenda in the cloak of religion.[29] This advice, with modifications, has provided a powerful and convenient base for the military in many armed conflicts throughout the world, although war has arguably nothing to do with right, justice, liberty or morality. On the other hand, 'religion is adept as politics in the art of self-justification'[30] and can thus be used to sharpen and justify conflicts.

Whilst many instrumentalist analysts claim that national interests (usually economic) have today driven out any religious or ideological concerns from foreign policy, thus leaving religion with little impact on 'realpolitik', most atrocities around the world are nonetheless still (mis-)attributed to religion, although it is usually admitted that religious issues *per se* are unlikely to cause armed conflict. Religious symbols, language and heritage are, according to instrumentalist observers, often exploited by secular leaders where the cause would not be undisputedly just, benign or good without the backing of the highest good known to humankind, namely religion. It is easy to spot instrumentalist analyses not only due to their salience within academia and political circles, but on a more fundamental note due to the language they employ. The role of religion is often expressed in terms such as exploit, use, abuse and misuse of religion, and most fundamentally, they refer to violent acts committed 'in the name of religion'.

There is a vast difference between committing a terrorist act, for example, for religious reasons and explaining it as being committed 'in the name of religion'. In other words, most academic and political analysts acknowledge violence 'in the name of religion', but rarely religious violence as a *sui generis* concept. This is mainly as a method of making the perceived irrational (religious violence) more rational (secular violence cloaked in religious terminology). This, as seen above, would be to misinterpret the power of religion, and would also be to fail to understand the violent potential of every religion.

Despite its every effort, the academic discipline of International Politics is decidedly conservative in its approach to violence, armed conflict and war, especially when religion or any of its tributaries are mentioned. The three perspectives or methodologies employed to explain the state of the contemporary world, as seen above, are similarly conservative. Of the three, primordialism and instrumentalism are closest in that they see conflicts with a religious element not only as inherently dangerous but also that religion may be 'the most potent – and certainly the least expensive – means of persuasion and justification'[31] in the contemporary world. Constructivism agrees with both to the extent that religion may make a conflict more intractable in that it can focus and magnify conflicts, but ultimately disagrees about the importance of religion since war rarely, if ever, is a purely religious affair. However, constructivism is more closely aligned with primordialism when it comes to taking religious beliefs seriously, which instrumentalism cannot do. Again taking the middle line, therefore, 'constructivists are not uncomfortable with the instrumentalist thesis that most contemporary conflicts are conflicts about power and wealth and not about religion'.[32] Whilst the terms 'primordialism' and 'instrumentalism' are problematic, it is possible to see why they are referred to as they are, the term 'constructivism', on the other hand, does not actually refer to *constructing* the discourse.

The problem with all three of these perspectives is that in their separate ways they aspire to explain the occurrence, reoccurrence and possible solution of violent armed conflicts. Unfortunately they do not contribute much to furthering understanding, and it is not possible to solve a religious conflict (whether primordial, constructivist or instrumentalist) merely by explaining what is perceived to be happening from a standpoint entrenched in its own assumptions. The instrumentalist perspective, for example, sees only one way to peace and that is that 'the flames of religious hatred are to be extinguished by the icy waters of force',[33] while for the primordialist the religious paradox (how a doctrine of love can be used for violence) will continue to bring violence in the world as long as there are different religions. Constructivists are better equipped to deal with issues of conflict transformation, but fail, nonetheless, to understand the subtleties of religious violence. In short, therefore, all three perspectives succeed relatively well in describing, or explaining, the phenomena but all three necessarily fail in providing a satisfactory solution to religious violence and armed conflict. The reason for failing, as argued here, is that these perspectives do not appreciate the causes and origins of the violence, and therefore do not truly understand the conflict. Using inappropriate (or nonexistent) understanding, therefore, frameworks for conflict transformation and resolution are created that in practice solve little. It is the aim of this book to show how a framework for conflict understanding, rather than conflict resolution, may be needed in order to achieve successful conflict transformation.

Notes

[1] G. Murray (1912), p.22 and (1946), p.8.
[2] T.R. Gurr and B. Harff (1994), p.2.
[3] J.L. Esposito (1995), p.33.
[4] J.G. Stoessinger, *Why* (1985), p.116.
[5] Speech by the Archbishop of Canterbury to the House of Lords, Friday 15th October 1999. Available online on http://www.archbishopofcanterbury.org/speeches/991015.html
[6] C. von Clausewitz, (1976), p75 and following refers to eg. p.605.
[7] M. Moodie and C.M. Parry in R.L. Pfaltzgraff Jr. and R.H. Schultz Jr. (n.d.), p.91. The two following quotes are *ibidem*.
[8] J. Dymond (1823), p.9.
[9] J. O'Brien and M. Palmer (1993), p.117.
[10] M. Kaldor and B. Vashee (1999), p.16.
[11] N. Machiavelli (1961), p.14.
[12] C.E.M. Joad (n.d.), p.95.
[13] A. McDermott (1988), p.195.
[14] The German priest Brocardus, in 1332, quoted in B. Lewis (1985), p.1.
[15] R. Hardin (1995), p.142.
[16] B. Hoffman and D. Claridge (1998), p.135.
[17] M. Atwood (1997), p.54.
[18] J.L. Esposito (1995), p.33.
[19] J.G. Stoessinger (1985), p.116.
[20] A. Rapoport (1995), p.62.
[21] Concept borrowed from E. Wyschogrod (1998).
[22] Jomini (1838), p.64. Free translation: Without doubt, religion is sometimes used as a political pretext or a tool, rather than as an issue of religion/dogmas. ... However, religion is not only a pretext it is also a powerful ally, for it serves the double goal of both exciting the ardour of the people and also creates a party.
[23] These terms borrowed from Andreas Hasenclever and Volker Rittberger (2000), although I am not in agreement with Hasenclever and Rittberger in all their conclusions.
[24] R. Hardin (1995), pp.149, 150; Abu Bakr on Islamic rules of war (632), Al-Tabari, I, p. 1850 quoted in B. Lewis (1987), p.212, writes "*Do not kill children! Do not kill children! Every soul is born with a natural disposition [to the true religion] and remains so until their tongue gives them power of expression. Then their parents make Jews or Christians of them.*"
[25] E. Carlton (1990), p.32.
[26] R.S. Appleby (2000), p.30.
[27] J.C. Bennett and H. Seifert (1977), p.88.
[28] N. Gibbs (2000), p.47.
[29] N. Machiavelli (1961), p.120.
[30] K. Cragg (1992), p.270.
[31] E. Carlton (1990), p.193.
[32] A. Hasenclever and V. Rittberger (2000), p.648.
[33] *ibid.* (2000), p.661.

Chapter 3

Correlates: Illustrative of Contemporary Perspectives

This chapter in certain ways marks the turning point as it proceeds from explaining to understanding. It also serves as an 'empirical interlude' in which the commonly accepted notions of religion and international relations receive a practical treatment. In other words, using real-world examples, the previously conceptual analyses are illustrated in order to simplify understanding and to add a practical dimension to the hitherto mostly theoretical and conceptual investigations by suggesting what the *correlates* are of religious armed conflict.

The strategic appraisal of the previous chapter is similar in that it portrays the various roles of religion in armed conflict, whether these are threats, dangers or possibilities. Here these are investigated in more detail, by exploring what types of religious conflict actually exist. In fact, the subject-matter of the present chapter has been the most common approach to the discourse on religion and violence on the international arena and numerous empirical, historical and political volumes (both popular and academic) have been devoted to the issues raised herein. It would, therefore, serve little purpose to try to emulate all this scholarship in one chapter and this is not intended. It is, however, important to ground any theoretical or conceptual investigation in reality. Therefore, the first part of the chapter will scratch the surface of the complex and varied phenomenon of different types of religious violence that are present on three distinct levels in the contemporary international world. The types raised are by no means exhaustive, but will serve merely as a pointer to the variety of religious violence. In the second part of the chapter, five of these types are further sifted out and each is illustrated by actual cases. This is as close to an ideographical investigation as this book comes. In three of the examples ongoing conflicts are used as examples and in the other two, examples from history are provided. Whereas the rationale for each will be explained below, the underlying argument is that religion is defined by its acts, or those of its adherents, rather than in the mere words of theologians, politicians, scholars or journalists. The last part of the chapter will highlight a number of problems and possibilities associated with the role of religion in various 'peace-building' initiatives, and I will raise such issues as religion as a third-party mediator and arbitrator and the concept of religious dialogue (in its three distinct forms) and knowledge dissemination.

Types of Religious Violence

Although the traditionalist approach to religion on the international arena as identified in the previous chapter alluded to many differing types of religious violence, it did not explicitly distinguish between them, nor did it attempt to offer an overview of the great variety of religious violence that exists on many levels in every society. This is the objective here. It is easy to claim, as was done in chapter two, that religion and armed conflict are often interlinked and inseparable. Such a statement, however, does not facilitate the understanding of this relationship, or what can possibly be done to alleviate its often destructive results. This section aims to present the more prevalent of the different ways in which religion unleashes its violent elements in society in general and on the international arena in particular.

Without judging the validity of the various approaches to religion and violence that were highlighted earlier, it can be argued that religion is in some way implicated in many armed conflicts throughout the world, ranging from full-scale ('total') war to so-called low intensity conflict (LIC). Of course, analysts disagree as to the extent of this relationship, whether religion is merely a contributory factor, an essential element or – indeed – neither. Due to the vast number of variables, it is not possible to explore all the varieties of religious violence in the contemporary world. Whilst this is acknowledged in the context of the intention of highlighting the more prevalent types existing on the present scene, it also means that many types are mentioned merely in passing, and most of them far too superficially for adequate interpretations and conclusions to be draw. At the outset, it is important to remember that no judgements are made as to what the causes of the conflicts or types of violence actually are, or if they are justified or legitimised, I merely portray how religious armed conflict is employed in the contemporary world. This means, for example, that here no distinction is made between the three perspectives of analysis explored earlier or whether religion is actually a genuine cause of conflict or not. Instead, the types of conflict are investigated as an aid to understanding how religion and armed conflict are perceived (for better or for worse) in the international system.

In short, religious violence exists on a three-tier division of the world, in any case for the purposes of observation and analysis. In this context, these are the individual level, the group or society level, and the state and international level. There are several types of religious violence that manifest themselves primarily within each of these three general areas or levels. By the process of escalation, however, it is nonetheless possible that a particular factor that may have started as an 'individual' expression of religious violence can be manifested as a societal – or group – issue and on rare occasions it may even become an international matter of concern, as will be illustrated. Certain elements, such as state policy or the actions of large corporations, invariably fall either into the second or the third category depending on situation.

Although the most common form of religious violence usually manifests itself in the individual sphere, it is not usually a potent enough expression to influence the international arena. Despite such violence often being detrimental on a personal level or within families, and as such deserving more attention, this is not my main concern here. However, as an illustration of the wide range of varieties of religious violence and the complexity of the issue, a number of manifestations within this tier should be briefly highlighted. Religion is often believed to be the main source of morals and ethics within most societies, though more clandestinely in some, as was argued previously. In the case of states or legislative bodies, morals and ethics (and thus their sense of right) are codified in rules, duties and laws. These rules can govern every part of life, and if anyone chooses to break one or more of these they are subjected to violence. On the individual level, however, religious violence (or the threat of it) is manifested in areas as wide-ranging as those pertaining to clothing, behaviour, sexuality, marriage, abortion, contraception, circumcision, education and employment, as well as many others.

Of course, whilst an individual faced with these kinds of religious violence may take his or her personal grievances to a higher plane, by methods including homicide, conversion, suicide (and thus often martyrdom) or membership of a subversive or in itself violent group, it is nonetheless primarily the case that religious violence on the individual level remains there. More interesting for the present purposes is where an individual *does* take either his or her grievance or the belief in question to the next level, namely the group – or societal – level. It is on this level that most expressions of religious violence are manifested by various forms of non-state political violence, the most prevalent of which, scholars seem to argue, is 'terrorism'. On this level, religious violence often pertains to issues of persecution (and thus also defence); gender relations and hierarchies that may manifest themselves as militant feminism, for example; immigration-related conflicts, such as segregation, discrimination and education, which also include manifestations of militant or violent nationalism or patriotism; and so forth. But this level also significantly includes areas such as political or ideological self-determination, the right to social benefits such as education, language and health-care, and the sense of righting a historical wrong. Virtually all types of sub- (or supra-) state religious violence finds a manifestation on this, the second, level.

The third level, however, is where manifestations of religious violence generally become most destructive and dangerous. It becomes significantly more dangerous in that legitimation and justification are most easily provided on this level, as the state codifies its religious values in laws that if not obeyed are punishable by penalties encoded in the same legislature. The notion of a 'fair trial', though noble, is inadequately futile in that it perpetuates the very values against which a crime has allegedly been committed. It is impossible for an individual first to be labelled a 'terrorist', for example, and then to be offered a 'fair trial'. On the state-level, and by default therefore on the state-centric international arena, religious violence may express itself in a number of ways, such as in domestic politics, particularly during election-campaigns; where there is a notion of a state-religion (either overtly or clandestinely); in issues of human rights and other so-called international legal instruments; within education, the curricula often indicate these expressions; issues relating to child-soldiers, women and gays in the military and so forth; and possibly most importantly (as I will return to later), the historical legacy.

Whereas manifestations of religious violence happen within the levels, it is where they meet that the most potent expressions are to be found, for example between an individual and the community (levels one and two), or between a state and a separatist group (levels three and two). It is unusual that an individual (level one) clashes with a state (level three) to any great extent, although personification of a cause (Nelson Mandela, the Dalai Lama, Ken Saro Wiwa, Usama bin Laden) or highly publicised events and individuals (Timothy McVeigh, Diane Pretty) may indeed bring an individual religious conflict to the state- or international level. Here, it may often be difficult to see the link to either religion or violence suffice it to say that religion often stands for the most fundamental beliefs of individuals and these may clash (conflict) with the legal view embodied by the state. It is in these 'border-areas' that it is interesting to note that most types of religious violence are manifested where a religious movement is opposed, rather than tolerated, although William Reade (1872) makes an eloquent counter-argument: 'Religion has little power when it works against the stream, but it can give streams a power which they would otherwise not possess, and it can unite their scattered waters into one majestic flood' (p.248). Both arguments are valid, in their own right, and have little impact on the present arguments *per se*, which are concerned with the varieties of religious violence.

Where religious violence differs most from purely secular violence is in the readily available legitimation by religions of any action or reaction, however violent or otherwise unjustifiable. Religion ensures that not all violence can be condemned, and even that it may become an obligation and a duty. This instant duty and legitimation make religious violence different and more dangerous than secular violence. Religious 'terrorism', for example, is – like religious violence in general – ultimately practised according to a belief in the right of the cause, and for the greater good of the community (or, indeed, the world). All 'terrorists', for example, are therefore fundamentally altruists, although in a world dominated by a media-constructed 'terrorism-discourse' this is rarely understood.

Due to the highly subjective nature of this 'terrorism discourse' in news media and fiction, 'terrorism' or sub-state political violence is usually regarded as constituting the largest collection of types of religious violence. It is important to point out that 'terrorism' does not constitute a single form of religious violence, since no definitions or interpretations of religious terrorism could ever be identical. Although 'each religion seems to generate a characteristic form of terror'[1] in respect of ends and means within each religion, this is often also the case within the same 'terrorist' organisation. In respect of the methodology employed, some advocate suicide-attacks, others employ the use of 'sleeper-cells' and again others are in need of an audience (either general or specialised). Further to this, the choice of weapons varies, often depending on what the religion in question prescribes (although other readily-available weapons would be 'safer'), as does the choice of victims, timing and subsequent 'redemption'. This ever-increasing range of variables and groups or individuals acting according to them has led conflict researchers to argue that religious 'terrorism' is the most prevalent form of (non-individual) violence in the world today. Despite such research and statistical reports to the contrary, there are nonetheless scholars who are adamant that religion and terrorism have very little to do with each other, or that it is very unlikely that religious differences *per se* will inspire violence. Rather than being a defence of religion it invariably appears that such arguments are either political exercises aimed at ameliorating already inflamed emotions or based on specious arguments of philosophy: for example, the studies of Peter Sherry (1977) and William Christian (1972), both of whom claim that religions aim to answer different questions and hence do not conflict.[2]

Disregarding philosophical argumentation for a moment, it is possible to ask, with John Hick, 'the straightforward question, "Are there any disagreements of belief between people of different religions?", [and] the answer is quite obviously "Yes"'.[3]

However, although there are disagreements of belief, the goals of most violent religious groups are similar, if not identical, namely the achievement of a better world: one of peace and harmony, of prosperity and security. As indicated earlier, this is why holy warriors, or those who strive for this goal, are not 'terrorists' as that would equate them with criminals, who are not altruists. This dream, or aspiration, for a conflict-free and perfect world is the basic tenet of apocalyptic or millenarian religious groups, for whom peace will inevitably come with the end of time as we now know it. Despite aspiring for peace and non-violence, it is often argued that without the use of violence all such movements are too abstract, futile and therefore ultimately ineffective. Like Chairman Mao, therefore, many movements believe that the only way to abolish war is through war. Indeed, it has been argued that a religion that forbids war and violence 'cannot make its way in the world'.[4] Therefore, as they take to violence they become closer to the divine and the cause is made sacred. As will be further illustrated below, with reference to the Nizaris (as an exemplar of a religious terrorist organisation), violence for such a cause then becomes the most supreme witness to God and the faith. Violent religious groups that are millenarian, apocalyptic or messianic differ from other non-state religious groups in that although both types agree that it is the end that is the ultimate goal, the means to reach that goal is often more important for the latter. This is because most religious groups that take to violence for a particular cause nonetheless need to retain (or create) some kind of political legitimacy or respectability if and when they achieve their goal. A religious government can therefore, for example, not employ *any* means to further its belief, for fear of being isolated or ostracised from the rest of the international community. However much they may loathe the international system they nonetheless need to be on some form of diplomatic or economic terms due to the *modus operandi* of the system itself, where it is not possible to be on the outside for any length of time as the 'rogue states' through history have shown. The same principle applies to non-state groups in relation to the state (and to an extent to other non-state and state entities). Many examples of 'previous' terrorist-groups could be given, although not entirely essential for the argument. This need to restrain the means of when and how violence is employed can be seen clearly, especially in respect of the cases of Sudan and Sri Lanka explored below.

The extent to which the means are restrained or restricted depends to a great degree on what the ends are. 'Terrorist' groups, for example, are often labelled as such merely because their ends are at odds with that of the system in which they operate, and therefore often include groups that are not considered 'terrorists' within another system. The African National Congress (ANC) is often referred to as an example of how a group that at one time were considered 'terrorists' subsequently received political recognition and the label was removed. However, to an extent the means employed by the groups will vary considerably depending on what the main objectives are.[5] In the case of the ANC, for example, great care has been taken to try to separate the political activism of the ANC from its violent and militant wing, the 'Spear of the Nation'. It can therefore be said that due to the levels of legitimacy and popular justification, the methodologies of 'terrorist' cells differ enormously depending on whether the goals of the group are economic;[6] for political recognition, self-determination or separatist/liberation;[7] to right a perceived historical wrong or injustice;[8] to re-establish a historical legacy;[9] to address a societal injustice or persecution;[10] for purely religious reasons, such as preparing for the second coming, or against cosmic enemies;[11] or indeed a range of dubious or more or less clearly defined objectives.[12] However, few – if any – 'terrorist' cells operate within a single sphere of activity, and then often draw upon both religious symbolism and secular rhetoric as and when convenient. In short, it is irrelevant that all of these (and more) objectives can be pursued with genuine religious faith, with religion as an instrument or without religion altogether. Religion may nevertheless be implicated in a variety of objectives, and whereas the means differ, religious rhetoric and language minimise the possibilities of a solution since such language is uncompromising and exclusive. In the same way, it does not really matter if 'terrorism' is defined philosophically, conceptually or using a tacit popular definition, as its effect is phenomenologically the same if we disregard individual characteristics.

Phenomenologically, the objectives and goals of any 'terrorist' group are the same, namely to improve the present situation and create a better society, as was highlighted earlier. Though not necessarily dogmatic, such millenarian, apocalyptic and messianic groups that take to violence – often as a last resort – to achieve a peaceful and harmonious world often employ religious symbols for good reasons. As mentioned, religion can honour just about any cause with legitimation and backing. This possibility is inherent in most religions, but even more so in those that are complete systems of life as they are sufficiently large not only to include genuine elements of violence, as will be investigated in chapter seven, but which can also entail 'loop-holes' that can be used by individuals and groups that may not have the noblest of intentions. The Prophet Muhammad's prohibition of fighting between Muslims, for example, could either be overcome by first denouncing the adversary as being false to the faith, or employing non-Muslim mercenaries or slaves to do the fighting on behalf of Muslim armies.

It is certainly true that although religious language and symbolism provide a solid, and often genuine, basis for violent action, it cannot always be assumed that such violence is genuinely religious, having evolved in a vacuum of outside factors. It is also true, however, that as religious conflict (in language, or 'reality') makes combatants of everyone, as seen previously, individual commitment to the cause is of little – if any – importance. Millenarian groups are experts at identifying portents both from foreign affairs and domestic politics. If proof was needed, which is not normally the case for religious *belief*, external events like wars, natural disasters and manmade catastrophes are invariably seen as portents for the imminent end of the world. Many such apocalyptic groups will thus take to violence to further the arrival of the 'New Time'. Once started as a consequence of tension relating to resources, territory or economics, any conflict can thus receive an 'unexpected' momentum from religious groups anticipating the end of the world. This momentum, often called the 'mechanisms' by war-scholars, over which politicians or military-personnel have little – if any – influence, may push the conflict past the point of no return. Whilst military analysts may refer to this as chance-events, following the Clausewitzian tradition, it is in reality neither chance nor unexpected. Reading between the lines of Clausewitz's great treatise on war, or possibly through the lens of religiously violent groups, Clausewitz himself referred to chance as the 'God of War'. Whilst perhaps reading too much into literary liberty and prose, the parallel is nonetheless striking.

Although not all expressions of religious identity lead to religious conflict, or that communal conflict inevitably pits religion against religion it is arguably true that throughout history religion has made a major contribution towards war and violence. Whilst it is primarily the violent logic that makes this relationship so volatile, it is nonetheless important to recognise that religion does have a significant influence in many peace-making activities throughout the world and showing this is the aim of the very brief exposé at the end of this chapter. Next, however, five brief 'case-studies' will illustrate several of the elements common to the types of religious violence that have been mentioned here.

Examples of Religious Violence

Any ideographical investigation of religious violence inevitably perches precariously on the edge of blatant bias and unconscious misinformation. It is impossible to be entirely neutral in any such discussion. Whilst I have therefore invested a great deal of thought to try to accommodate this fact here, and to avoid falling into this ideographical 'trap' so common amongst researchers, it is important to remember that the five types of religious violence illustrated in the present chapter are exactly that, examples. No political agenda, ideological predisposition or religious cause has been a determinant of the choices made in establishing these illustrations. This does not mean, however, that the choices are random or spontaneous. In fact, the opposite is true. Five distinct types of religious violence are extracted from the more general description in the first part of this chapter, and these illustrations are briefly outlined below.

The first illustration deals with non-state political violence, or 'terrorism'. This is arguably the most common type of religious violence, and today possibly most relevant, but also the concept most fraught with danger. Any choice of a so-called terrorist organisation or group as an illustration of 'religious terrorism' would inevitably betray a particular bias or preference for one cause or another. Even labelling various groups as 'terrorist'-groups for the purpose of illustration makes the same judgements, and will have certain consequences. As previously argued, this is often not acknowledged. Here, however, it is not only acknowledged but a solution to this difficulty has been actively sought. This has meant that the case chosen to 'represent' religious terrorism has been the subject of many hours of scrutiny. In order to benefit from a number of advantages, such as remaining relatively neutral, phenomenologically up-to-date and simple, I am opting to illustrate the concept of 'terrorism' by considering a long-since pacified religious sect, with no political or ideological influence today, namely the Nizaris, active in the Middle Ages. However, doing so faces several disadvantages, such as losing a sense of current relevance (including contemporary issues of capitalism, globalisation, and so forth) and not accommodating the inherently changing nature of the concept. It is believed, however, that by using the Nizaris as an illustration of many elements of contemporary 'terrorism' it becomes nomothetically applicable, although primarily ideographic in form.

Secondly, the concept of 'political religion' is illustrated. Here, the notion of violence due to violent politicised religion on a state-level is exemplified by the contemporary conflict in the Sudan, where *sharia*-law has led to violence, discrimination and persecution on religious grounds. The intention of this example is to show how genuine belief in a state-religion (in this case Islam) can lead to violence if there are other, opposing, ideologies within the state. In the Sudan, the various religious minorities (mostly Christians) have been faced with violence, and in turn resorted to violence, under various regimes during most of the past two decades. Again, I am not making a value-judgement as to the legitimacy either of the policies of the majority-backed regime or the reactions of the minority groups in the country, but merely illustrating how genuine belief in a political religion often leads to violence and armed conflict.

The third illustration picks up on a concept that is superficially similar to the concept of the Sudan, but – as will be highlighted – is vitally different. This is the concept of 'religious politics' where state-politics are inspired, motivated and justified by religious ideals and principles. The religiously motivated political violence of the present civil war in Sri Lanka is taken as an example. Although many of the agendas of this war are largely secular (ranging from self-determination and class to linguistics and education), the conflict is vastly complicated by religious narratives and allegiance (fictional and not) to a particular religious system. In this example, as various regimes have overtly followed extremist Buddhist principles, this is the main rationale for choosing it as an illustration of a type of religious violence.

Fourthly, violence and conflict that is justified by reference to a pre-existing religious identity is illustrated by an incident that started the war in (British) India in 1857, namely the so-called '*Sepoy* Mutiny' in the ranks of the British Army. This mutiny is generally believed to have started the great war of 1857-1858, which underwrites contemporary notions of identity, independence and sense of 'Indian-hood'. My reason for choosing this example, although it is not contemporary today, is primarily due to its clarity. Out of a multitude of possible examples to illustrate this type of religious violence, which in reality is defensive violence (in that it is the pre-existing faith that is being defended against an outside force), the incident relating to the introduction of a new type of ammunition in India almost 150 years ago makes a fascinating illustration.

The final example illustrates how a conflict can be created and perpetuated by the imposition of new external religious values, identities and narratives. Chosen as an example of this is the protracted civil war in Myanmar (Burma). Although one of the fiercest conflicts in the world, with thousands of casualties every year, I argue here that it is nonetheless fought largely due to a recently invented narrative of religious identity. Of course, although it would be ludicrous to suggest that the civil war of Myanmar is based entirely on a fictitious sense of identity, it is nonetheless that particular aspect of the conflict that is extracted, isolated and ultimately offered as an example of how this provides a breeding ground for religious violence.

Whether one believes that the ancient Greeks invented the concept of 'holy war' (*Ieros Polemos*); that there were no 'holy wars' prior to the Prophet Muhammad, since in other religions war was previously an anomaly; or – indeed – one sides with those scholars who contrary to this believe that prior to Jesus no 'holy wars' were fought; it is none the less true that as a practical (rather than theoretical) phenomenon, religion has transformed international relations. No religious tradition can escape its inherent violent element, and the issue is not really whether religion can act either as a violent or as a peacemaking force. Indeed, these aspects of religion are two sides of the same coin on the international arena. As a precursor to the following case studies, however, it must be remembered that for many religionists, the issue is not between non-violence and violence, but between justified and unjustified violence.

The First Terrorists: The Assassins

There is relatively little satisfactory research concerning the 'Assassins'.[13] Although often considered as the first (religious) terrorists, the myths and legends surrounding these fierce and dreaded killers and their legendary leader the 'Old Man of the Mountains' have often obscured their true nature. This is neither the time nor the place to rectify this by re-writing history; all I am seeking is to pull out certain elements that are exemplary of contemporary religious terrorism and political violence. Amongst these are the aims and objectives of the 'Assassins' and the means they employed to achieve those goals, but also what motivated them and how they were perceived in their own time. Further to this, the narratives relating to the 'Assassins' have perpetuated and solidified them as 'terrorists' in the same way as modern narratives create similar frameworks for contemporary groups. By highlighting how they were perceived, and why, it is intended that an understanding of how narratives work on the international arena will further the possibilities for successful conflict transformation. Furthermore, if some of the myths and legends are dispelled, and misinformation clarified, this will be a welcome bonus for a group that have been largely misunderstood for a millennium.

Much of the information that exists about the 'Assassins' is derived from sources that are historically unreliable, or deliberately misleading. Part of the problem, of course, is that these people lived in the remote regions of Central Asia, almost a millennium ago, but more important is the fact that the majority of the observers were Sunni-Muslim scholars, the archenemies of the 'Assassins', who often set out with the calculated intention of discrediting them. When they first became known in Europe in the twelfth and thirteenth centuries C.E. it was in the accounts of returning Crusaders, travellers such as Marco Polo, who had – in turn – picked up morsels and fragments from various arguably unreliable sources in the Middle East and Central Asia. Recently, scholarship and research has begun to show an interest in this fascinating but 'evasive' sect of Islam but since the primary sources are virtually non-existent and the secondary sources are unreliable at best, it is a perilous task. Often the 'Assassins' are mentioned in passing using often misleading references, but rarely as a subject in their own right. There are a few exceptions to this, among which Bernard Lewis' (1985) comprehensive account often occupies the central position as 'authoritative'. Worth mentioning is also Farhad Daftary's (1990) mammoth (both in content and size) piece of scholarship. Neither, however, can be considered as 'recent'.

The 'Assassins' is the name by which this group of Nizari Ismailis (the Nizaris are a sub-branch of the Ismailis, which in turn is a sub-branch of Shi'ism, the second main branch of Islam, next to Sunni) came to be known in Europe by the above-mentioned accounts of returning Crusaders and travellers. Whilst the word is of dubious etymology, and did not exist in any European language prior to these accounts, it has received its present meaning from the methods employed by the followers of this sect. At first, it was the unrelenting loyalty of the 'Assassins' that struck a cord with the romantic Europeans. However, it soon became their religio-political zeal and murderous tactics that drew the attention of Crusaders, politicians and poets alike. By the early fourteenth century, therefore, the name, and associated concept, had entered (to stay) in the vernacular of European poets and writers, such as Dante Alighieri.[14] It is still unclear how the Nizaris came to be known as the 'Assassins' although the most common perspective today, as it was seven hundred years ago (for purposes of disinformation), was that the observers believed that the fanatical zeal and devotion so unique amongst the Nizaris was due to the ingestion of drugs, and in particular hashish. Hence, one etymological root of 'assassin' is believed to stem from various forms of *hashshashin*, or 'drug-takers'.[15] Whereas most information during the last half-millennium has stemmed from deliberate disinformation, ignorance and Western ethnocentrism, most serious contemporary analyses of the Assassins, however, admit that there are numerous possible etymologies of the word and none that has been made convincingly authoritative.

The etymological root of the sect's name as being related to hashish was intentionally derogatory. There is no independent evidence verifying whether or not the 'Assassins' were hashish consumers (*hashishi*), habitual hashish consumers (*hashashash*) or a variety of forms (in both Arabic and Persian). Occasionally, therefore, it has been argued that it was the *actions* of these men that inspired the usage, namely that the term was used as an allegory for a madman, or irresponsible person, rather than the actual etymological root of the word. It is significant, however, that many legends pertaining to the 'Assassins' mention a rather interesting methodology used by the 'Assassins' that involved drugs. Marco Polo, in his somewhat fictional accounts of his travels in Asia, mentions this particular usage, as did many other poets and writers. Whether these accounts were describing the actual practice of the 'Assassins' or a fiction that has been perpetuated through usage is unclear, but largely irrelevant, as will be seen. The particular usage of drugs referred to here relates to the secret 'gardens of paradise'. In the late thirteenth century, Marco Polo relates the story of 'the Old Man of the Mountains', the leader of the Assassins, allegedly recreating the Qur'anic image of paradise in a secret valley in the mountains. This paradise, which in accordance with the paradise of the Qur'an included rivers of wine, milk and honey, luxuries of all kinds, and of course beautiful women 'accomplished in the arts of singing, playing upon all sorts of musical instruments, dancing, and especially those of dalliance and amorous allurement'[16] was not for his own pleasure, but it had a very specific purpose. The young men who were chosen for the greatest of religious duties and privileges, namely martyrdom, were allegedly drugged and in an unconscious state taken to the secret paradise, where they would awake. For a few days, their every desire would be fulfilled, as stated in the Qur'an, before they again would be drugged unconscious and removed from 'paradise'. Back in the material world these men would relate the stories of where they had been, and of what they had experienced, and they would long to go back to 'paradise'. They had little desire to continue to live on earth now that they had been to paradise, which they knew they had seen and experienced, so it was no lie or mere literary fiction. Thus they became ready to sacrifice themselves for the cause, in order that they could return to paradise as heroes, forever. Marco Polo's account, and countless similar others throughout history affirmed the belief that these Assassins were drug users, as no man in his right mind would willingly give up his life for an abstract cause. Even from a pious, God-fearing European perspective it was difficult to see how anyone would sacrifice their own life in such a way unless they were under the influence of drugs.

This particular element of the Nizari heritage is often used as one of the parallels to contemporary groups involved in political violence, and 'terrorism' such as Hamas. 'Mock funerals' and images of paradise for the martyrs-to-be are common within the Hamas, and are often used for 'educational purposes', although today much use is made of video-imaging, rather than drugs. Another parallel sometimes drawn between the Nizaris and contemporary 'terrorism' relates to their leader, the legendary (and somewhat mythical) 'Old Man of the Mountains'. In the days when the Al-Qai'da network retreated into the Afghan mountains under the leadership of Usama bin Laden, during the autumn of 2001, some over-zealous journalists even compared him to Hasan-i-Sabbah, the feared leader of the 'Assassins' in the eleventh century C.E. Such comparisons, however, are superficial, as Usama bin Laden is a Sunni, and Hasan-i-Sabbah a Shi'ite, and so forth. It must also be remembered that not all scholars agree that Hasan-i-Sabbah was the 'Old Man of the Mountains' feared by Crusaders, princes and politicians alike. Some insist that the Crusaders' *vetulus de montanis* ('Old Man of the Mountains') was a later leader of the 'Assassins', namely Rashid al-Din Sinan.

A more fundamental parallel between the Nizaris and contemporary religious terrorists is, of course, their belief in martyrdom, as touched upon above. It is clear that the Nizari 'Assassins' went on their missions with the intention of *not* escaping with their life once the task (the assassination) had been accomplished. The Nizaris may in fact have glorified the pursuit of such a task, and anticipated virtually non-existent chances of survival, as heroic and desirable. Martyrdom is one of the few instances of wilful death that most religions agree on. The main reason why religion throughout the ages (starting with religious history's 'first' martyr Samson; cf. Bible: Judges 16:30) has inspired its confessors to sacrifice their own lives is, as Jon Davis argues, because in order to really become true and valid for many believers, 'religions have to become graphic and to have their noise, taste and smell, their virility, endlessly reinforced by replays, large and small, of their story'.[17] Hence, according to Davis, martyrdom is a fact. Religion is at risk of being over-intellectualised, whereas for believers it is living the faith that matters, and if this 'living' includes dying, then so be it. Martyrdom, as such, is not a rush towards death, but towards *real* life. The deeply held admiration for martyrs within all message-giving religions can be emphasised with regard as much to the Nizaris, as it can for present-day martyrs. There are few things that people are willing to die for that are abstract, so any conceptualisation of religion must also necessarily recognise that it is the acts of the believers, not merely their words, which make religion true and as such constitute 'true witness' to the religion. Whatever the roots of martyrdom, whether it is the need for ritual sacrifice, the re-enactment of a memory of an important figure, such as Jesus, or true realisation of the religion, it is none the less an area that unfortunately is much neglected in scholarly research, and from which many important elements of violent religion can be learned.

Martyrdom suggests that the only witness that is needed for an act is god, where the conviction is on the part of the believer, not of the observer. However, as most modern analysts of 'terrorism' have failed to see the difference between religious 'terrorism' and purely political 'terrorism' they have invariably insisted on the need for an external audience. This is allegedly the 'third party' necessary for 'terrorism' to become what it is. Since the Munich Olympics, the role of media has been much researched and criticised in relation to its coverage of 'terrorism' in that analysts have argued that without the coverage, that is the audience, 'terrorism' would not have a stage to perform its violent acts, and would thus cease. Where there is a religious dimension to the violence, however, the only witness (or audience) to the attack may be god, or fellow believers. Hence, there has been a decline of groups announcing responsibility for 'terrorist' attacks, whereas after purely political attacks often two or three separate groups will announce their involvement, merely to highlight their own plight and cause. This is as yet something that 'terrorism discourse' needs to come to terms with, as seen by seemingly 'throw-away' comments from otherwise thorough research-institutes such as saying that the target audience for the Japanese sect Aum Shinrikyo were 'space aliens'. There is an interesting parallel with the Nizaris, however. The Nizari 'Assassins' had no intention to survive their missions, as seen above. Therefore they deliberately chose to carry out their assassinations at a very close proximity to the victim (although weapons vary in regard to sects and time, daggers, bludgeons and nooses have all been used) and in as public a place and time as possible. This was not only due to the fact that they would be immediately apprehended and killed by the guards of the prominent victim, but it also indicates a further interesting parallel with modern 'terrorism', namely wanting an audience. Furthermore, it was also believed that other groups, not associated with the 'Assassins', *per se*, claimed that they were, in order to instil terror in surrounding people. The audience of the real 'Assassins' were, for these *pseudo*-'Assassins', a vital asset in furthering their own interests. Here, the final parallel to be drawn between the Nizaris and contemporary religious 'terrorists', becomes clear, namely the element of terror.

Whatever definition of 'terrorism' one chooses to employ at any particular point in time, the etymological root of the word still has significance, namely that the act of 'terrorism' is intended to create terror and fear. The Nizaris were far from being the first to assign religious credence to assassinations, or make murder a religious duty. They were neither the first, nor the last to employ their religious duty for political means (namely the creation and sustaining of a political 'state'). However, where they are usually considered to be the first religious 'terrorists' is in 'the planned, systematic and long-term use of terror as a political weapon …[which] was the method that Hasan [-i-Sabbah] chose – the method, it may well be, that he invented'.[18] The 'Assassins' were the most feared sect active in the Middle Ages, and this was what ensured their longevity. This fear created and furthered other legends and stories relating to their ends and means, and of their 'mystical' fortress at Alamut. Many of these myths are still perpetuated by scholars with little interest in historical accuracy. Some commentators of Dante's reference to '*lo perfido assassin*' have taken it to mean 'hired murderer',[19] for example, whilst there is little evidence that they were actually cutthroats for hire, or that their services were for sale. Having said that, other scholars have indicated that some Seljuq princes did indeed make use of them as hired assassins, or even paid protection-money to the 'Assassins'. A further legend, that is likely to be based in fact, and one that has poignant parallels with contemporary 'terrorist' organisations is the cellular structure of the Nizaris. Modern 'terrorism' discourse is reluctantly impressed by the way that most (if not all) terrorist groups are split into several small and independent cells. These cells are often specialised as to tasks or area, and even cells within the same organisation are often completely unaware of where other cells are, and who is a member. This ensures the survivability of the organisation as a whole, and raises the odds for a 'successful' mission. Some cells are so-called 'sleeper cells' whose members are totally integrated in the host-society, and do not practise any form of 'terrorism' until an instruction is received. Whilst it is often believed that this is a relatively new practice, the 'Assassins' perfected this methodology to an art. 'Assassins-to-be' were as children often placed as servants with potential victims, and grew up within the family, earning the trust of the 'notable' person, until instructed to assassinate the victim who therefore did not expect to be attacked by the 'devoted' servant.

The Nizaris provide a fascinating insight into religious martyrology, and religious violence, and deserve a more comprehensive examination, something that unfortunately is impossible in this book. Not only do their means and ends provide many possibilities of comparison with contemporary religious groups involved in political violence, the Nizari 'Assassins' also show two further interesting factors that may be of importance and relevance to conflict transformation. Firstly, this ancient movement, in its different facets, almost succeeded in their attempt to unite the whole population of the Islamic world, irrespective of social status or creed, and secondly that the movement experienced a complete and fundamental change in both means and ends many hundred years ago. Today, therefore, the few remaining 'Assassins' are far removed from violence and 'terrorism'. Their present-day leader, HH Aga Khan VI, is a renowned philanthropist and humanitarian and from his home in Europe he heads the non-denominational and international humanitarian charity and development agency the Aga Khan Foundation, part of the Aga Khan Development Network, and various other worldwide philanthropic and educational organisations within the network.

Political Religion: Holy War in the Sudan

There is considerable debate whether it is 'terrorism' or state-violence that is posing the greatest 'threat to international peace and security', or – indeed – whether the two can be taken as separate phenomena at all. As highlighted above, the label terrorist not only depends on who is doing the labelling, but such labels can – and do – frequently change according to how the world changes. It has largely been accepted within the academy, that the semi-secular liberal Protestantism of the West has shaped 'international' conceptions of right and wrong through the imposition of international laws, documents on human rights, and economic conditions compatible with these values. This is, however, not the general practice of politicians or other activists in the

West. Much violence is thus experienced in connection with this; between the 'west and the rest'. Although such violence frequently employs religious symbols and language, the agendas are ultimately political. The case of the Sudan highlights that genuinely political religion also can lead to violence, despite the religion striving for peace, as highlighted earlier. The Sudan, certainly, illustrates how religion is a force for both good and evil, although here, the particular issue under investigation is the violent side of religion.

The Sudan is the largest country in Africa, bordering nine other countries and the Red Sea, and with almost 600 indigenous groups and some 400 distinct languages spoken it is one of the most ethnically and religiously diverse countries on the continent. Due to this, it comes as no surprise that ethnic and religious conflict has been commonplace in the country, no less since independence from British (-Egyptian) colonial rule in 1956. The third civil war, or rather the third *wave* of fighting, since independence, erupted in 1983 and is along the 'classic' African fault-line of an Islamic/Arabic north and a Christian or pagan south. In this section, I will illustrate the concept of 'political religion' by a brief exposé of this religious conflict.

Since independence there has been a trend of re-Islamisation in the country, as it is believed that Islam was generally neglected during colonial rule. With various levels of success, leaders have tried to establish a pure Islamic republic and implement the *sharia* (Islamic law) as the only law of the land, controlling all aspects of society. As John Esposito argues, Sudan's implementation of the *sharia* was very much a practical process and 'in contrast to Libya and Pakistan, where Islamic punishments were legalized but seldom carried out, amputations for theft became common in the Sudan'.[20] This has left the contemporary Sudan one of the world's three 'ultra-Islamic' states, in league with Iran and Afghanistan, which makes it incompatible (in the eyes of many outside observers) with any other belief-system. The Sudan is made up of two-thirds Muslims (who mainly reside in the north) and the rest Christians, animists and other traditional faiths. The prolonged war has meant that millions of refugees are on the move within the country and this, in turn, has meant that the *sharia*, which in effect can only be practised in the north, now often applies to non-Muslims as well.

Relatively recently, the *al-Ikhwan al-Muslimun* (Muslim Brotherhood), through its more political wing the National Islamic Front (NIF), in the north declared a state of *jihad* in the south which arguably 'transformed the civil war from a mere fratricide into a war between Muslims and non-Muslims'.[21] If a genuine *jihad* is declared, Islamic law insists that it is the duty of every able-bodied Muslim to join in the struggle. As was highlighted with regard to the Nizaris, in the previous section, to die in such a cosmic battle is the highest form of witness to the religion. The incompatibility of divine truths, which will be explored in chapter six, has thus made the polity of the Sudan extremely fragile.

The relationship between politics and religion has been turbulent, at best, during the past two decades in the Sudan. Islam, being a 'comprehensive' religion, stipulates rules and practices for every situation in life and addresses all issues of concern in the world. Therefore, since Islam is divinely revealed, meaning that the scriptures and laws have been given unaltered by *Allah*, there cannot be a difference between the secular and the religious in an Islamic society. It is therefore the vocation of every Muslim to follow and obey *Allah*'s will in every situation encountered in life. In order to successfully apply the inalterable and binding texts of the Qur'an and the *Sunna* (the texts of prophetic guidance) to society, an intricate system of *fiqh* ('jurisprudence') is in force in Islamic society, to give *ijtihad* ('interpretation') of the *sharia*. As the *sharia* is in theory immutable, having been given by *Allah*, the NIF regime in the Sudan had relative success in its efforts of realising the necessity of making Islamic law the main source of national legislature in the 1980s.

One feature of this system, in which the *sharia* is made national law, is that a large part of the Islamic jurisprudence is *shura* ('consultation'), which can be explained as 'the expression of the will of the democratic majority',[22] as the NIF charter states. However, if the state is based on such divine law that stipulates how all aspects of society and politics are to be conducted, 'then democracy must logically be curtailed'[23] and non-religious laws must necessarily conform with the *sharia*. When the Sudan's 286 laws were reviewed in 1977, 38 were found to be inconsistent with Islam and were subsequently altered in order to be consistent with the *sharia*. As the concept of *riba* (charging and paying interest), for example, is forbidden according to the *sharia*, such laws as the Banking Act, the Bills of Exchange Act and the Bankruptcy Act were removed or altered by the reform of 1977. Also necessary in an Islamic state, invariably labelled as 'barbaric' by Western observers and Human Rights activists, are the *hudud* ('punishments') for breaking Islamic laws as these are stipulated in the *sharia*. These include cross-amputation (that is, amputation of right hand and left foot), flogging, stoning, crucifixion, and beheading and they – together with other punishments – are applied to all crimes ranging from petty theft to apostasy, according to strict guidelines.

In the latter half of the 1980s, the south of the country was given relative autonomy under Saddiq el-Mahdi, who was elected president in 1986. Mahdi relaxed the strict imposition of the *sharia* and the country resumed its severed diplomatic and trade relationships with the international community. The provision of autonomy for the south meant in practice that the *sharia*, and thus related punishments, would only apply to Muslims and that Christians and other 'responsible' faiths (that is *al-millal al-kitabiyya* –the Religions of the Book) would be governed by their own laws in their own communities. This relaxation could not by definition be unconditional as the monotheistic religion of Islam only allows one truth, namely the Islamic truth. Christians were therefore to be governed by Islamic law, but not on equal terms with Muslims, where there was an overwhelming majority of Christians, and similar provisions were also in force for the Jews and Sabians. Atheists, animists or those believing in other, that is 'irresponsible' religions (*dhawi al-millal al-mahalliya*), have no status whatsoever in Islamic law and would therefore be governed by the *sharia*. Islam cannot, by definition, conceive of a 'non-religious' citizen. As the civil war continued with renewed intensity, the NIF retook power in 1990 led by Hassan Abdullah al-Turabi (leader of the NIF) and General Omar Hassan Ahmad al-Bashir (leader of the Sudanese military) who later became the executive president in the Sudan. This duo once again enforced the *sharia* throughout the country, with the accompanying withdrawal of diplomatic and economic ties with many countries.

During the 1990s, the civil war forced refugees to mix throughout the country, and the 'relative autonomy' of the south was therefore a notion of the past. Now, the *sharia* applies to all citizens of the Sudan and this has caused the international community to express much 'concern over the violation of human rights caused by the imposition of Islamic law on non-Muslims'.[24] Whilst it is true that the only legally mature person according to the *sharia* is a *compos mentis* Muslim male, Islam is fundamentally a humane, tolerant, flexible and peaceful, albeit competitive religion, but not unconditionally so. The religion offers guidance and support in every aspect of life, not only in the spiritual but also in the social dimension and regulations are in force governing family-, criminal-, contract- and international-law. A secular, and therefore by definition false, alternative such as the contemporary international conception of Human Rights, which is ultimately Western-inspired, must by definition be unacceptable to strict Muslims (so-called 'fundamentalists') following the true path of *Allah*, as laid down in the *sharia*. These points raises many issues, most of which will be explored at some length in the next chapter.

The war in the Sudan is probably still one of the most vicious and costly in Africa and peace is impossible as long as there are conflicting religious truths, as I will explore further in chapter six. The civil war in the Sudan is a good illustration of 'political religion', but it must be remembered that it is merely an example. Countless similar examples can be found throughout the world. 'Political religion', in this case political Islam, is necessarily incompatible with other faiths as religious peace is only possible if one truth 'backs down' and admits defeat. In the Sudan, as in most conflicts all around the world, this seems highly unlikely, though by no means impossible.

'Religious Politics': Sri Lanka's Civil War

It is incontestable that genuine religious belief motivates politics. This is not the same as genuine political religion, as I highlighted in relation to the Sudan. Religious politics, on the other hand, refers to predominantly secular politics that may receive an increased momentum, added justification and solidified mobilisation from religious ideals. Here, I illustrate this by the example of Sri Lanka, where fundamentally secular politics of nationalism and 'ethnicity' have become coloured by religious terminology, symbolism, history and mythology. In turn, a genuine religious conflict is apparent, although it was not entirely religious from the beginning. The civil war in Sri Lanka can thus probably not be referred to as a genuinely 'holy war', like the instances of violence described in the two previous sections, as the rewards of victory and valour are not essentially spiritual. Whereas for some individuals the rewards are no doubt perceived to be in the after-life, in the next life or at least not in the present space-time realm, the main issue of concern here is state-violence, and as such individual perceptions that in effect are acts of 'terrorism' are not investigated in the present exposé of the Sri Lankan case.

Marco Polo allegedly called Sri Lanka ('Zeilan') paradise on earth, the most beautiful country in the world, and throughout history he has not been alone. Visitors and citizens alike have always thought of it as paradise. However, a fierce civil war is tearing the country apart. The last wave of fighting started, as did the Sudanese conflict described previously, in 1983 with renewed fighting between the majority ethno-political group, the Sinhalese, and one of the country's several minorities, the Tamils. In short, the present conflict is a struggle by the Tamils to establish a separate, independent 'homeland' in the northeast of the island. This is the idea of the state of Eelam, pursued mainly by the LTTE (Liberation Tigers of Tamil Eelam, usually referred to as 'the [Tamil] Tigers'). However, as with any conflict, the Sri Lankan conflict is far more complex than that, with history, politics, education and religion being skewed and perverted by all parties and factions involved, to make this particular conflict one of the fiercest in the world today. It would, of course, prove impossible to adequately simplify a narrative of a conflict where more than 100,000 human beings have died, and more than two million people have been forced to leave their homes. This is therefore merely an attempt to provide a brief description of the role of religion in this conflict, as an illustration of 'religious politics'.

Like many before and after him, Mani Dixit, India's former High Commissioner to Sri Lanka, argues that the roots of the present conflict in Sri Lanka lie in British colonial rule. Throughout the empire, policies of *divide et impera* ('divide and rule') were implemented, which in Sri Lanka left the Sinhalese majority feeling 'discriminated against and unfairly treated',[25] as the Tamil minority were granted far more privileges by the British colonial administration. Whilst Sri Lanka (or Ceylon as it was known until 1972) was thought of as the model colony, and even initially provided the only example of peaceful and orderly transfer of power, the prejudices and antagonisms that had been cultivated during British rule turned Sri Lanka into an exemplar of ethno-religious conflict.

In newly independent Sri Lanka, the Sinhalese re-took control of the power-structure and in matters of politics, as emphasised in the election-campaigns, 'Tamils came under increasing pressure to pay the price of their past role in the colonial power structure'.[26] Issues of religion and ethnicity, therefore, became of utmost importance in the first half of the 1950s and culminated in the general election of 1956, in which S.W.R.D. Bandaranaike was elected Prime Minister. The events surrounding Bandaranaike's politics are generally believed to be the start of the civil war in Sri Lanka, as he was an unscrupulous demagogue. Sri Lankan nationalism that, understandably, had been the focal point of Sri Lankan politics after independence took a drastic turn for the worse under Bandaranaike who abandoned nationalistic pluralism in favour of a highly divisive 'Sinhala Only' policy.

A factor that greatly affected the divisive ethnic policies under Bandaranaike, and also under subsequent governments, is the Sinhalese sense that their ethnic identity is closely inter-linked with the dominant religion in the country, Buddhism. So much so, in fact, that Bandaranaike abandoned Christianity in preference for Buddhism as he entered politics, for both legal and historical reasons. Whilst the *Mahavamsa*-chronicles, written around the sixth century C.E., first established that the Buddhist nature of the Sinhala nation and the Sinhalese people stemmed from the third century B.C.E., it was arguably the Portuguese import of Roman Catholicism in the 16th century C.E. which brought religious zealotry and intolerance to the country. Some analysts and historians even argue that in the present conflict religion is one of the most important factors. In this context it is important to note, however, that such arguments do not refer to Buddhism as a peaceful 'teaching', but as a political force 'espoused by Sri Lankans of the late nineteenth and the twentieth centuries, [which] has contributed to the current ethnic conflict and collective violence in Sri Lanka'.[27] That is to say, Buddhism is used to provide justification for political agendas and the conflict is arguably not a 'proper' religious conflict as 'it [religion] does not define the divisions between the people in the current conflict'.[28] However, there is a religious element in the conflict that cannot be ignored, both in the perceived and in the factual dimension. In fact, most analysts admit that a religious conflict *does* exist in Sri Lanka that predates the present ethnic conflict.

There has been a trend among foreign observers (both academic and journalistic) to 'create' a 'proper' religious war by using arguments such as 'Sinhala Buddhist' versus 'Tamil Hindus'. Whilst this certainly applies in the majority of cases, the distinction is not quite that simple, and although the figures from the 1981 census seem rather ambiguous the trend at least is quite clear. With that in mind, it must also be made clear that in the run-up to the general election of 1956 religion and ethnicity were the most contentious issues, and subsequently won Bandaranaike the position as Sri Lanka's fourth Prime Minister. The Sri Lanka Freedom Party (SLFP), led by Bandaranaike, converted Sri Lanka into a Sinhalese Buddhist state. This not only meant that national symbols such as the flag and national anthem changed, but also that Sinhala was made the only official language and that the Tamils, in effect, lost all civil and political rights. Bandaranaike's 'Sinhala Only' policy was implemented in all aspects of society, and turned Sri Lanka from a peaceful multi-ethnic, multi-religious and multi-lingual society into a violent and antagonistic state. Religion (that is, Buddhism) was very much on the political agenda, or – rather – the political agendas were sharpened by religion, and many politically active monks and clergy ran religio-political organisations and parties, and in many cases dictated policies to the government. Whilst it is quite clear that Bandaranaike was not a Buddhist monk himself, as is sometimes claimed, he was ironically enough assassinated by one in 1959. The Buddhist monk who carried out the assassination was supported by one of the most influential Buddhist political organisations in the country at the time (the *Eksath Bikkhu Paramuna* – EBP) allegedly because Bandaranaike 'had not moved Sri Lanka far enough towards becoming a sufficiently assertive Buddhist State and society'.[29] As a result of this perversion of Buddhist principles, public support for 'religious politics' dropped drastically, and monks were thus not very politically active in the election of 1960. However, in line with another Buddhist teaching, the seed of religious antagonism was nonetheless already sown.

Throughout the history of Sri Lanka, from the *Mahavamsa* and the *Chulavansa* to the present day, Buddhism has had a strong link with Sinhala nationalism. Today a large number of Buddhist organisations and movements are active in the country to 'protect' and 'foster' the religion. Ranging from a number of Buddhist political parties and a strong lobbying-body to university unions and grass-root councils, the link between Buddhism as a 'religion' and the Sinhala ethnic identity has made such terms as 'religio-nationalism' apt in describing the country. It is observed by certain scholars that the Buddhist *religious* identity was in fact blending and becoming one with the Sinhala *ethnic* identity already in the third century B.C.E., as mentioned above. Such arguments are usually presented when it is necessary to justify the continuation of the ethnic conflict according to a narrative of 'ancient hatred'. In Sri Lanka, the Buddhist lobby is arguing that since the beginning of time in the country (remarkably, excluding the aboriginal Veddha-people[30]), after the Sinhalese race first established the island as a Sinhalese nation, history shows the Sinhalese as 'waging war against the Damilas

[Tamils] to restore Buddhism to its proper position'.[31] The extremist left-wing nationalist group *Janatha Vimukti Peramuna* (JVP) therefore used religious politics to bring about a change in society, as Buddhism and the Sinhalese ethnicity 'could not flourish without a sovereign territory, which was the motherland of Sri Lanka',[32] according to JVP radical monks. Such arguments of the late 1980s implied that, although independent, the country was not properly sovereign until it was a homogenous Sinhala Buddhist state.

The role of religious narratives in the Sri Lankan conflict is very important, and they have been used, re-used, abused and misused on countless occasions, probably since the times of the *Mahavamsa* and even earlier, to achieve political goals or strengthen political agendas. High Commissioner Dixit recollects an incident at his official residence in Colombo in June 1987, in which a Buddhist monk 'produced an enlarged photograph of a Buddhist monk immolating himself in fire in Saigon in the late sixties or early seventies'[33] and threatened similar – or worse – violence if India did not reconsider its policies on Sri Lanka. Whilst entirely against Buddhist principles, especially for clergy, 'religious politics' was a potent reminder of the coalescence of religion and ethnicity in Sri Lanka. Another incident, which for some weeks saturated the local (Sinhala and Colombo based) English newspapers in the very early 1990s was the apparent massacre, by the LTTE, of hundreds of civilians in jungle-villages in the northeast of the country. Allegedly, buses were ambushed, and all passengers except Sinhala Buddhists were let go. The Buddhists were subsequently killed and left to burn along the road as a warning, or a statement. Ethnicity, in this case, was not an issue, since those Sinhalese who were Muslims, Christians or Hindus were spared. The Tigers allegedly killed Buddhist monks and destroyed temples and other Buddhist pilgrimage-sites. The government, JVP and other politically active groups were able to use such ancient Buddhist concepts as *mlecca* (lit. 'savage') to justify 'revenge' and violence towards 'those committing heinous crimes against Buddhism'[34] and this usually sanctifies violence and hatred in the most peaceful of minds.

Sri Lanka, as explained, has seen religion being used in the most 'unorthodox' way to sanctify ethnic conflict in the country. Religious politics have been commonplace during the last half-century, to incite or justify violence, to sanctify a cause or to rally support, but it should be noted that the religious politics explained so far, in the Sri Lanka case, are severely affected by bias. That is, religious politics are, by the nature of the conflict, only 'successfully' practised by the Sinhalese. The Tamil ethnic identity does not have a similar affiliation to a specific religion as the Sinhalese do to Buddhism, although a bare majority of Sri Lanka Tamils are Hindu, many are also Christian or Muslim. In creating a Tamil homeland, other ethnic characteristics, such as race, tradition and language have played a far greater role. Whilst the propaganda-apparatus for the Tamil Eelam homeland, the *Tamil Nation*, is more overtly bias than governmental organs, it provides something of a balance to the Buddhist 'fundamentalism' described above. The *Tamil Nation* writes that 'there is no religious conflict between the Hindus and the Buddhists. Sinhala Buddhists are making fiery attempts … to portray the national liberation struggle of the Tamils as a mere religious conflict'[35] and continues by arguing that the religious politics of Sri Lanka are mere exercises for 'pretending that Buddhists and Buddhism are being attacked by Hindu Tamils'[36] and as such justify violence.

The above, albeit brief, use of the current conflict in Sri Lanka as a practical illustration of 'religious politics' has contributed to show how the previously theoretical concepts can be applied in practice. As a conclusion to the Sri Lankan conflict it is possible to argue that as long as religious narratives are used to justify violence, the very existence of violence is inevitable, as seen by President Chandrika Kumaratunge's failed attempt in 1995 at devolution of the Tamil 'controlled' parts of the island. For the Tigers only complete independence is sufficient, and for the Sinhalese Buddhist lobby no compromising provisions whatsoever are permissible. Of course, in Kumaratunge's case, her heritage also works against her, as she is the daughter of S.W.R.D. Bandaranaike, and has continued to implement many of her father's doctrines and policies. Though the peace-process was looking hopeful at the end of 2002, events during 2003 show that the struggle in Sri Lanka is far from over.

Pre-existing Religious Narratives: The *Sepoy* Mutiny in British India

It is sometimes argued that there is no present, or future, without a past in issues pertaining to identity. This is certainly true in the case highlighted next. Religion is well known for being able to incite people, mobilise them and prepare them to fight, to the end if necessary. If people are to rebel against the law, society and rank, with the only individual reward being death, they prefer to die for a cause. Religion provides such instant justification. In the following illustration, elements both of genuine religious belief and of religion being employed as a political tool can be discerned in relation to the Indian sub-continent. Here, it is an insurgent group that arguably brings about the fall of the dominant system that is investigated. Although not 'terrorism', *per se*, the actions of this particular sub-state group (the *sepoys*) can be thought of in terms of being rebellious, mutinous, revolutionary and ultimately threatening and terrorising, like other similar groups, whether termed 'terrorism' or not.

In the mid-nineteenth century there was much cause for grievance, unrest and antagonism in the ranks of the native soldiers of the British Empire in India. Although the *sepoys* (native infantry-men) were the focus of most of the cruel and degrading actions by British (and other European) officers, I will merely pick up on one particular point in order to illustrate how a pre-existing religious narrative can be used as a justification for violent conflict. Whilst the method of isolating an incident, and in effect taking it out of context, might be criticised, I am not attempting to provide any kind of explanation for either the historic sequence of events, their implications or even the truthfulness of the narrative. By choosing one out of the multitudes of tributary events, which interlinked to finally change the reign from 'the Company'[37] to the British Crown (and ultimately bring the 'Raj' to independence), it is my intention to provide a representative illustration of how a pre-existing ethno-religious identity can be 're-created' and thus further justified. The event chosen, therefore, is described by many historians to be the least trivial, and actually the single most important in the war in 1857, namely the so-called 'cartridge incident'.

To understand the importance and significance of this incident, it is important to have a little knowledge about the weapons used in British India during the 19th century. Until the 1850s, the army had, on the whole, been using standard smoothbore muskets, the so-called 'Brown Bess'. The officers mainly used rifles, because despite them being slower to load (this was usually done by a servant in any case), they were far more accurate over long distances. A new rifle with a three-groove bore was, however, under development by James P. Lee, at the Enfield arsenal in England, which would replace both the old two-groove rifles (used mainly by officers) *and* the standard musket, as it would be fast to load and shoot accurately, even at a long distance. The new weapon was loaded differently from the earlier rifle, where a charge of gunpowder was first rammed down the muzzle followed by a bullet (which was wrapped in greasy cloth to assist in the smooth loading). The new .303 calibre Lee-Enfield rifle, as it came to be known, made loading easier by combining both powder-charge and bullet in a single cartridge. This cartridge was composed of paper which, for both preservative and lubrication purposes, was heavily greased. During testing in 1853, tallow was found to last longer as a lubricant than the previously used mixture of vegetable oil and wax. To load the rifle, the end of the cartridge had to be torn off, and as James Farrell's fictional character Captain Hudson explains: 'in army drill we teach the men to do this with their teeth'.[38] The *sepoys* felt defiled and degraded by this because if the tallow was made up of beef-fat it would mean that the Hindus lost their caste and if it contained pork-lard, it would similarly be *haram* (or a religious sin) for the Muslim *sepoys*, if it touched their lips.

The truth of the contents of the tallow was never resolved, and is still under much debate by historians. It is, however, true that several of the British officers did understand the problem and ordered the contractors in Calcutta, who were making the cartridges under licence from Enfield, to use mutton or goat-fat in preparing the tallow. However, there are also reports that the Enfield trial cartridges were, in fact, greased with beef- and pork-tallow, and since it was the cheapest tallow available in India at the time, it is not improbable that such fat was used. In either case, this section is not concerned, as stated above, with the 'truth' of the matter but rather with what ethno-religious narrative was invented as a result.

Several historians refer to a specific incident in relation to the above cartridges, which allegedly occurred at the end of January 1857 and ignited the 'Great *Sepoy* War'. A low-caste untouchable *khalassi* (a camp-follower, usually a tent-pitcher or a labourer) asked a high-caste Brahmin *sepoy* for a drink of water from the latter's *lotah* (water-pot). According to Hindu faith, the *sepoy* naturally refused, as this would defile his *lotah* and thus degrade the Brahmin caste. The *khalassi* is then alleged to have said: 'You will soon lose your caste altogether'[39] as before long the Europeans will make *sepoys* 'bite cartridges covered with the fat of pigs and cows',[40] which would mean complete loss of caste for the Brahmin. Historians argue that news of this incident – whether fictional or not – quickly spread through the ranks of the native *sepoy* regiments and, in effect, started the 'mutiny', in early May 1857.

Although it was 'proved' by the British that the new cartridges had not been made using any (potentially) defiling substances, the whole issue of the cartridges became the very symbol of the struggle against the Company. The *sepoys* used their religion (Hinduism and Islam) to justify their refusal to touch the cartridges. As a particular issue was needed to focus the *sepoy* grievances towards the British, the 'cartridge-incident' was invented around the pre-existing religious identity, to justify going to armed action against an enemy that would otherwise be 'out of bounds'. From being a class struggle, between the native 'barbarians' and the 'civilised' Europeans, the struggle was swung around, using this created imagery into an ethno-religious struggle of truly cosmic characteristics. It could be argued that the whole issue of the cartridges was relatively unimportant had it been merely an issue of the technicality of ammunition making. Such a perspective is strengthened by accounts of those present at the time. Colonel Carmichael-Smyth is quoted as saying that none of the *sepoys* gave any reason for refusing to take the cartridges other than saying 'that they would get a bad name'.[41] The relative unimportance of the actual issue is further exemplified in other accounts where the *sepoys* allegedly were willing to concede that 'if all the regiment[s] will take [the] cartridges I will'.[42] Out of the 90 men whom Colonel Carmichael-Smyth ordered to take the cartridges (during a parade) five men (allegedly two Hindus and three Muslims) actually accepted the order and took the cartridges.

As the religious differences (as they had become) escalated, the war finally broke out in the early months of 1857. In British accounts it is often referred to as the '*Sepoy* Mutiny',[43] whilst other sources (Karl Marx notably being one) refer to the war as 'the first War of Indian Independence', or the 'Great *Sepoy* Rebellion'. Illustrating arguments that the 'cartridge issue' was merely created out of an ethnic identity, which was itself thereby further justified, Lieutenant Hugh Gough (at the time, later General Sir Hugh Gough) of the 3rd Light Cavalry recorded that as the situation got worse and broke out into armed conflict the *sepoys* 'helped themselves to the ammunition – regardless of its being the "unclean cartridges"'.[44] Further to Hugh Gough's account, however, the insurgency was nonetheless of ethno-religious character as illustrated by the placards that were raised across India at the time, 'calling upon all true Mussulmans [Muslims] to rise and slaughter the English'.[45]

The issue of 'unclean' or 'defiling' cartridges thus epitomised a threat to the religious identity of the *sepoys* (and later the *sowars* – cavalrymen – and also civilians) and focused the struggle into one of religion and identity rather than class and rank. Whatever the 'truth' of the story in reality, it was the 'imagined threat to their religion that caused so many Hindu and Mahommedan sepoys to break out into revolt'.[46] It has furthermore been argued that the war that thus started by conflicting narratives about ammunition almost a century and a half ago has been revived and re-interpreted to justify the contemporary ethno-religious identity of the Indian people. Whilst British historians (with a few notable exceptions) often describe the whole incident as 'a mistake, based on the superstitions of ignorant people',[47] Indian historians often refer to it as proving the heroism of the *sepoys* in starting the struggle against European imperialism. Despite this, there are nonetheless also Indian accounts of the incident as being invented. A native officer, Subedar Sita Ram, recollects that he refused to believe the alleged truth of the story, as it was too extraordinary and believed it to be 'a story invented to inflame the minds of the people',[48] which further strengthens the argument that the incident was largely invented to achieve a particular goal. The 'cartridge incident' has, to some extent, become a landmark in the justification of Indian ethnic identity, and therefore an important narrative when justifying contemporary ethnic conflicts in the Indian sub-continent, and therefore also an apt example for this book.

Imposed Religious Narratives: The Conflict of the Karens in Myanmar

It can be argued that, especially in conflict situations, the relationship between identity, legitimacy and religion becomes increasingly important. However, although religious identity commands believers to fight and die for the Truth, such an identity is not necessarily an example of 'ancient hatred'. During the Cold War, the world became used to the concept of 'proxy wars' in which the superpowers did not confront each other directly, but through their satellite- (or proxy-) states. This practice, however, has long been pursued in the 'name of religion', although not always with the same explicit conscious rationale. Religious missions, and proselytising, have throughout history often inadvertently brought violence and suffering to every corner of the world. In some cases, the violence has been offensive, where the 'new' subjects are given the relatively simple choice to convert or die, and in other contexts it has been purely defensive, protecting the existing believers and faith from the outside force threatening their survival. On occasions, the new religion has been adopted with such fervour that it generates its own violence. Such is the case for the Karen ethnic community in Myanmar, which was introduced to Christianity – and wholeheartedly adopted it – less than two centuries ago. In Myanmar, this new religious identity has led to one of the bloodiest civil wars in modern history, and it is included as an illustration here, to show that when religious narratives are employed, compromise – and thus conflict resolution – is near impossible. The religious identity of the Karens that was imposed (often forcibly) by outside powers, with hidden agendas, less than two centuries ago have proved to be a virtually insoluble situation today.

Before proceeding to outline briefly the next case study, it is important that a linguistic note of clarification is included as to prevent misunderstanding. This note concerns the name of the people and place under investigation. The country in question will be referred to as Myanmar. This is the native name for the country and probably derives from a 'corruption' of *myo-ma* (roughly translated as land of the 'people' or 'race'), which is a far more likely explanation than that *Myan-ma* is the written form of *Bam-ma*, meaning *Brahma* or god according to the narrative of the national etymology. The name could also derive from the Chinese name for Myanmar, namely *Mien* meaning roughly the same as *myo* (people/race). Officially, Myanmar reverted to the traditional name from the English word 'Burma' (derived from the name of the dominant ethnic group, the Burman) on 19 June 1989. The second consideration to be remembered is that there is considerable confusion in the literature regarding the use of the terms 'Burman' and 'Burmese'. In English, most writers have used 'Burmese' to refer to all citizens of the country regardless of ethnic affiliation, and 'Burman' to refer to the largest, and dominant, ethnic group. Other writers have done the opposite using the terms interchangeably in the anticipation that the text determines which of the concepts is meant. Here, however, the perceivably more 'proper' usage is employed: 'Burman' will refer to the dominant ethnic group and 'Burmese' to all citizens of the country that will be referred to as Myanmar, since 'Burma' in effect excludes non-Burmans, except when reasons of history requires the name '(British) Burma' to be used. It is hoped that the distinction will be clear from the context.

The war now raging in Myanmar is one of the worst in the contemporary world and has been ongoing non-stop since 1947 (and possibly even before then). As an illustration of how religious narratives are used to justify armed conflict, it is impossible to deal with the whole Myanmar case, as at least 35 warring factions have been identified. Therefore, the 'main' conflict is chosen as an illustration here, and will be 'isolated' from the overall context of the war in Myanmar. As with the *sepoy* incident, this is a dangerous methodology if it claims to provide a description of the entire conflict. However, as in the previous section, this is not my intention but rather to illustrate how an externally imposed religious identity is used in justifying conflict. The chosen issue is the conflict between the government, which is predominantly Burman in ethnicity, against the largest of the minority ethnic groups, the Karens.

Myanmar Naingngandaw, or the Union of Myanmar, as the country is officially known, is in fact a federation of seven states and seven divisions – or provinces – in which more than 70 ethnic groups compete for land and resources in an area the size of the UK. The majority group, the Burmans, were made dominant at the end of British colonial rule, in the late 1940s. With more than one million 'members', the Karen form the second largest ethnic group in the country.

Myanmar was not a unified entity before the British conquered the land, and like most Asian civilisations it was not based on the Western Westphalian system of states, but rather a 'feudal'-like system of kingdoms. In three Anglo-Burmese wars the British gradually conquered the region beginning with the Karens in the south in 1826. Throughout the rest of the British conquests in the region, the Karen provided loyal co-operation and support, and the British 'successfully' completed the process by conquering the kingdom of Ava in the north in 1886.

Because of the 'privilege' of being the first group in the region to be colonised, the Karens subsequently enjoyed highly developed education, political, economic and social systems. Not only were such developments part of the British colonial administration's policies, but the American Baptist Mission, established by Judson in 1813, also created a very 'Western' education-system, and in the capital a university was set up for 'the Higher Education of the Karens'.[49] Due to this and other reasons, the Karens became the most advanced group in the region on all levels, ranging from education and politics to economics and military, where it is believed that more than "two-thirds of the British Military in Burma were made up of Karens'.[50] In the case of British Burma, therefore, Donald Horowitz's system of classification would make the Karens the 'advanced ethnic group', whilst the Burmans could definitely be seen as the 'backward ethnic group'.[51] Despite all this the Burmans were made the dominant group on independence, but more as a matter of locality, however, as the city of Rangoon (Yangon) was on Burman territory. This city was made the capital of British Burma due to its strategic location and its harbour potential.

Throughout British rule the Karens were loyal to the British and even provided a regiment, known as the 'Burma Rifles', which helped quench insurgencies and wars throughout the empire. In the Second World War, the Karens fought alongside the British against the Japanese, whilst the Burmans, for example, fought with the Japanese against the British. The reward for the Karens by the British for this unceasing loyalty was set to be autonomy and separate independence for the Karen state. They did attain a substantial level of autonomy but ultimately they 'suffered horribly for their loyalty'[52] and felt betrayed by the British as the Union of Burma became independent in 1948, without any provisions for the Karens, leading to the complete loss of their autonomy.

Whilst theoretically achieving some political separatism in 1951, as a Karen State (within the Union of Myanmar), this meant little change in practice.

The essence of the above brief exposé is that arguably the very reason for the present war, the Karen identity, was very hard – if at all possible – to define prior to the British arrival. At the time of the first wave of British conquest of Myanmar, the Karens had themselves not long been conquered by the Burmans. However, whilst the process of assimilating the Karens into Burmans had begun, it was in its early stages, and far from complete. The British colonial administration exploited this and, according to some scholars, did in fact create a previously non-existent Karen identity. With the use of the American (and other) missionaries, this was done in a bid to prevent Burmans from becoming powerful enough to threaten British rule, exactly the same methodology as pursued with regard to the Sinhalese in the earlier illustration.

The Karens, celebrating the (then in practice non-existent) Karen State in December 1917 (and again in September 1945), referred to the British both as their 'guardian angels' and 'liberators' who protected them from the Burmans and 'pleaded for the continuance of British control'.[53] Using their newly created identity, they rose to the cause of separatism and the struggle for independence. It can easily be argued that the war in Myanmar is fought on the basis of religious identity. However, if an identity such as the Karen's is – in fact – invented to serve the interest of another pre-existing identity, that of the British in this case, the question arises as to whether the war can be truly justified on religious or ethnic grounds. As illustrated here, it is possible to wage a fierce war, like the one in Myanmar, killing more than 2,000 people every year, based on the notion of a religious identity created a mere 150 years ago, *ex nihilo*. Some historians argue that it was, in fact, the introduction of Christianity that became the 'unifying element' behind the Karens and 'they associated their new religion [Christianity] with a powerful sense of ethnic identity'[54] which had – to a large extent – been non-existent until then. Though they kept some traditional aspects of their spirituality (such as natural animism, ancestral *lae*, etc.) Christianity, being monolithic, insisted on certain elements, including monotheism, scripture and (allegedly) pacifism. However, when Burmese Buddhist monks joined the fighting against the British forces, during the third 'Anglo-Burmese War' in 1885-1886, there are accounts of the Karens 'turning their pacification into religious and ethnic warfare'.[55] Arguably, still fresh in memory were the earlier Burman attempts to convert the Karens to Buddhism and they would thus go to any lengths to protect their new religious identity. An American Baptist missionary, reported at the time that the Karens had never before been so anxious to fight, and that 'this is ... welding the Karens into a nation'. Of course, he might not be the best of analysts as he belonged to the 'old school' of missionaries: 'The whole thing is doing good for the Karen. This will put virility into our Christianity'.[56]

One of the problems faced by the new Karen ethnic identity, created out of British administrative interests and American proselytising, was not only that it was new to the scene, it was also created using Western or Euro-American moulds of identity. With respect to the present illustration, therefore, the narrative used to create the Karen identity was incompatible with the surrounding narratives to such an extent that conflict was inevitable. In the West any one person can arguably only belong to one ethnic identity. One is either one or the other; a combination is neither 'proper' nor even possible. Outside the West one finds that it is indeed possible to belong to two, or even several, ethnic identities simultaneously. It is even possible to switch between identities, or 'manipulate' them, to match the occasion or desire. The Karens, though in the process of being converted to Buddhism in the late eighteenth and early nineteenth centuries, would probably have retained such traditional beliefs as *bgha* (ancestral spirit), *lae* (personal spirit) and *Y'wa* (natural animism), as did the Mongols. However, with the introduction of Christianity, with its missions and schools, the 'heathen' Karens were converted into pious Christians. With this, traditional beliefs and faiths were largely suppressed, and the otherwise present 'mixture' of ethnic identities was prohibited. It can therefore be argued that the narratives created concerning the ethnic identity of the Karens were largely responsible for forming the basis of an inevitable conflict, which could possibly have been avoided had such narratives not existed. Where religious identities – and narratives thereof – are not really an issue, foreign import of ethnic bias might actually be a source of tension and conflict.

Types of Peaceful Religion

Religion is, of course, not always or even necessarily a violent force in international politics. Indeed, an important aspect of religion and conflict is where religion is a peace-making, rather than a war-mongering, force. There is not only a tendency in academia and popular discourse to focus on the prominence of conflict or war in the history and present of religions, there is also an epistemological imbalance in studies pertaining to these issues as a result. Although comparatively few books are written on the subject of religion and war, even fewer are written on the subject on religion and peace. It must be remembered that although this study pertains to the logic of religious violence and not religious peace, thus focusing on the violent elements inherent in religion, there are similarly peaceful elements within every religion. Indeed, every religion strives for ultimate and absolute peace. To illustrate the ambivalence of religion and violence, but also for balance of argument I highlight certain aspects of non-violent religious belief on the international arena, without elaborating further on these here.

Religious dialogue, in respect of conflict situations, can be sub-divided into three main types, namely intra-religious, inter-religious and religious-secular dialogue. The first usually refers to dialogue within a particular religious tradition, between liberals and conservatives, fundamentalists and modernists, and so forth. The second type of dialogue is between two or more religious traditions, usually on different levels, such as between schools, communities or religious leadership. The last type of religious dialogue is usually neglected in contemporary discourse relating to dialogue, and this is dialogue between religion and secularity. This type is also apparent on various levels, ranging from individual to governments or political leadership.

Recently, as more and more analyses have been concerned with the relationship between religion and armed conflict, so too scholars have begun to investigate the peaceful activities in which religion has an influence. As with most academic disciplines, there will always be elements that are contrary to the majority belief, and that is where research of religion as a tool of peace has been located. Two relatively recent works highlight this ambivalent nature of religion and war on the one hand and religion and peace on the other; namely R. Scott Appleby's aptly titled *The Ambivalence of the Sacred* (2000) and Mark Gopin's *Between Eden and Armageddon* (2000). Both of these, and a few other contemporary academics, highlight a range of peace-making activities that are influenced by religion, including 'preventive diplomacy, education and training, election monitoring, conflict mediation, non-violent protest and advocacy for structural reform, and withdrawing or providing moral legitimacy for a government in times of crises'.[57] These examples offer an insight into how a religious body can act where there is no opposing religious body on the scene. Where that is the case, dialogue might be necessary. Dialogue is, however, a problematic concept within many religious systems. The very concept of dialogue may itself prove a major concession for a religion, and sometimes a concession not worth agreeing to if deemed to jeopardise the integrity of the faith itself. This is due to the ontological basis that in order to have dialogue there must be 'an Other' to have such dialogue with, and by agreeing to dialogue, therefore, one has not only already conceded that the Other exists but that it is a legitimate and moral counterpart to oneself. Inter-faith dialogue is, according to such religious arguments, 'a foreign, evil and Western idea that has no basis in Islam',[58] for example, though Islam is by no means unique in such a belief. Of course, as noted above, religion is only a useful tool for mobilisation where the religion is opposed to another (religious) system, or else it would be a futile and ineffective tool for rallying support. In the same way, the times where religious dialogue would be of most use is where the religious system is opposed to another, or dialogue would be futile. This is where religious dialogue today faces its biggest problem.

This fundamental problem is also related to the nature of knowledge and is summed up by Stanley Samartha when he claims that 'If all religions are "true", dialogue is hardly necessary. If only one religion is "true", dialogue is impossible'.[59] Religious dialogue seems, by this account, to be doomed to failure, whether it refers to dialogue within religious traditions, or the contemporary buzzword of 'inter-faith' dialogue. Although liberal religionists may be willing to concede that believers of other religions may have valid and rational beliefs and it is therefore possible to have dialogue with them, there is always an element of the superiority-inferiority dichotomy, according to scholars like Samartha who see problems of religious pluralism and dialogue. Where dialogue may be of significant value in conflict transformation is in highlighting a common denominator in differing religions. Within the three large (traditionally) monotheistic religions, for example, dialogue may cover significant mileage in acknowledging the 'same' god, or the existence of Jesus (though not necessarily his position within the Christian trinity). On an even more basic level, dialogue may be able to highlight the non-violent element of religion in times of conflict. Although referred to by different religious teachers, and by different words, the concept of *ahimsa* is arguably the highest of religions. This, of course, is on condition that it is not further qualified, for example by adding concerns about morality, divinity or any number of other exclusive and absolutist elements inevitable within religion. Even Mohandas Gandhi, renowned for his non-violence (*ahimsa*) believed that both cowardice and treason, for example, were worse than taking up arms. Therefore, in order to prevent these 'vices' violence was not only a right, but also a duty, as Gandhi says: 'where there is only a choice between cowardice and violence, I would advise violence'.[60]

Gandhi's strong principles of *ahimsa* were, for him, inferior to his principles of truth and courage, and true *ahimsa* was only possible through the attainment of the two latter. Similarly, the non-violence adhered to by most religionists (and secularists) in the contemporary world is subordinated to concerns of perceived right and wrong, morality, justice and legality. When non-violence becomes a subsidiary to political or religious agendas, perceived as an obstacle to so-called 'peace and security' and not as a viable option in world politics, the types of religious violence highlighted earlier in this chapter become a fact. Whilst in legend, at least, it is possible to create a completely non-violent state, as King Ashoka did when embracing Buddhism following the bloody battle of Kalinya (and in effect creating the first Buddhist state), this, though desirable, may not be a plausible alternative in reality. Even Buddhist violence exists, as seen above, and is usually justified on grounds of defence of the teaching or for the common goal of peace and harmony, despite most Western analysts (and others) claiming that Buddhism never has been violent and never could be, and the odd argument that the only way to prevent World War III is to spread Buddhism around the world. But as with most millenarian and apocalyptic groups, as highlighted in the first part of this chapter, even the pursuit of peace and harmony often takes a violent path.

The ambivalence of religion in respect to war and peace should be more than obvious through even a superficial observation of the contemporary international arena. Experiences of the twentieth century show that religion does offer a number of possibilities for conflict transformation, and several recent attempts have shown how both truth and reconciliation committees around the world and forums for dialogue, for example, have had considerable success. The relative failure of 'inter-faith' initiatives lies in the difficulties raised above relating to the impossibility of neutral interaction in issues of religious dialogue. Another difficulty of religious 'peace-making' is that it necessarily requires an explicit denomination (though not necessarily religious), or at least an explicit affiliation to an identity. In religious research, especially in areas of conflict and tension, this is often impossible as individuals and groups often prefer to remain religiously anonymous, for fear of discrimination, persecution, bias and misleading assumptions. Such decisions, though prudent, and often due to a rational strategic or legal reasoning, complicate the task not only for the researcher but also for the possibility of dialogue, or other religious conflict transformation initiatives. Here, understanding is vital, as mere explanations of the situations will not overcome this difficulty, and religion can be useful in providing such understanding and thus acting as a force of social stability.

Apart from providing a sense of social stability, religion also has the ability to offer a (mostly) party-politically independent influence on a politically tense situation, or provide a calming influence. This influence exists and is affirmed, regardless of whether the religion in question is 'true' or not, although it can be argued – contrary to this – that certain problems regarding religion and violence can never be resolved 'by superficial pronouncements about justifiable or unjustifiable, malignant or benign violence'.[61] Even where such pronouncements are not 'superficial', it is none the less true that where religion is concerned questions of legitimacy, and 'truth-hood' are always apparent at one or another level. This is by far the most challenging aspect of religious peace-making initiatives. A religion generally needs to reaffirm itself to its adherents (and to itself) by assuming some sort of superiority, truth-value or moral or ethical right. Finding a common basic tenet, as was indicated above with the birth of Jesus being a possible example, is likewise steeped in difficulty. It is sometimes felt that such a common tenet, useful for dialogue between religions, within traditions and in relations of religions to the secular world, could be a version of 'the Golden Rule' under which you do to others as you wish to be done to yourself. Apart from this 'rule' assuming an ontological superiority that this is neither the time nor the place to discuss (it is only applicable where the person applying it is of an equally sound and moral mind as 'I', and does not have any adverse, insurgent, fundamentalist or 'wrong' worldviews), it also does not mean that the outcome necessarily will be 'favourable': 'We love our neighbour as ourself. But loving one's self does not mean sparing one's self'.[62]

Where religion can cover most ground, however, is probably in its reaffirmation of peace, love, compassion and harmony. It is certainly difficult, from a religious perspective at least, to grasp these concepts without also referring to (the usually evil) 'Other', in relation to whom the religion or identity is in fact usually not only clarified but also created. Furthermore, it must also be remembered that religions have very different interpretations of what peace, compassion, and so forth entail, and more importantly for whom, and how to attain such a state of harmony. Although the phenomenological logic of peace persists within all religious traditions, it is in practice often a contradictory phenomenon. It is not true that religious peace and secular peace are only marginally distinguished, as has been argued recently by some scholars.

Notes

[1] W. Reich (1998), p.120.
[2] P. Sherry (1977), see p.171; W.A. Christian (1972), see, especially, pp.14, 29.
[3] J. Hick (1985b), p.88.
[4] P.T. Forsyth (1916), p.43.
[5] The examples referred to in this paragraph (see notes 6-12) are merely for illustrative purposes, and as there are more than 500 'international terrorist organisations' identified today, a number which furthermore is constantly changing, examples are in abundance.
[6] For example, the Sendero Luminoso (Peru), Chukaku-Ha (Japan), Red Army Faction (Germany), etc. (See n.5).
[7] For example, the ETA (Basque Country), PKK (Kurdistan), ASALA (Armenia), LTTE (Sri Lanka), etc. (See n.5).
[8] For example, the Algetsk Wolves (Georgia), Yukoko Seiwa-kai (Japan), Justice Commandos for the Armenian Genocide (Turkey), etc. (See n.5).
[9] For example, the Kahane Chai (Israel), TIKKO (Turkey), Jamaat ul-Fuqra (USA), etc. (See n.5).
[10] For example, the Guerrilla Army of the Poor (Guatemala), MAVI – Northern Epirus Liberation Front (Albania/Greece), Jewish Defense League (USA), Frenad 187 (El Salvador), etc. (See n.5).
[11] For example, the Aum Shinrikyo (Japan), Amal (Lebanon), M3 (Peru), Hamas (Palestine), Hezb'allah (Lebanon), etc. (See n.5).
[12] For example, the Poultry Liberation Organisation (UK), Hambre (Honduras), Furious Rebellion (Greece), Armed Phalanx (Italy), etc. (See n.5).
[13] For convenience and for the benefit of those readers unfamiliar with Islamic references, the Nizaris will often, though not always, be used interchangeably with their more familiar name the 'Assassins', in inverted commas as it is acknowledged that this term is loaded, and often infers negative connotations. Cf. D.C. Rapoport (1984), p664n20. The word assassins (without ' '), as used in common vernacular, refers to the concept of political murder to which the 'Assassins' have lent their name.
[14] Dante (1994), *The Divine Comedy*, 'the Inferno', Canto 19:49-50.
[15] M. Juergensmeyer (2000), p.80.
[16] Marco Polo (1997), p.39.
[17] J. Davis (1999), p.203.
[18] B. Lewis (1967), pp.129 and 130 respectively.
[19] Dante (1994) Canto 19:49-50; See, for example, C.S. Singleton's commentary to Dante's *Inferno* (1970), p.333.
[20] J.L. Esposito (1995), p.89.
[21] A.M. Abdelmoula (1998), p.13.
[22] A.M. Abdelmoula (1998), p.4.
[23] R.S. O'Fahey (1995), p.41.
[24] J.L. Esposito (1995), p.90.
[25] J.N. Dixit (1998), p.10.
[26] *ibid.*
[27] S.J. Tambiah (1992).
[28] K.M. de Silva (1998), p.41.
[29] J.N. Dixit (1998), p.11.
[30] See G. de S.G. Punchihewa (1989), for a fascinating account of the Veddhas.
[31] S.J. Tambiah (1992), p.135.
[32] S.J. Tambiah (1992), p.99.
[33] J.N. Dixit (1998), p.110.
[34] S.J. Tambiah (1992), p.95.

[35] M. Neiminathan (1998), p.5.
[36] *ibid.* p.5.
[37] By 'the Company' is meant the British East India Company, which was the administrative and legislative ruling body in British India until 1858.
[38] J.G. Farrell (1973).
[39] C. Hibbert (1973), p.63.
[40] J.A.B. Palmer (1966), p.15.
[41] C. Hibbert (1973), p.78.
[42] *ibid.* p.78.
[43] The pejorative connotation of the word is acknowledged, as is the rather favourable impression given by 'rebellion'. The Hindustani word *ghadr* might be a better term, as it has neither pejorative nor favourable connotations. In short, it "*does not convey the same meaning that 'mutiny' conveys to English ears.*" C. Hibbert (1973), p.62. In this text, the terms are used interchangeably.
[44] H. Gough (1897), p.35.
[45] N.A. Chick in C. Hibbert (1973), p.30.
[46] J. Lunt (1970), p.157.
[47] T. Shibutani and K.M. Kwan (1975), p.448.
[48] Subedar Sita Ram in J. Lunt (1970), p.163.
[49] D.G.E. Hall, *A History of Southeast Asia* (1968), p.736.
[50] N. Tarling (1966), p.92.
[51] D.L. Horowitz (1985), p.148.
[52] D.G.E. Hall (1968), p.820.
[53] N. Tarling (1992), p.214.
[54] D.C. Hellman (1976), p.166.
[55] N. Tarling (1992), p.125.
[56] Both quotes from J.F. Cady (1958), p.139.
[57] R.S. Appleby (2000), p.211.
[58] Unknown (2001), p.13.
[59] S.J. Samartha (1974), p.x.
[60] J.V. Bondurant (1958) p.28; S. Radakrishnan (1961) p.90; M. Juergensmeyer (2002) pp.ix, 13.
[61] P. Tournier (1978), p.4.
[62] P.T. Forsyth (1916), p.13.

Chapter 4

Prerequisites: Philosophical Prerequisites for Contemporary Perspectives

Certain basic issues need to be investigated properly in order to understand the 'Questions/Problems' that were analysed earlier, and illustrated empirically in the previous chapter. Many of these have been alluded to, but have not been investigated in depth. It is my belief that the prevalent social scientist perceptions of the role of religion in armed conflict that have been explored previously mean very little if not understood in conjunction with the underlying issues ranging from semantics to varying (academic and practical) epistemologies. The present chapter, therefore, aims to explore the philosophical *prerequisites* for the kind of explaining that has been the focus thus far and for the understanding that is being approached. In other words, it is not the prerequisites necessary for the actual events of religion and war to occur that are under investigation, but the prerequisites that make the discourse of the contemporary perspectives possible.

The relationship between religion and armed conflict, as it has been framed thus far, may be criticised as undoubtedly smacking of both ethnocentrism and blatant bias. Throughout the previous chapters, it may appear that the word 'religion' has been thrown around without apparent thought or due consideration, as were other terms, such as those related to the academic discipline variously called International Relations, International Politics and International Studies (and in the United States, invariably 'Political Science'). Indeed, many concepts and phenomena may have been quickly dismissed without necessary qualification and often there has been a seemingly dangerous use of lacking due care and attention. This is not only acknowledged, but was also a conscious practice for two main reasons: first, because this is by far the most prevalent methodology within the Western academy, political scene and society in general; second, if this is recognised it is possible to work on a framework that does not suffer the same defects. Many of the hitherto unexplored concepts and notions, that were so apparently crudely used in earlier chapters, are unpacked and explored at some depth in this chapter.

Definitional Prerequisites

Questions were raised earlier as to the usage of certain terms and concepts. The sometimes casual use of terms such as 'religion' was defended as being consciously employed to uncover the hidden agendas implicit in contemporary discourse. These agendas are not so often consciously ignored as unconsciously assumed without question. It is not uncommon within the academy that as in chapter 2, unquestioned definitions, which are often not explicitly explained, are used. Rather than facilitating analyses, such dismissive use of definitions often impedes understanding. The first prerequisite for understanding, therefore, deals with definitional issues.

Often, an implicit or tacit definition may prove more useful than an explicit definition at the outset of an analysis as it forces the reader to adopt his or her own definition of the terms used. This may be a functional tool for removing restrictive limits on the research, but before any points of fundamental importance can be made, the concepts must be subjected to an explicit exploration lest there be misunderstanding detrimental to the conclusions. Within the boundaries of this book, therefore, it is important that some concepts are explicitly explored, and the most fundamental of these definitional enquiries is one which has led to much brooding and furrowed brows among scholars throughout history – an acceptable definition of religion. This is the first concept to be explored and conceptualised. The second definitional exploration pertains in part to the name of the academic discipline of International Relations, and as opposed to the first, no conceptualisation or problematisation is attempted, but rather a simplification of these – and other – terms. Finally, considerable weight is placed here on the difference between the process of explanation and understanding, an exploration of the definitional issues concerning these will be offered.

Definition, Conceptualisation and Use of the Term 'Religion'

An issue that has confounded scholars from all disciplines throughout history is the search for a satisfactory definition of religion, and despite several recent impressive attempts, none has been found. Or, rather, depending on what perspective you take, there are too many definitions. Although often considered vital, any pursuit of an all-encompassing definition is invariably disparaged. Indeed, the lack of a nomothetical definition is often advanced as a case for ideographic research within the social sciences, and similarly the tacit acceptance of a definition within the theological or religious disciplines consistently favours singular analyses. Although theologians often fail in comparative research as their definition of religion is necessarily based within their own confessional tradition, this is also the case in the political sciences where a definition is often only sought superficially.

One difficulty with a general definition of religion rather than a definition of a particular religion is that 'religion' contains too many divergent phenomena, and this has led to a number of simplistic definitions that are often criticised for being *too* general. These overly general definitions, in turn, not only include otherwise decidedly non-religious phenomena but can also exclude otherwise included phenomena. An illustration of this could be the general – if somewhat facile – definition of religion as 'belief in god' that includes purportedly secular phenomena such as variants of Nationalsozialism or Communism but excludes Theravada Buddhism, for example. Disparities like this have led scholars (mainly theologians and other religious scholars) to formulate a range of definitions, none of which seem to be completely satisfactory.

Wilfred Cantwell Smith suggested that the nomothetical noun 'religion' ought to bc dismissed from scholarly usage in preference for ideographical terms or the adjective 'religious'. Although there is some mileage in such a suggestion, this did not happen by the late 1980s as Cantwell Smith predicted, and understandably so.[1] Religion, according to such a view, is invariably too vague or general for successful reasoning and it may therefore often make more sense not to try to fit every religious concept into the one word 'religion'. Many societies, both 'primitive' and 'civilised', do not have a word corresponding to the Western (secularised) concept of 'religion', or at least not conceptualised in the same way, where the same concept may refer to both one's own religion and an opposing group's contradictory religion. Religion in most societies refers to faith, whereas in the scholastically influenced West, it pertains more to identity. By this reasoning, it is therefore easy from a Western analytical point of view to argue that the main source of demarcation and tension between groups is religious identity. It is, in the Western analytical tradition, possible to talk about religions in the plural when comparing various phenomena, whereas this would clearly be perceived as blasphemous if there is only one (true) religion, as Ibn Khaldun suggested.[2]

This leads to the issue of whether it is possible to comprehend a religion. The issue is two-fold and one part refers to whether the human believer is even capable of grasping divine truth. This part will not be investigated, other than in passing. What is of more interest here is whether it is possible to understand a religious system as an outsider (secular or religious). From a religious point of view, one must be a believer of a particular religion in order to understand it; understanding is impossible without belief. For a believer, the outsider's conception is inadequate to the point of futility; it is completely inconceivable. From a Religious Studies perspective, on the other hand, this raises the question of whether it is not possible to 'learn a religion' as one 'learns a language' or at least comprehend the meaning of one or more religions other than one's own (or, in the case of secular observers, the possibility of comprehending religion at all). There is, of course, the further view that a non-faith specific position is the only possible standpoint for a completely unconditional understanding, as this provides a much needed perspective, taking 'the radical secularity of contemporary culture as a starting point for theological speculation'.[3] That such understanding is at all possible may, of course, also be questioned.

Although it is difficult to agree with arguments that students of religion necessarily adopt one out of only three perspectives on religion, knowingly or not, ('mirror', 'window' or '2-way mirror'), it is possible to argue that there exists only a relatively scant number of varying methodologies that have been used by scholars throughout history in their quest for a satisfying definition of religion. In previous chapters, the implicit variant was employed. The case for avoiding an explicit definition altogether can be made in the name of flexibility. Allowing the reader to employ his or her own tacit understanding of religion may be very useful. On the other hand, this vagueness does offer greater scope of misunderstanding (deliberate or not) and an explicit definition therefore seems an apt methodology. As noted, however, although the explicit approach to a definition has been the one most frequently employed by observers it does pose a number of problems. Most of these problems relate to an explicit definition being either too general or, paradoxically, too specific.

Explicit definitions are usually of two general categories; one is relatively specific, and the other relies on 'family resemblances'. In reality there is not much difference between these, as both offer an explicit definition. The latter tends to find a number of common traits in various religions, such as belief in something supernatural, the existence of doctrine, ritual and a church or following, together with a particular history and language. These traits, or 'family resemblances', are usually constant, but some variation does occur, as for Ludwig Wittgenstein from whom the term is derived. Although Wittgenstein's analysis referred to games, it may be equally well applied to religion. Nothing is common to *all* religions, but there is 'a complicated network of similarities overlapping and criss-crossing: sometimes overall similarities, sometimes similarities in detail'.[4] Such common traits make the term 'religion' usable in common parlance, and it is the family resemblances that thus permit a general understanding of 'religion'. Where an explicit definition is made without reference to common characteristics, the definition usually has so-called Tillichian attributes, referring to Paul Tillich's conviction that religion pertains to 'ultimate concerns'. Although for Tillich ultimacy did not have to be supernatural, many subsequent adoptions of definitions of 'ultimate concern / devotion / transformation' do contain sacred, holy or supernatural characteristics.[5]

A number of scholars who have attempted to circumvent the definitional problems of trying to establish family resemblances or of expressing religion in terms of ultimate concerns have in the interests of simplicity focussed on the linguistic basis of the word in order to reach an explicit definition. This is a methodology fraught with danger since the word 'religion' is 'of doubtful etymology' as the Oxford English Dictionary states, and has been used 'in a great variety of senses, even by a single writer, without precision'.[6] Although the modern word 'religion' is thought to derive from the Latin *religio*, there is not even consensus as to the root of that word. The two most common etymological roots, however, are both from Latin, namely *relegere* and *religare*, meaning 'to read again' and 'to bind (back)' respectively. The latter of these, 'to bind (back)', is the later and now the most prevalent. The linguistic definition is by far the most naïve, albeit simple, characterisation of religion. It is simple because it not only provides a semantic meaning, but it is also apt for contemporary empirical observation of religion, which recognises religion's ability to 'bind' people. It is, of course, important to be aware of the semantics and etymology of the word, but not to attribute more weight to them than appropriate.

It may be argued that religion is primarily a practical phenomenon and not a theoretical one, and that there is a danger of over-intellectualising both religion and believers. It may be necessary, however, to explicitly conceptualise the phenomenon of religion for the relationship between religion and violence to be understood. Here, therefore, the phenomena of religion will be conceptualised not only for the purposes of this book but also as a prerequisite for a framework of understanding conflict. As seen in chapter two, the lack of a satisfactory understanding of the concept of religion makes misunderstanding of events all the more likely. This is particularly the case where either religion is defined on a case-by-case basis (in which case the analyses are not applicable to other conflicts) or where a 'new' or unsatisfactory definition is applied to modern conflicts (in which case 'religion' might not be properly understood). Internationally, most modern analyses fail to satisfactorily define religion, as the definitions are inevitably rooted in the scholar's own paradigm. By applying a Western perception of religion to another tradition, the conclusions will invariably be tainted and even blatantly wrong. However, although it is vital to conceptualise religion, as will be seen, there is always a possibility that the concept of religion thus becomes violated, and loses its unique meaning, which is why religion, claims Radakrishnan, 'is suspicious of enquiry and criticism. The fear of knowledge is as old as the Garden of Eden'.[7]

This sense of being a unique discourse, which religion insists on being, also makes definition difficult and subsequent analyses and research often suffer as a result. The definition of religion that is employed in security analyses and research has an especially great impact on the conclusions of such research, as security is self-referential to the extreme. By categorising religion as a security issue it inevitably becomes one. How religion is defined is therefore of great importance, but this is a practice that often fails to achieve a satisfactory middle ground between being too exclusive or too inclusive. Indeed, this failure is one of the major downfalls of most disciplines' perspective of religion, especially in relation to issues of relevance to this study. Inadequate definitions often do more to hamper understanding of conflicts than they contribute to explaining them. As I believe understanding to be of more importance than explaining, it is my express purpose to advocate a notion of abstract, or conceptualised, religion.

An interesting approach to this is that of Benson Saler (1993), who proposes and (rather successfully) argues for the benefits of explicitly conceptualising religion in scholarly research (p.214). Saler's approach is impressive, to say the least, but does nonetheless not go as far as is proposed here. Building on such an explicit conceptualisation of religion and also on nomothetical theorisation as advocated by Wilfred Cantwell Smith for whom no religion is, in itself, an intelligible entity of research, but not agreeing wholly with either, the case is made for a conceptualisation of religion as an abstraction. Although acknowledging that religion for the believer is mainly a practical series of experimental experiences and not a theoretical exercise, it is argued here that religion as a *concept* must be abstracted in order to understand its role in violence, terrorism and armed conflict.

Without doubt, the vast majority of observation, study and research within most disciplines and in all contexts tends to focus on a notion of 'world religions', whether for a nomothetical or for an ideographical analysis. When using this notion, which pertains to the number of adherents of usually four to six so-called 'main' religions, it is made implicit, and sometimes explicit, that the number of adherents of a religion is somehow relevant to the validity of the belief. Such arguments are by far the most common within academia, and with a few exceptions this has come to mean a vast body of literature dealing with various aspects (and comparisons) of Buddhism, Christianity, Islam and Hinduism, whilst scant attention has been given to religions with few adherents. In most analyses, Judaism is also added to the category of 'world religion', although it does not have a large following. The rationale for this, although somewhat tenuous, is that 'it contains historical preconditions decisive for understanding Christianity and Islamism [sic], and because of its historic and autonomous significance for the development of the modern economic ethic of the Occident – a significance [that is] partly real and partly alleged'.[8] Although the same case can be made for other religious traditions, such as Zoroastrianism, these are not commonly associated with the category 'world religion'. On the international political arena, it is clear that Judaism asserts its alleged status as a 'world religion' due to its influence over mainly American politics (both domestic and foreign). The main problem with the perception of 'world religion' as being more important than other, so-called 'lesser' or 'minor' religions is that it implies that a small circle would be less infinite than a large one, for example, or that conviction guarantees truth. Both of which are obvious fallacies.

In any case, the choice of which religions to include and which to exclude from scholarly research is often merely a political exercise, whether consciously or not. This is, of course, understandable and no less so within the discipline of International Politics and related areas, since religion and political affairs can be inseparable and interlinked, as Gandhi – for example – argued. Taken further, the perspective that the very choice of religion has an impact on the definitional aspect of religion makes Albert Camus's (1953, p.115) claim that politics in fact *is* religion more understandable, as it implies that in order to make a conscious decision of which religions to include in research, one is admitting that knowledge itself is not universal but always limited to both time and space. This leads, in turn, to scholarship being unable to function outside its own epistemology, and Bochenski's (1965, p.vi) failure to find a generally applicable logic of all religions rather than one is therefore understandable, albeit regrettable.

It is easy to follow how the concept of 'world religion' has an impact on the international politics the discourse aims to explain. If religion is perceived as a threat and if Islam, for example, is identified as a religion, logic would then indicate that Islam is a threat without any further qualification. One may, however, agree two-fold that neither religion in general nor religions in particular are intelligible entities for research. First, when choosing a particular religion as an illustration for a secular argument, 'religion' will be identified with that issue, and secondly when explaining a secular notion from a religious perspective, the arguments and conclusions are influenced by the traditions on which they are founded. As this often disregards the truths of religion, it becomes one of the main strengths of an argument for the conceptualisation of religion, rather than pluralism. Although aiming to be wide-ranging in scope, pluralism nonetheless makes choices about which truths are more valid (more 'true') than others and thus more suitable for inclusion in the study, whether by personal or political reasoning.

The case for 'abstract religion' can thus be made by reference to truth. In essence, it does not matter what a religion entails as long as the adherents of that particular faith believe it to be the embodiment of (religious) truth. It is not religion *per se* that is important, rather it is the belief that matters, and it is important to understand this in relation to religions' roles on the international stage, as will be seen. The conceptualisation proposed here, therefore, does not make the size and spread of a religion a criterion for the 'truth-hood' of religion. Furthermore, it does not use a phenomenological distinction between truth and untruth, and it is with this qualification that this study may become controversial *in extremis*. By not acknowledging any superiority of claim of truth, but regarding all religious truth as equal, it places a traditional institutional religion with several million adherents on a par with a coven of only a handful of adherents. Similarly the truth of the Temple of Set is as equal a truth as that of the Roman Catholic Church; the World Church of the Creator is neither more nor less truthful than Sunni Islam; Theravada Buddhism and Wicca proclaim different truths but are equally true; Christian Protestantism and Sufism are equal as to truth and value.

There are no criteria for measuring the value or truth of a religion, as any approach will inevitably be coloured by a belief that one's own faith is the norm. The only possible way to approach an abstraction of religion may therefore be from a non-confessional or non-theological standpoint, as these carry with them inherent preconceptions of the issues at hand, which would serve as obstacles for a successful conceptualisation of religion. From a Christian point of view it would obviously not only be blasphemous to acknowledge the truth of Satanism, but also deeply offensive. However, by using the same argument, it would be offensive from a Satanist point of view to have Christian ideals, values and claims of truth subjected to one's faith. It is offensive to an exclusivist monotheistic religion (such as Islam, Judaism and Christianity) when a mystic religion (such as Hinduism and Buddhism) claims that every religion is equally valid, as the variety of religion merely shows that there are many paths to a common goal.

A caveat must be made at this stage, however, that in striving to be as unbiased as possible towards any particular religious belief, in not accepting that 'truth-hood' or commitment increases with size and thus arguing for the equality of truth (in essence, though not necessarily in content) of all religions in order to avoid intellectual ethnocentrism, this book may be criticised for exactly that. This may be the case since, although it confronts the obstacles of definitions, for example, these very obstacles become stumbling blocks on many levels, ultimately because the epistemology requires the vocabulary of concepts to be derived from a 'Western' philosophical tradition.

It is proposed, therefore, that both for the purposes of the arguments presented here and the wider aim of understanding religious differences on the international arena, wherever 'religion' is employed it refers to a notion of 'abstract religion'. This, in turn, as described above, refers to truth. Although examples and illustrations are given for the more 'well known' religions in the world, this is done for the analytical purpose of facilitating understanding of the concepts at hand and not for bias as to 'truth-hood'. It is believed that the concepts can be applied to any 'religion' with equal accuracy. It is with respect to this that the definition may be thought to be Tillichian (see above) as religion is defined as pertaining to ultimate and absolute truths, which for many 'religionists' would be deemed to have to do with theism, and so forth. However, belief, knowledge, faith or 'mere' adherence to a 'religion' does not automatically, necessarily, inevitably or prevalently mean an acceptance of supernatural, theistic or spiritual matters. According to this definition, it is thus possible not only to have both theistic and atheistic religions, but also secular, philosophical and scientific religions.

Whereas this conceptualisation of religion is inclusive of all systems of philosophy that pertain to ultimate truth, the analytical category applied herein is not generally one of individual commitment, although this is its basic tenet, but of 'family resemblances' of religion. This category is inclusive of institutional religion, historical/traditional religion, 'primitive' religion and so forth without bias as to the content of the particular truth, or to the number of 'adherents'. Of course, it would be beneficial to keep an explicit definition of religion in abeyance for the purposes of research, but this would, to an extent, limit the understandings necessary for my present purposes. Therefore, although the definition will be somewhat altered by a number of qualifications in the concluding framework, an attempt at a functional definition, though not only for the specific purposes of the research, is offered.

This definition is, however, an abstraction and thus applicable primarily as an analytical and methodological tool to facilitate understanding of the hypotheses at hand. The conceptualisation may thus not always be applicable in common parlance or with reference to all concepts that would fall into the proposed definition of religion. Although ethnocentric in that it is introspect (only in 'Western' philosophical traditions is it possible a) to use the word religion and b) to call it an abstraction) the definition can – as an aid to understanding – be applied universally to all religions. This means that Communism, Liberal Democracy (to an extent) and other systems of thought can be included, whereas loyalty to one's employer, marque of car or brand of whisky usually is not, although exceptions have been known. It may be useful to keep John Rawls' claim in mind that 'the merit of any definition depends upon the soundness of the theory that results; by itself a definition cannot settle any fundamental question'.[9]

Definition and Use of Other Words and Concepts

Continuing on definitions, we now proceed to a significantly lesser investigation. Whilst the discussion of 'abstract religion' has implications not only for this book, but also in the wider application of academia and the world in general, this second definitional query pertains mainly to a particular academic discipline, namely International Relations / International Politics. Thus far, terms such as international politics / relations / studies have been employed without much explanation and seemingly indiscriminate use of terms (and capital/lower case) has been made. As with religion, this was a conscious attempt to imitate a discipline that is failing in its ambition to be reflective and introspective. As with many academic disciplines, this one suffers from a fundamental identity crisis and in order to successfully explore its relation to religion it needs to be 'un-packed' and somewhat 'problematised'. It is near impossible to attempt to understand the explanations investigated in the previous chapter if the meaning of International Relations, and its usages, are not understood. This is my main aim here.

I do not intend to conceptualise International Politics, as was my object with the definitional investigation of religion above. Here, the exercise is merely explanatory, as meanings of the concepts employed have not been satisfactorily explored, but have relied upon the implicit or tacit definitions the reader has had to employ.

There is an obvious difference between the relationship of actors on the international arena and the theories of such relations in the academic discourse concerning these. As with all academic disciplines, the latter is used in title case (International Relations, International Politics, etc), whereas the former – the actual international world – is used with lower case (international relations, international politics, etc.). Therefore, as Martin Hollis and Steve Smith state 'International Relations is a discipline, where theories about international relations compete. These, for the most part, are theories about international relations (hence the small letters), although we may occasionally take note of theories about the conduct of the discipline itself (i.e. theories of International Relations)'.[10] Furthermore, although the adherents of each are convinced of a fundamental difference, the present research uses the disciplines International Relations, International Politics and International Studies interchangeably, arguing that they are synonymous. Where necessary, further qualifications are made where this is of importance to the argument, or where a term differs in use between the academic discipline and common usage.

International Relations is about telling the world about the world, and although the discipline is self-professedly striving to move away from questions concerning only peace and war, the fact remains that the world is a violent place where armed conflict is in abundance on every continent (except Antarctica, perhaps) around the world. Of course, in an academic context it is possible to debate what the conceptual definition of a violent armed conflict is, what a war is and what, for example, 'terrorism' entails, but in practice such definitional queries seem rather trivial. One of the fundamental difficulties with conflict theory is this very lack of an acceptable definition of conflict. To overcome this theoretical pitfall and as human suffering cannot be measured, the tautological approach is taken, namely that a conflict involving arms is an 'armed conflict'.

Although my narrative is intended to be as value-neutral as possible, it should also be noted that language, to an extent, resembles the legal notion of 'strict liability', where intent is not necessary in order to cause offence. Whoever wants to find a particular term or phrase derogatory or pejorative will, for such is the ambivalent beauty of language.

Whilst the narrative is in English it must be made clear that some of the concepts are derived from other languages and cultures and do not allow for proper translations. Wherever possible systems of transliteration have been employed rather than translation. Transliteration does, of course, pose many problems ranging from meaning-carrying morphemes (as in Sanskrit and Pali) that are often lost in the transliteration-process to the lack of standardised systems for many languages (such as Arabic). With this comes the further complicating factor that not only are non-Anglophonic terms often transliterated or transcribed in a variety of ways, authors invariably use the concepts differently. As Western analysts sometimes do not pick up such distinctions, it may therefore make the translation more difficult if only one source is used as the authority on the term. To illustrate this, take the Arabic concept often transliterated as *jahiliyya* or *jāhilīyah*. Whilst it may be prudent to use as few diacritics as possible this does not solve the difficulty as to meaning. Superficially, the range of meanings often conveys a similar connotation of a state of ignorance (of divine guidance for mankind), or (pagan) pre-Islamic Arabia. However, whereas the religiously traditionalist revolutionary Qutb employed the term as a negative concept, the secular Ba'athist Arab nationalist Al-Arsuzi saw the term as a positive concept referring to the time before the coming of Islam. A third main way of employing this term is the 'fundamentalist' stand, as espoused by Faraj and others, taking it to mean the un-Islamic world as a whole. If we accept that either of these is the true authority, any analyst will necessarily reject the other sources and problems of translation are evident. The controversies surrounding the term and concept of *jihad* are even more intricate and complicated, and are therefore not used as an illustration here, but wherever the concept is used its usage is clarified.

Of course, similar arguments could be made about the Anglophonic concept of 'violence', for example, or 'war'. In many respects there is general consensus that violence is the opposite of 'force', for example, in that it is a sign of weakness (force being a sign of strength) and illegitimate (where force is legitimate). However, arguably 'not all violence can be condemned, because it is in holy acts of violence that man reveals his noblest aspirations',[11] although this contradicts the Kantian notion that war creates more evil than it destroys. As will be highlighted in the following sections, the solution is not merely to frame the definition in purportedly value-neutral language, and say that war, for example, is 'collective killing for collective purposes', whilst violence is individual, or that it takes many forms, some legitimate and some not. Throughout this book, a tacit, implicit, definition of 'violence' is preferred, wherever possible; 'political violence' is used as a less value-laden or judgemental word for 'terrorism'; the definition of 'armed conflict' is taken tautologically as any conflict involving arms (weaponry); and 'religion' has, as investigated in the previous section, a very specific application and use throughout.

Distinction between 'Explaining' and 'Understanding'

The last of the definitional prerequisites deals with a fundamental distinction in this book, namely that between explanation and understanding. As with the conceptualisation of religion, this is an area where a gap in the existing body of knowledge may be filled. This distinction is not merely semantic but also has a profound impact on conflict transformation in most instances and in relation to religious conflicts in particular. As such, although this differs vastly from conventional thinking on the matters, it is also believed that a framework that utilises this distinction can cover much ground.

Although distinctions between explaining and understanding have been made in the past, these are usually either based on language, as the grammatical forms of the terms differ (something is explained in order to be understood), or on the insider-outsider dichotomy (something is explained from the outside, but understood from the inside). Following such distinctions, therefore, disciplines relating to international relations have traditionally sought to explain the events of the world, whereas theological studies have been primarily for the purposes of understanding the faith. As has been argued previously, this usually means that it is not possible for an outsider to understand a particular religion, other than his/her own, however well the history and facts are known. To fully understand doctrines of religion it would furthermore be necessary to have the 'right intention'. Within International Relations, it has likewise often been necessary merely to explain what occurs in a particular situation as it is generally impossible to completely become the enemy and thus understand his/her actions. Although it has recently been recognised that the goal of international relations may, in fact, be to understand, rather than to explain, this is realised in discourse only and very rarely in practice. Whilst regrettable, this stance is none the less understandable, and prevalent throughout the study and practice of international politics.

It is true, of course, that the distinction between explaining and understanding is more often than not thought to be artificial and specious. However, this may only be superficially true as the various studies grappling with the distinction show. Such studies illustrate that explicitly proving the contrast between the concepts has not been a simple task, which it arguably would be if the arguments were purely baseless. Most distinctions derive from Wilhelm Dilthey's attempts to define the concepts, but although his distinctions contain many valuable points, they do not go far enough for the present distinction. It is true that the ideal of explaining a phenomenon is now gradually becoming replaced with the ideal of understanding it, but that process has not yet matured sufficiently to be commonly accepted.

Schematically, this book progresses from explanation to understanding and this will become increasingly clear as the distinction between the concepts is clarified. At the end, therefore, as a framework for understanding conflict is more explicitly analysed, it will be apparent that it will not work on a basis of explanation but only on one of understanding. The distinction is not as simple as is most frequently argued, namely that explaining is from the outside, and understanding from the inside, as touched upon above. Such a distinction makes the two concepts too simplistic in that it infers that explanation is a nomothetical practice and understanding is an ideographical one. Although there is some mileage in this argument, it nonetheless makes it impossible to understand events in general, or as conceptualised phenomena. Indeed, it has been claimed that any form of conceptualisation (of 'religion', for example) blocks the very progress of understanding. Here, the opposite is proposed, namely that it is vital to conceptualise and phenomenalise concepts in order to achieve satisfactory understanding that will ultimately enable a transformation of the methodologies employed to deal with religion and armed conflict.

Whereas the human desire to explain phenomena and events may be a universal characteristic of human nature, understanding certainly is not. As is frequently illustrated in media and politics, for example, it is possible to explain a certain 'terrorist-attack' as exactly that, but this does little to further understanding of the issues pertaining to the attack. Indeed, the word 'terrorism' is itself a term convenient for explanation, but also one that inhibits genuine understanding. The only reaction to terrorism must necessarily be 'counter-terrorism', with all the difficulties that entails. 'Counter-terrorism' may include, for example, launching an attack that, had it been the action rather than the re-action, would have been regarded as 'terrorism' itself. Unless 'terrorism' is understood, therefore, it will be impossible to combat it successfully. The international system continuously reaffirms its unequivocal condemnation of 'terrorism', but has yet to reach agreement on how to define 'terrorism', who a 'terrorist' is, or what a 'terrorist' act is. These arguments will be reiterated and investigated further in the next section.

Of course, it is important to remember that any conceptualisation is only useful so far as it relates to reality. It may therefore serve a purpose at this point to clarify that, although the common usage of the terms explanation and understanding is easy to comprehend, it has little relevance in the present conceptualisation. The former term refers to the meaning of what is occurring and the latter to how or why the particular event is taking place. In short, therefore, in popular usage, both concepts (explanation and understanding) refer to 'intelligibilifying'[12] or making something clear. Where such a seemingly superficial distinction differs from the more conceptual one proposed here is that both concepts are, in fact, levels of explanation. In other words, such a basic distinction is actually not a distinction at all, as it equates explanation with understanding, but rather a teleological 'stretching' of the same concept. The one, as it were, presupposes the other. In the context of the present distinction, both would therefore fall under the same category, namely that of explanation. Martin Hollis and Steve Smith's distinction,[13] for example, is an excellent example of this since although it began the debate within International Politics throughout the 1990s regarding the need to understand rather than merely explain, it has not really lived up to its own ideal. This is because their distinction is rather superficial, as although it claims that understanding pertains to motives and intentions of actors it nonetheless does so from an explanatory standpoint. In practical reality, of course, it is frowned upon whenever anyone proposes the importance of genuine understanding of the enemy, or advocates a view that such understanding is possible. This is not to say that one should necessarily become the enemy, and thus being able to understand from the inside rather than explain from the outside, but that it is vital that the possibility is recognised that it is feasible to understand from the outside. Nevertheless, claiming to understand the motives of Al-Qa'ida (to pick one of many possible examples) is today as taboo as men and women eating together in not so ancient Hawaii.

In this context, it is sometimes argued that on an intellectual level it is necessary to understand, even to disagree. Although this is a fine ideal, it rarely works in practice, since it is easier to disagree than to understand. Within the modern Western analytical tradition, almost Hegalian importance is placed on the perceived superiority of reason, and non-intellectual knowledge is often pejoratively demoted to the arts, for example, and religion. In attempts to explain the world, therefore, it becomes easier, if not necessary, to argue that religion and politics must inevitably be in conflict, as incompatible loyalties are often compromised in situations where both phenomena are implicated. Recent attempts at changing the perspectives of Western political science have come up with the more radical analytical view that religious interpretations cannot be separated from politics. Such a view does not, however, go as far as the predominantly Eastern view that there is, in fact, no contradiction at all between religion and politics, and that although politics is the clear duty of religion, both are interlinked, often beyond distinction. Although far from being reconciled with the latter, the former view is today becoming an increasingly popular choice amongst political scientists striving to be perceived as less ethnocentrically Western in their approach and more open to 'outside' discourses.

This again raises the issue of narratives, pertaining to how, why and by whom something is described. Whilst narratives certainly embody explanations they do more than that, since they also embody understandings. Western culture, including academia and international law, is permeated and patterned by religion, more so, in fact, than most analysts within the tradition want to admit. The understandings of the world that they describe are thus intersubjective, in that they necessarily presuppose a number of underlying shared, or common, bases. From these intersubjective paradigms, discourses are made possible that both describe and inform international relations, such as those that were characterised earlier.

This distinction – between explanation and understanding – is often rejected by scholars for a variety of reasons, as alluded to above. Sometimes, in a bid to simplify their analyses, scholars have been known to disregard any distinction whatsoever and use the terms interchangeably. Explanation, it may be claimed, is a less problematic and controversial concept than understanding in that it is less subjective. Although it may be right to say that explanation is often less subjective than understanding, it does not follow from this either that explanation is any kind of value-free exercise or that the two concepts can be equated. As was mentioned above, explanations are as made up of narratives as understandings are, and taken further, it is even possible to argue that genuine understandings are less affected by value-judgements than are explanations. To an extent, this is due to the fact that to understand issues in war, for example, there is a need for more than simply factual truths, there is also a need for 'more or less truths' or even myths. Popular academic and scientific explanations of conflict generally disregard all 'mechanisms' of conflict that are not purely analytical, or that cannot be satisfactorily categorised. What is left over is often referred to as 'the human factor', 'chance elements' or what Carl von Clausewitz would call 'friction', and these little-known aspects of conflicts have been invariably ignored, and as they are largely unknown, their importance is thus often underrated. In order to understand what motivates an individual to act in a certain way, it is paramount that his or her fears and needs are appreciated, on his or her own terms, not in the context of a process or system that may – in fact – be epitomising those very fears.

It is with this that I anticipate bridging most gaps in existing research. The most common perspective of all stages and levels of armed conflict, and in particular religious armed conflict, is that of explanation. Where known, the factual truths are presented as objectively as thought possible, although by so doing the media – for example – are already framing the conflict, and may actually be creating the conflict. What is perceivably worse is that explanations are not, as stated above, value-neutral and are often no more than political exercises. It must be remembered that, although understanding is neither the first nor the last step, I nonetheless believe it to be vital for any successful conflict management, where other approaches have invariably failed. Basing a practically applicable approach to conflict transformation on the distinction between explanation and understanding is the ultimate practical goal of this study, and although there are other more academic applications, the world is nonetheless one primarily of international relations, not International Relations.

In relation to the conceptualisation of religion that was explored at some length earlier, it is sometimes proposed that the Dilthian distinction between explanation and understanding may be better substituted for another approach. Such an approach takes religion to be understood and interpreted in relation to its meaning, rather than explained in reference to the causality behind the events. This distinction does not in actuality offer a better approach, as although it advocates the importance of understanding rather than explanation (as in Hollis and Smith's approach highlighted above) and acknowledges a link between explanation and causality, it nonetheless fails to achieve genuine understanding. Although it is important to understand the usage of a religious statement, rather than its meaning, as is argued by many theologians, it is none the less important to realise that religious language is often more easily grasped than the concepts it pertains to, and many analysts have thus (consciously or unconsciously) chosen the easier way to analyse the phenomena. This, however, is exactly what is meant by 'intelligibilifying', namely making the phenomena clear through the use of the popular concepts of understanding and explanation.

Assumptions, Presuppositions and Bias

The second prerequisite that is necessary to understand who attempts the explanations explored in chapter two relates to assumptions, presuppositions and bias. Here I explore some of the underlying assumptions that facilitate the general/common perspectives analysed earlier. Such assumptions include threat perception, the alleged desirability of a secular international society and an analysis of how the Judeo-Christian basis of international law, economic system and society of states is not necessarily a possible option in a multi-religious world. It is not my intention either to pinpoint all the assumptions and presuppositions that make Western academia – in particular – create the discourses seen previously, or to attempt a thorough exploration leading to judgement of how discourses *should* be created. On a very basic level, the rationale here is to show that assumptions, presuppositions and bias exist and that in order to successfully overcome the obstacles they present it is necessary to acknowledge their existence.

Even a superficial reading of chapter two would indicate that the issues concerning religion and armed conflict are contentious not only due to the 'facts' that are employed but rather more by the stand-point of those who employ these 'facts'. This is perhaps most true in disciplines concerned with risk assessment and threat perception. Earlier, I implied that many of the 'problems' of religion are problems merely due to the particular background of the international system. For example, to a highly religious society the threat will often not be 'fundamental religion' but rather its opposite, namely secularisation. Secularisation, on the other hand, is the perceived solution to the problem of religious conflict according to analysts in societies (such as the West) where non-religious life is seen as the optimal political system.

Apart from a number of legal documents to the contrary, there is nothing inherently secular about any domestic system of politics, or indeed about any international political system. Although some systems are avowedly atheistic, this does not invariably mean that they are irreligious. The old adage that Marxism is a religion, whose credo is that it has no god and Marx is its prophet, proves this well. It has already been suggested that the international system of states, or the modern state system, is built on largely Western notions of international law derived from the treaties of Westphalia in the 17th century. The international system, according to which all except the most hardened of 'rogue' states operate, is based on the Western conception of law, morals and ethics. In turn, these are invariably derived from the Judeo-Christian tradition. Although there are difficulties with combining these two religious traditions into one, it is believed that it serves no purpose to analyse them as two separate entities at the current juncture. The laws of every society are based upon the moral and ethical guidelines laid down by the religion of that particular country, or group of people. The pragmatic laws and duties are thus justified by divine sanction, whether explicitly through the rule of a Buddhist 'God-King' or more clandestinely by the incorporation of a divine sanction in the history, tradition or 'ritual' of the juridical system in question. This is true whatever the size or background of the society. On a domestic level, states may therefore proclaim to be religious or secular political entities, but both are nonetheless rooted in particular concepts of 'Right'.

Without digressing too far into the often obstructing fundamentals of the international society (or, in any case, International Relations Theory), such as the possibility of it existing at all, the above argument can similarly be successfully made that international society is largely based on religion, as is every society. The difficulty on the international arena is that the basis is rooted in a very particular historical tradition. Whilst this is the case even in smaller societies, the complications are all the greater in relation to the anarchical international system, where there are a number of very large and influential religious traditions that conflict with the one that has informed the legal basis of relations. Like every society, Western culture – and therefore international law – is 'permeated and patterned'[14] by religion more so than is usually admitted.

It should be made clear that every academic and practical discourse is necessarily influenced by its own specific background and history. A discourse cannot possibly be 'neutral' in that it is never completely free of assumptions, bias and presuppositions, or – indeed – of value judgements and connotations. The weakest link in the chain of academic discourse is usually its failure, consciously or not, to acknowledge its own heritage and the influence that has on the ideas that are presented. John Mearsheimer's attempt at reversing this trend is the 'policy-informs-discourse' cycle.[15] In short, this refers to the idea that although the discourse is meant to describe a particular phenomenon neutrally, that phenomenon is altered by the discourse, which in turn alters the discourse in a never-ending cycle. On the international arena the main actors in this, apart from academics and other analysts, are the media. Framing a conflict as a religious conflict, for example, may therefore indeed create such a conflict and the policy is therefore altered to deal with a religious conflict, which is then reported on as being a religious conflict, and so forth. Although this practice may be either conscious or unconscious the effects are largely the same.

The debates within the academy during the last decade in relation to this, however, are unfortunately only superficially introspective. In reality, of course, the assumptions lie somewhat deeper than this. Without much thought, for example, scholars are often considered as neutral analysts or observers of the world (and therefore called in as experts in news broadcasts, for example), despite the fact that the very possibility of such analyses depends upon a certain value-system. Although religion is usually considered to be at the core of a country's or society's value-system, it is far too often neglected that there are similar assumptions upon which academia and research are founded. Indeed, it may be impossible to pursue any scholarly study of religion, in this case, without certain presuppositions. Purportedly simple tasks show, with a bit of probing, that there is no such thing as a value-neutral approach to this type of research. Even the very act of identifying religious belief, already prior to identifying different religions *per se*, contains presuppositions of the societal heritage of the researcher or observer, which invariably leads to academic ethnocentrism. Taken further, of course, this then informs policy and the assumptions become 'inherent' in society. The answer, however, is not to deny that there are underlying assumptions that in some way influence or inform the discourse, but rather to acknowledge their existence and realise their impact.

Acknowledging the assumptions and presuppositions may then facilitate understanding of the possible implications of the discourse. Rather than being distraught about the often obvious failures of such concepts as Universal Human Rights, the Just War tradition or the International Laws of War, a better approach might thus be to acknowledge the ethnocentric heritage of these concepts and therefore why they may not be wholly accepted outside their own spheres of interest. Likewise, it is important to realise that the inherent bias in any discourse is not only based on the use of language. Although language is a vital part in the conceptualisation of bias and assumptions, it is nonetheless true that most underlying presuppositions are dependant on language only inasmuch as they need a medium to be disseminated. The assumptions, therefore, precede language, but require language in order to be shared and communicated. This means that a careful re-wording of a particular argument may still not receive the intended response, since the underlying assumptions are not addressed. Language is, however, an important first step in overcoming some of the main obstacles imposed by assumptions and presuppositions. Unfortunately, however, the majority of works of International Relations advocate the view that the use of language is of little, if any, relevance within the field. Martin Hollis and Steve Smith, again, provide a convenient summary of the position of most scholars within the discipline: 'Luckily, theories of international relations need not grapple with the nature of language in any depth'.[16] Setting out with such a mindset unfortunately means that few attempts are made at using neutral language or even acknowledging that language in itself is not neutral. Perhaps if the opposite practice were employed, there would be less blatant bias and complicating assumptions and presuppositions.

As proposed here, there is a case not only for acknowledging that there are certain assumptions in every discourse that influences that particular discussion, but also for actively confronting the presuppositions that are inherent in any society, in its language, symbolism and historical and philosophical heritage. Again, the case for conceptualised religion may be one practical and proactive response to dealing with these assumptions. Earlier in this chapter the distinction between philosophical and practical religion was alluded to. The latter being 'popular' religion and the former the type of conceptualisation advocated here. Although there are ethnocentric difficulties even with this type of distinction it may be argued that philosophical religion makes no presuppositions or assumptions about religious truth, whereas this would be the very object of practical religion, or philosophy of theology.

Many of the assumptions that surface through the use of language are based deeper than that. Often, assumptions are rooted in the historical and philosophical traditions of a particular culture or society. Sometimes explicitly, but more often not, the concepts and notions according to which society created its values were developed during a period of importance, be it of glory or of chaos, in the history of the society. Using the specific vocabulary of each, political Judaism, Zionism, for example, takes its strength from the age-long persecution and pogroms of the Jews whilst Islamism does likewise from the glorious days of Islam. Similarly, Laws of War are derived from the difficulties faced by societies in the wake of hundreds of years of European war, and individual Human Rights from the pursuit of freedom and independence during the French Revolution and the American War of Independence. History, therefore, is important in order to understand any society, but in conjunction with this it must be remembered that scholars and observers obviously have the liberty to be unhistorical, especially in religious comparison, and this needs to be acknowledged as well, or further assumptions are created. In the case of the study of religions, in particular, relating the history of a particular religion must be pursued in the narrative form of language, as mere chronological lists are not sufficient to portray a true picture of the religion. Such narratives will necessarily be based on assumptions and presuppositions. Despite the sometimes admittedly unhistorical historicising, religion is nonetheless often considered to be one of the most fundamental aspects of a society's value-system and it is therefore vital to have a grasp of the history of a religion in order to understand that religion, and thus the society in question. Such understanding can be hindered by *not* acknowledging the assumptions and presuppositions inherent in any discourse.

It may be seen as a spurious argument, and somewhat semantic, to labour the importance of acknowledging the assumptions, presuppositions and bias inherent in every society. However, the failure to do so within most contemporary academic disciplines and practices has grave consequences, especially within the areas of media, politics, and conflict transformation. The exceptions to this failure to look beyond the immediate discourse are few and far between, but they do exist, as shown by the discipline of Critical Linguistics and in the research of such groups as the Glasgow University Mass Media Unit, which has long focussed on more than 'face-value' news, for example. Within the news-media in particular, but significantly also within the academy, the use both of negative terms and concepts, such as 'non-Western' or 'non-Christian', and a 'we–they' dichotomy, often reinforces and solidifies existing assumptions and presuppositions. Returning to language as the main vehicle for such bias to become apparent, therefore, it is sometimes passionately argued that such terms should be banished from popular and specific usage.

Changing the vocabulary to this extent in order to remove many of the obstacles to conflict transformation and peace is a noble endeavour, though probably futile in its idealism. Of most significance to the present research, and to its further field of inquiry is the concept of 'terrorism'. On many levels, 'terrorism' is one of the fundamental phenomena under investigation in this book. However, wherever referred to by using this term it is only for rhetorical purposes, and this should be kept in mind throughout (stylistically, the term is not always kept within apostrophes, but this is invariably the ultimate intent). The assumptions, presuppositions and bias that are entailed within 'terrorism discourse' are often damaging to the extreme, due to its referential invalidity; it means nothing. 'Terrorism discourse' is creating a 'reality' that blends 'the media's sensational stories, old mythical stereotypes, and a burning sense of moral wrath',[17] but contributes little, if anything, to the understanding of logic of 'terrorism' and how to overcome the threatening and dangerous aspects of it. Although 'terrorism' has never been satisfactorily defined, this is not due to lack of effort, but rather due to a fundamental misunderstanding of different cultures' epistemological and ontological heritages as will be explained in the next section. The international system regularly reaffirms its condemnation of 'terrorism', in UN Security Council Resolutions and other instruments. All this without being able to define what a 'terrorist' is, or what his or her actions entail. Depending on one's perspective, just about anyone or anything may be considered a 'terrorist' act at any given time.

One of the main difficulties with 'terrorism' discourse, both academically and practically, is the lack of a satisfactory way of dealing with situations referred to as 'terrorism'. The only possible 'solution' to 'terrorism' is necessarily 'counter-terrorism', but this concept possibly means even less than the concept of 'terrorism'. Idealistic opposites to 'terrorism' as for example 'joyism', are probably not applicable in political reality, although the effort is admirable. When referring to political violence as 'terrorism' it is important to remember the old cliché that 'one person's terrorist is another person's freedom fighter'. When labelling any person a 'terrorist', or any phenomenon 'terrorism', the assumptions and presuppositions inherent in that discourse are sure to make an enemy of whoever is on the receiving side of such circular rhetoric, whilst contributing little to understanding the phenomenon. The 'terrorist' is ultimately and inevitably an altruist, believing (rightly or wrongly) that he or she is acting for the greater good in the struggle against evil. Labelling his or her act as 'terrorism' would indicate it as being a criminal act, and therefore bad, rather than good. Although the abolition of the term 'terrorism' would not solve all difficulties faced by the discourse of political violence, as advocated here, it would contribute to removing the main impediments to conflict transformation. As such, this is not seen as futile idealism, but as vital for deep understanding of the socio-political world of today. Here, whenever the term 'terrorism' is included, it is either to produce a certain reaction or to facilitate popular and lay understanding. It is, however, never used as the unqualified concept so common in the media, politics and academia today. Where an explicit qualification is not provided, this is nonetheless the tacit understanding.

A facilitating factor in identifying, acknowledging and ultimately minimising assumptions and presuppositions is their relative superficiality. Most assumptions stem from ignorance, or a lack of knowledge, whereas an ontology, for example, is much more fundamental. Presuppositions, of course, are of two main variants, where one is almost synonymous with assumptions and the other resembles an epistemology in that it is rather more fundamental, and not as clearly decipherable. Amongst the latter are concepts that are taken for granted in popular perception, and unfortunately also in most academic research, even after the issues have been made apparent. Examples of this might be that religious fundamentalism presupposes *writing* and Christianity, being a baptising faith, presupposes *water*.

Ontological Considerations

The last so-called prerequisite for the earlier perceptions entails an investigation of the epistemology and ontology that are permissive of such explanation. There are certain epistemological and ontological considerations that need to be highlighted. These relate to the nature of knowledge (ontology) and how it is influenced by the way it is istemology). The notion of a 'threat to international peace and security' efly touched upon above is highlighted here on an ontological level. It is o talk about such a threat if one a) realises that international peace and and b) that it is worth protecting, hence anything else being a threat and section depends heavily on a sub-branch of the Narrativist school of lations.

Another ontological notion that I highlight here refers, again, to the concept of 'religion'. In addition to the conceptualisation of religion at the beginning of this chapter, the idea that the concept does not necessarily exist in all cultures as a separate and researchable notion was touched upon. This can be seen for example in Ibn Khaldun's early categorisation of rational and traditional sciences. Whereas religion is undoubtedly part of the traditional sciences, it cannot be researched as a separate phenomenon and it would thus be impossible to investigate the notion not only of another religion but also of many religions and even 'abstract' religion.

Certain concepts developed for a particular purpose often have a negative, albeit unintentional, effect that at times is not only a source of violence and conflict, but is often dangerous in ways opposed to the very concept itself. This is investigated in respect of concepts of identity, pluralism and notions of multi-religious societies. Research into conflicts pertaining to ethnic or religious identity often perpetuates these conflicts. This conclusion is reached by questioning the allegiance to certain ontological and epistemological arguments such as the possibility of only having one identity. In the West this is seen not only as desirable but also without alternative, whereas in many Eastern cultures an individual can have several identities depending on the context and situation. Notions of identity-conflict were alien to many of these cultures, but Western researchers have often imposed such conflict on them.

These three illustrations of the underlying epistemological and ontological considerations must be seen as merely examples, and there are other – often better – cases that could be highlighted. However, it is important that some illustrations are employed to exemplify what makes the explanations explored in chapter two permissible. As those explanations refer to armed conflict and the role that religion plays in this and on the international arena in general, the foundations of these explanatory discourses are of great importance.

First, therefore, the notion of a 'threat to international peace and security' was *explained* earlier. Very briefly it was then mentioned in relation to the assumptions and presuppositions in the previous section. This notion is far from simple, and is often more complicated than those who use the phrase care to admit. Joseba Zulaika and William Douglass do, however, point out that in contemporary discourse at least, 'the perception of threat, in particular, is notoriously subjective'[18] and this is true inasmuch as whoever perceives the threat is defining it by his or her own assumptions and heritage, as pointed out in the previous section. But whereas a threat on the individual level is based on basic perception, on a conceptual level, threats are also defined by the intersubjective paradigm to which they relate. Again, what this means is that in order even to perceive a threat to 'international peace and security' it is necessary both to agree that such a phenomenon exists and that it is worth protecting. If it did not exist, there could not possibly be a threat against it. Similarly, if it indeed does exist it must be seen as a valuable concept that should be safeguarded, or there would be no threat against it.

Such an argument can be extended to include the more fundamental issue as to whether there actually is an international system *per se*. If the international system is taken as a construct of formerly imperial or colonial Western states, according to their perception of 'proper' politics, it is clear that there will be dissenting voices making themselves audible at regular intervals of international history. Indeed, it could even be possible to raise the objection that the very term 'international' system presupposes nations, that is states, and therefore excludes non-nation, or sub-state, groups. A threat to the peace and security of such a system, therefore, does not merely entail the complexities of threat perception, but also the common understanding of the desirability of an 'international' system of states. In addition, the questions relating to its peace and security further complicate the issues, as these two concepts are self-referential *in extremis*. If something is considered a security-issue it immediately becomes one.

It is possible to see how this argument could be thought to be merely academic, but my belief is rather that it is vital to understand why the underlying paradigms matter to enable new methodologies to be successfully applied throughout research into these fields, and in a range of practical areas related to these, such as risk assessment and conflict transformation. Of course, as religion not only teaches a theoretical view of the world, but also a genuine pattern of life the practical application of threat perception is all the more relevant, but only if its permissive bases are acknowledged.

The second epistemological phenomenon draws heavily on the basis of the conceptualisation of religion. The perception of 'religion' is not necessarily equal between different cultures. Indeed, it is more often the exception, rather than the rule, that understandings of the concepts concur. Even within allegedly similar, or the same, religious traditions, the definitions and perceptions differ widely. It is from this basis that one of the epistemological bases of this book is its perspective that it is possible to conceptualise religion, and make it into an abstract phenomenon for the purposes of research. Even in religiously liberal cultures, where freedom of religion often implies pluralism and the right to choose religion (or not), it is difficult to perceive religion as a researchable notion in its own right. In less religiously liberal cultures, where religion is of more importance, perceived to have more historical value, or is of a more 'advanced' stage, this becomes even more difficult, if not impossible. Indeed, there are not many things people are willing to die for that are abstract.

Where 'religion' can be perceived outside of one's own worldview, it is nonetheless on a vastly different level from one's own faith. If liberal about religious views, one can discuss another religion, but never discuss it on the same level as one's own belief, or indeed believe it to be on a par with one's own belief. In several language-systems, therefore, there are constructs (many of them relatively new) that would allow for such argumentation. Arabic, for example, does have words for religion, creed, faith, belief, denomination (like *dīn* and *milla*) and a range of variants of the roots. Indeed, these words can even carry plural forms (*adyān* and *milal,* respectively, in this example), and a variety of negative forms (for example, *lā-dīnī*, *lā-dīnīya*, etc.). The Arabic word for the religion of Islam (*silm* and *islam*), however, cannot. Similarly one can talk about God (*Allah*) as the one and only, or of pagan gods (*alih*), but these two concepts are far from equal. Whilst Arabic is used as an example here, every language has similar distinctions, as in English where there is a tacit distinction, for example, between 'God' and 'god'.

This underlying distinction in every tradition, once made apparent through language, influences research and knowledge by the way the knowledge is perceived, even prior to the commencement of the analysis. In Ibn Khaldun's early treatise on the philosophy of history the rational and traditional sciences are categorised. Religion falls into the category of the traditional sciences, but cannot be researched as a separate phenomenon. It is not possible to research other religious beliefs than Islam, according to Ibn Khaldun, if one is a Muslim. Similarly, it is impossible for a non-Muslim to research and understand Islam. It would be impossible, therefore, not only to investigate other religions than Islam (in the case of a Muslim), but also to comprehend and investigate a conceptual perception of religion, or 'abstract' religion, as advocated earlier in this chapter.

Coupled with the idea that very few cultures (if any) have a value-neutral approach to the study of religious ideas, and in particular those with contemporary socio-political influences, is the difficulty associated with how scholars and observers within the various traditions have attempted to overcome this. In the Western philosophical tradition, within which I somewhat reluctantly find myself, the rise of the discipline (and associated research) of Comparative Religion is a misnomer. Very little has been learnt by Western scholars of so-called 'non-Western' religions due to the obstacles created by unawareness of the epistemology and ontology within which they were rooted. Apparently without any irony, Alfred Martin, for example, believes that 'it was the discovery of other Bibles than the Old and New Testaments that gave birth to the science of comparative religion'.[19]

The last of the epistemological and ontological considerations to be raised here is in many ways the practical exemplification of what happens when the above two obstacles are not realised, but also a consideration in its own right. For these purposes, this last concept will be referred to as 'ethno-religious narratives', but it must be remembered that in these, religion and ethnicity often form inseparable and indiscernible entities. This concept is arguably the foundation of most ethno-religious conflicts around the contemporary world, and is the basis for all of the strategic dangers as presented in the 'strategic appraisal' at the beginning. Some conflict analysts often take the 'easy' way out by referring to 'ancient hatreds' as the cause of conflict, where the (real) underlying cause may be elusive. Such a perspective, although not alone, poses a grave danger as it not only enables the dangers outlined in chapter two to exist, but also hampers successful conflict transformation. The concept of 'ethno-religious narratives' works in two main ways, case specific and what will be called 'underlying permissive'.

The case-specific application of 'ethno-religious narratives' is used to mobilise peoples, rally support and justify – or explain – a particular cause. It is often the case that history is invented, or re-invented, along religious and ethnic fault-lines to achieve political goals. Amongst some scholars it is indeed recognised that the religious conflicts that are seen as some of today's major threats to 'international peace and security' (bearing the qualifications made above in mind) are often due to invented (or created) narratives, usually regarding the struggle for the restoration of an imagined (or fictitious) past, or to achieve particular political ends. Whatever happened in the past, be it good or bad, becomes sacred, and was reverenced by later adherents, revivalists or reformers. Of course, this is far from being a modern phenomenon, although the modernisation does play an important part in allowing 'ethno-religious narratives' to dominate analysis of religious (and ethnic) conflict in the contemporary world. As the religious identities that enable conflicts with extraordinary dangers are often formed *ex nihilo*, or at least 'on the flimsy basis of an imagined past'[20] the implications are obviously threatening to 'international peace and security' (again, remembering the above qualifications). However, explanations of conflict based on such ethno-religious identities are not only tacitly allowed in the international system, they are also positively condoned. This is the concept of the 'underlying permissive' ontology, which allows religious conflict to exist, and thus that the dangers described earlier are present on the international arena.

Earlier, the cycle advocated by scholar John Mearsheimer was briefly outlined. This cycle suggests that policy informs the discourse that is supposed to describe the policy and that this in fact shapes both policy and discourse. A somewhat corrupted version of this 'policy-informs-discourse' cycle can be applied to the present discussion. When narratives of ethno-religiosity are used to explain and analyse one of the multitude of contemporary religious (or ethnic) conflicts, it could thus be argued that this tends 'to lead people who had not previously thought in those terms to explain their own behaviour "ethnically" and perhaps even start seeing their "ethnic" difference from their neighbor [sic]'.[21] This argument is equally apt if replaced by 'religiosity'. Indeed, it is often impossible to separate the two concepts, especially in situations of conflict. Analysis of such a conflict would thus use 'ethno-religious' narratives to explain the conflict, which in turn would fortify and solidify the 'religiosity-factor'. Justifying conflicts on religious grounds would therefore mean justifying them in narratives and stories that the intellectuals and elite of such a society are required to forge, create or otherwise provide. In situations where the identities are forged according to a somewhat created history or mythology, the all-important role of the historian or academic, for example, is to prove that the narrative is true and 'what is alleged to have happened did happen'.[22] This in itself sounds almost fictional and one can see the resemblance to Ken Kesey's Chief in 'One Flew Over the Cuckoo's Nest': '...it's the truth even if it didn't happen'.[23]

Now, the dangers and threats outlined in the beginning are very real indeed and these dangers are often enabled by the use, abuse and – indeed – misuse of 'ethno-religious narratives'. Prior to that the inherent subjectivity of such concepts as 'threats to international peace and security' was investigated, followed by a short outline of the impediments to neutrality posed by the epistemological bases of such concepts as religion within different philosophical and historical traditions. There is, however, still an additional aspect that further complicates research and practice into religious armed conflict. Whilst accepting that all identities are created using narratives of history, and that 'historical accuracy is a weapon'[24] potent enough to pit neighbour against neighbour and friend against friend, I will conclude this chapter by offering a further consideration in relation to epistemology and ontology.

This is the concept of ethnocentrism, which has only recently begun to interest scholars. Rather than attempting to judge or justify ethnocentrism, my aim is to highlight its existence and the importance of acknowledging that it does exist, rather than trying to overcome it. Such an endeavour would probably prove futile, as there is arguably no such thing as a non-ethnocentric discourse. To expect and realise its existence and influence, however, is a different matter. Whilst it would be impossible for the researcher to reach correct conclusions if he or she was dishonest or prejudiced it is probably equally true that no conclusions can escape a degree of prejudice since anyone's perspective is invariably confirmed by definitional fiat. Indeed, it may not be possible to pursue any scholarly study of religion without presuppositions, and hence prejudice. Bearing this acknowledgement, albeit no resolution, regarding ethnocentrism in mind, it is now possible to briefly highlight how *not* acknowledging the ethnocentric epistemology may have serious consequences.

The management of religious conflicts is the main security concern in the 'new world order' following the end of the Cold War. Such a statement is 'true' since the international community 'is now predominantly in agreement as to the nature of proper government'[25] and such an agreement must necessarily entail agreement as to certain concepts of threats, of which 'religion' is one. It is this view that has been contested throughout this chapter. An ontological obstacle posed by such a view is that according to the Western concept of identity, which due to religio-historical reasons is highly monolithic, any person 'must belong to one, and only one "ethnic" unit'.[26] Consequently, this means that the intellectual and popular 'hype' of ethnicity today, emanating from such Western foundations, means that multiculturalism – in the ethnic sense of the word – is not possible. As contemporary narratives thus could be said to be monolithic in principle – albeit differing in content, form and fact – conflicts become inevitable as one truth-claiming narrative is posed against another, opposite truth-claiming narrative.

Whilst recognising the growing importance of such concepts as narratives, ethnicity, religion and identity in International Relations – and as a practice – it is necessary to recognise that religious conflicts are still viewed from a problematic perspective. Narratives explaining ethno-religious conflict are often Western creations and when these are used in order to try to explain 'multi-ethnicity' within a state, for example, the narratives are nonetheless concerned with how members of different ethno-religious identities can cohabit. Such 'cohabitational' theories do not lead to greater harmony, peace or security, but rather enforce and solidify the differences. According to Western mindsets, so-called 'non-Western' notions of ethnicity, for example, are often 'vague', as a person can have one, two or several ethnic identities as and when it is suitable, simultaneously or combining fragments of each wherever necessary. Asian notions of ethnicity, although the concept itself is rather alien, can – for example – be manipulated and act as a flexible tool, rather than as a trap.

Although history, and its 're-invention' serves a highly important role, as was outlined above, it is possible to agree with arguments that a person's ethno-religious identity is 'a theoretical, not an instinctive notion. If you have it, you learned it in your own lifetime, you did not somehow learn it at the Battle of Kosovo in 1389'.[27] The very existence of the Western perception of 'ethno-religious narratives' is providing a breeding-ground for further and protracted religious conflicts in an already inflamed world. It is thus important to understand that the arguments presented throughout chapter two are largely made possible by the existence of certain prerequisites that have been explored throughout this chapter. The Western contribution of some kind of ethno-religious 'awareness' to the international arena has often added a complicating factor to international affairs. Inadvertently such narratives, aimed at promoting and achieving harmony, peace and security, have had the opposite effect. Without understanding the underlying ontology and epistemology of Western approaches to conflict transformation and international relations, there is scant possibility of reaching a more peaceful world. Many Western concepts have been exported throughout the world, by military, economic, humanitarian and religious methods (and in the last century undoubtedly by mass media, too) that are often incompatible with the existing systems and traditions of which suffering, armed conflict and war are often the inevitable conclusion. Such newly introduced concepts are thus scarcely desirable imports.

Although religious narratives are not merely constructs, however, as will be seen below, the solution to the conflicts around the world where religion plays a part is certainly not to label everything as religious without thought of the consequences. Religion has a peculiar ability to create, support and further the identity of groups and individuals. This ability is sometimes seen as the link between religion and conflict, a relationship that will be explored and developed at some detail throughout the remainder of this book.

Notes

[1] W. Cantwell Smith (1962), pp.17, 195.
[2] Ibn Khaldun II:387, III:40, 43.
[3] R. Rubenstein in H.P. Fry (1996), p.55.
[4] L. Wittgenstein (1953), §66, see also §67 where the term 'family resemblances' is coined. See, for example, also J.M. Bochenski (1965), p.10; H. Suganami (1996), p.192.
[5] P. Tillich (1958), see, e.g., pp.11-12.
[6] W. Cantwell Smith (1962), p.19.
[7] S. Radakrishnan (1961), p.33.
[8] M. Weber (1991), p.267.
[9] J. Rawls (1973), p.130.
[10] M. Hollis and S. Smith (1990), p.10.
[11] P. Tournier (1978), p.115.
[12] The term (and much of its usage) is derived from H. Suganami (2000), p.3.
[13] M. Hollis and S. Smith (1990).
[14] D.S. El-Alami in D. Cohn-Sherbok and D.S. El-Alami (2001), p.184.
[15] See, J. Mearscheimer (1990).
[16] M. Hollis and S. Smith (1990), p.69.
[17] J. Zulaika and W.A. Douglass (1996), p.ix.
[18] J. Zulaika and W.A. Douglass (1996), p.8.
[19] A.W. Martin (1975), p.ix.
[20] S. Hoffman (1998), p.226.
[21] R.K. Dentan (1976), p.79.
[22] E. Wyschogrod (1998), p.2.
[23] K. Kesey (1962), p.13.
[24] J.W. Björkman (1988), p.5.
[25] P. Janke (1994), p.vii.
[26] R.K. Dentan (1976), p.72.
[27] R. Hardin (1995), p.150.

Chapter 5

Causation: Historical Causation of Contemporary Perspectives

In this chapter I will investigate the underlying causes of the arguments noted so far; that is the *causation* of the discourse. Though it may not be advisable to speculate about causes, this is nevertheless attempted in order to try to reach an understanding of why the relationship between religion and international relations is prevalently perceived as 'incompatible', with a view to highlighting how such a perspective can come to be altered to facilitate conflict transformation. Using the distinction explored earlier, schematically the book has now left 'explaining' and entered the realm of 'understanding'. The chapter has two sections, one dealing with the logical or rational cause of the arguments and the other with the historical cause behind the ontology permissive of such arguments.

In international politics, the explicitly secular heritage of the Peace of Westphalia (1648) means that the international system is largely unable to deal with religious violence, which by the very definition of the system is highly irrational and (apart from the tautology of violence in itself) also dangerous, and thus a 'threat to international peace and security'. Because international relations cannot acknowledge religion as a rational actor, religious belief is invariably seen as a tool or an instrument for political (and/or secular) agendas, which are perceived to be rational. This is the basis for most contemporary conflict resolution techniques. The 'opposing' side of the argument is usually presented from the religious perspective, which claims that there may be a genuine difference of belief. In such a conflict, it is argued, at least one of the parties is influenced by religion, and religion is seen as a rational actor in its own right. Both perspectives, however, fail to provide a satisfactory base for a framework of conflict transformation in that neither offers a sound understanding of the causes of the issue.

Where conflict/peace research conventionally includes religion, it invariably occupies one of two main positions, derived from the above perspectives, which in turn are based on an historical ontology no more than 350 years old. The first position, as outlined at length earlier, takes the position in conflict research that religion is an irrational threat to international peace and security. The other perspective, mainly within peace research, argues that religions can work together to ameliorate, limit or resolve conflicts. Both positions are arguably applicable in all conflicts, but especially those in which a religious dimension can be identified. Both perspectives are, however, based on Western notions stemming from the end of the Thirty Years War, that exclude religion from the public (political) sphere, and therefore necessarily perceive religion as a threat. The Westphalian convention declares that the only way to a peaceful international society is to completely remove religion from any position of international influence. Although this has proved to be a futile exercise, it is still the prevalent position on the international arena. More recent attempts at resolving the issue of religion and conflict have, however, been focused on the efforts of society (that is, peaceful 'international society') not to strive for secularisation of the public sphere, but rather a re-discovery of religious issues. It is clear that each of these 'peace-making' positions derives from the above distinction between conflict-research and peace-research, when it comes to the issue of religion and armed conflict.

Rationality: Rational Actor Model vs. Religious Rationality

First, I will highlight why religion does not fit the Rational Actor Model (also known as Rational Choice Theory) and what this means for the arguments presented above. The Rational Actor Model is today the most common perception within circles of international relations (and other social and economic sciences), both on a practical and on an academic level. This model assumes that an actor's decision-making process is greatly influenced (and often *only* influenced) by personal, political and ultimately economic gains. Within political decision-making it is important to be able to predict the outcome of an action by knowing how the 'enemy' will respond. Such intelligence ensures the desired outcome of deterrence, threat and direct action, for example. The problem lies in the fact that religion does not follow the same 'rationality' as international politics. The major reason for this is that for religious actors, political agendas, economic profit and even personal survival are often of lesser importance than, say, the survival of the values upheld by the religion, its moral 'high-ground' or its truth.

However, religion is inherently rational, although this rationality differs from strictly political rationality. For example, although religious actions are carried out with the view of a reward or some sort of gain, as is the secular political act, religious rewards are often only claimed in the afterlife. The examples of this are countless, and includes the Nizari 'Assassins', certain Shi'a groups in Lebanon, Hezb'allah and Hamas from the Muslim world, the Branch Davidians, adherents of Jim Jones in Jonestown and WCOTC from the Christian world, and so on. Of course, as every religious tradition makes some sort of similar claim on its adherents, the examples do not end there, but include everything from Sinhala Buddhist fundamentalists to Sikh separatists.

Although the section is concerned with logic and rationality, any logician would be disappointed, if not left with a sense of being conned into reading the research. This is because the logic used is not any kind of formal logic. I use no formal propositions or formulae, nor are there any signs of mathematical equations. It should also be noted that although similar in many ways, the rationality I refer to is not the theory of Rationalism – the third main theory of International Relations – which pertains to the functioning of the 'anarchical' international society, and espoused by the late Hedley Bull, and others. Instead, the logic here is of popular heritage for general readability and understanding. Whilst scholarship concerning religion and 'formal' logic or rationality is relatively rare, with only a few logicians dabbling with theology, or vice versa, research into popular logic is even less frequent. It is a shame that works with such promising titles as Lawrence Young's *Rational Choice Theory and Religion*[1] should, in so many ways, be inadequate in addressing the fundamental issues of religion and rational choice, which are significant for our present purposes. Although these two concepts (religion and rational choice) have very little to do with religious economics, Young's volume is useful in that it does highlight the major problem with much of Rational Choice Theory and religion, namely that it is based on economic models of rationality. Even gender-related research, which is usually renowned for unconventional approaches to conventional scholarship, bases its research into religion and rationality on economics. Although rational choice research has influenced economics and politics for a long time, rationality research – though not necessarily formal Rational Choice Theory or 'contractarian' rationality, for example – may be equally important for the understanding of religious actors.

From a political science perspective, it is invariably argued that religion is irrational, and essentially entails 'nonrational emotive factors'.[2] This 'political myth' ensures that religion is an unwelcome actor on the international arena, where the importance of being a rational actor is placed above all other characteristics of the players. This, of course, has serious implications both for conflict management and resolution, and ultimately for conflict transformation, where rationality however it is defined, is central. There is, however, nothing that makes religion inherently contradictory to rationality. Indeed, if rationality is defined as serving the highest interests known, religion may be *more* rational than political affairs, economics or any range of social sciences, and it has even been argued that rationality and religion cannot – in fact – be separated. Being rational, on the international arena, entails the calm calculation of interests, of gains and losses and of the market equilibrium. Any action will have its unavoidable re-action, and this influences the kind of moves that are generally 'allowed' on the international arena. Where such 'international' rationality differs from individual rationality is that it not only involves groups of states, societies and communities, but also a vast number of individuals. The rational method of conducting international affairs, therefore, is by way of economic relationships. Such market economies that are the base of international politics work best, as Michael Doyle has shown, if the political system supporting it is of a liberal democratic kind. This is because in Liberal Democracies, the *individuals* have a say, and although not all may be 'rational' in the strict sense, most are. Liberal Democratic states, therefore, seldom – if ever – wage war against each other, although they may wage war against non-Liberal Democratic states.

The international system of states expects and requires the actors within that system to be rational actors. This is known as the Rational Actor Model (RAM), and arguably 'most contemporary analysts (as well as laymen) proceed predominantly – albeit most often implicitly – in terms of this framework'.[3] It is applicable in international relations so that the actions of all actors may be predicted prior to them taking place, and as such facilitating an action, preventative measures or one's own counter-action. This so-called *realpolitik*, or Realism, has undermined interest in any alternative rationality, such as that provided by religions. It is important that one's opponents fit the Rational Actor Model, so that their actions can be determined prior to them taking place in order for deterrence, for example, to be effective. When faced with deterrence, it is likely that a rational actor would not proceed further, whereas an irrational actor, so it is believed, will not be deterred by traditional means. Throughout the Cold War, the two superpowers were bitter enemies, but they both none the less complied with the RAM, and although escalation led to the concept of MAD (Mutually Assured Destruction), the 'rationality' of both actors prevented a direct war from breaking out. This is because, although both powers were ideologically opposed, they nevertheless adhered to the same intersubjective paradigm, or shared worldview. In inter-state relations, a state must assume that its adversary shares its worldview of peace and war lest any moves or counter-moves be essentially futile. Of course, where this view of all actors on the international arena as following the RAM fails is where an alternative type of rationality is applied, because it is indeed hard 'to deter a group that is seeking to bring on Armageddon'.[4]

Whilst the social scientist (here including the economic and political disciplines) interpretation of rationality, and thus a rational actor, is basically concerned with economic, political – or in any case secular – benefit, its ultimate criterion is ensuring that individual human needs are met (although 'individual' in this sense is not necessarily taken to mean the same as the 'legal person'). Religious rationality, on the other hand, usually defines rationality as conduct that is morally right. A rational actor, in this sense, would act according to his or her morals, which are generally – though not always – defined by adherence to a religious system of belief. Defining morality in this way is of course not incompatible in any way with arguments that rationality pertains to 'happiness' and ultimately to 'goodness'. Although these definitions to an extent may apply to the secular RAM as well, religious rationality does not guarantee that the individual's life is spared. From the social scientist perspective, the most basic criterion for determining rationality would be individual survival, whilst in religion, 'the interests of the individual are subordinated to those of the group',[5] after the 'well-being' of the community, the faith, Truth or god. Despite this, there is no necessary conflict between religion and reason, as on several levels religious rationality nonetheless serves the interests of the individual, as does secular rationality, although for the latter, the rewards must be in this space-time. Religious rewards may come in a potential after-life (determining the choice between heaven or hell, favourable or unfavourable reincarnation, and so forth), whereas the ultimate *irrationality* for secular rationality would be to end one's own life. The most basic human need, according to secularists, is life, and religious 'rationality' would counteract that need.

The distinction between 'secular rationality' and 'religious rationality' made above is rather simplistic, of course, but it does highlight a main difficulty of the Rational Actor Model where religion is concerned. For a religious believer, individual life is often thought of as greatly inferior to the faith. Deciding to die for the religion, as Albert Camus (1953) explains, is because the Truth of that faith is considered more important to the individual, and for the common good, than his or her own life (p.21). Whilst a suicide-attack for a religious belief will thus appear as irrational and without any logic to a secular observer, it is usually carried out with the most profound inner logic. Here, the RAM of secular international politics is left without recourse. There is nothing that could be construed as logical in the act not only of taking 'innocent' lives, but also of an act that will ultimately kill the perpetrator. Secular observers often cannot comprehend how ending one's own life can be rational, or what kind of logic can justify the destruction of others' lives as furthering one's own peace and security. Inevitably, therefore, misunderstandings ensue when religious actors do not act in accordance with the RAM, although the acts in themselves were religiously rational in that both rewards and motives may be supplied, although generally of a transcendental or 'supernatural' character.

Whilst the only personal compensation for a martyr may be to have fulfilled, or at least furthered, a transcendental goal that is unbound by time or space, the political horizon is proximate and relies on an identifiable or calculable time-span. Political rationality, therefore, must identify goals that are attainable not only within the lifespan of the individual, but also that do not compromise his or her perceived well-being, or basic needs. It is true, of course, that arguably no human issue can be regarded as *exclusively* religious, in that it cannot arise from a vacuum or be unrelated to other events or factors. Genuine religious rationality may therefore be compromised in the minds of the believers to incorporate some kind of secular pragmatism in dealings with everyday life. It is not a sound practice, for example, to cross a busy motorway on foot, despite being convinced of one's salvation, or to preach one's religion in an extremely intolerant country where it may lead to incarceration or worse. However, in instances of cosmic war, for example, day-to-day pragmatism is often suspended in the struggle for religion, and it is then that religion usually enters the political arena.

As religious violence does not fit the RAM of international politics, the system finds that there is an apparent 'problem' in dealing with religion. Traditionally there have been two main ways of dealing with this 'problem', though neither is very satisfactory. Taking its cue from the Westphalian heritage of international relations, one of the solutions to the incompatibility of religion with secular RAM is simply to remove religion from the 'public sphere', so that actors are to be secular when they are in public. Any actions, therefore, *will* be in concordance with the Rational Actor Model even if the actors themselves justify their acts as being religious. As with the perspectives highlighted in chapter three, therefore, religion is merely an instrument for a political agenda, or 'a plaything of politics'.[6] There are, according to this view, no genuine religious motives for violence, for example, and all actors are rational in that all they seek is to maximise their economic profits, gain political control or improve their market-status. This is a simple enough method to circumvent a problem as complex as the one of religion and violence on the international arena; there is no religion in the 'public sphere'. The second methodology for coping with the issue of religion and the RAM has come further in its removal from the Westphalian system, and its solution is simply to rationalise religion. The most common form of doing this is by 'politicising' religion (as was the case with the Sudan explored earlier). This method does not remove religion from the political scene, but rather makes sure that it belongs there by moulding religious traditions according to political systems. Whilst this would arguably be very easy for many religions, as they already constitute a form of political system, the difficulty lies in that the kind of political system religions naturally espouse includes politics, whereas the secular argument for this type of rationalisation is that religion should be subordinated to politics. Politicising religions in this way puts them at the core of the civilisations that both Samuel Huntington and Sayyed Qutb refer to as clashing. Ultimately, however, neither method manages to resolve the problem of genuine religious rationality being incompatible with a secular perception of the rational actor and rational choice.

A third position, which is advocated here, is the need for genuine understanding of religion in relation to rationality and logic. Such understanding would ensure that whilst not acting in accordance with the secular RAM, religions and their adherents are highly logical and rational. Understanding this, in turn, would mean that the logic of religious violence could be understood, and this is vital for conflict transformation in theory and practice. Whilst religion may not conform to the same economic, 'market-place' type rationality as the secular political system, it is not helpful to claim that 'any meaningful discussion on the nature of religion must begin with a recognition that nonrational experience exists at the core of all religions'.[7] Instead, attempting to understand the rationality of – and logic behind – religious actors' beliefs, definitions and alternatives, although any such discussion of religion may be controversial, would cover more ground. It is doubtful, however, claims Magnus Ranstorp, 'that the U.S. or any Western government are adequately prepared to meet this challenge'.[8]

Rather than accepting a core irrationality in religion, any framework for conflict transformation must build on the premise that, on the contrary, there is an inherent logic to religious violence, although this logic – or rationality – is not necessarily based on the same intersubjective paradigms as its secular counterpart. Strategists, who are never too far removed from the so-called Clausewitzian tradition, argue that no war is started without clear intentions, methodologies and goals, although the course of the war is not predetermined due to incalculable 'mechanisms' as was touched upon previously. On this, both the secular Rational Actor Model and religious rationality agree, in that no actor would enter into a war unless certain of victory. However, whereas the former would insist that this certainty could only be derived from technical and numerical superiority on the battlefield, the latter believes that it is possible for just a handful of combatants to bring a super-power to its knees by having divine legitimation on its side, as virtually all the 500 or so wars since the beginning of the 18th century have shown. In the conventional strategic sense, the inferior group would have no chance of 'winning', whilst any number of possible examples from the world of 'terrorist' organisations show that this is not the rationality subscribed to by religiously motivated violent groups. In this context, it is important to remember that secular and religious rationality are not contradictory but rather complementary. In bridging the inevitable gap between the two, however, more of a multidisciplinary approach must be employed than the rather disciplinarily singular attempts offered by conflict resolution experts, politicians, journalists and academics today.

By accepting that much can be learned from taking a multidisciplinary approach to the issue of global religious violence, it is possible to overcome the perceived irrationality of religious actors. Certain aspects of a religious actor's rationalising of his or her acts *do* fit the secular RAM, such as the much cited and paraphrased theorem that war is merely the continuation of policy. On the other hand, other aspects of the actor's rationalisation conform to strictly religious ideas, rather than those of the secular Rational Choice Theory, such as that violence is always justified and rationalised in decadent or immoral times, or the idea of a paradisial reward in the after-life. Realising, for example, that this ideal does not change, and is the same today as it was hundreds (or thousands) of years ago, may be the first step in identifying certain aspects of religious rationality. Combined, the two approaches may highlight how an act that is perceived to be irrational in that there is no economic profit or individual gain, such as the action of a suicide-bomber, may none the less prove to be a completely rational act, although the rewards 'might come now, in a future condition of the perfect society of brotherhood, or after death'[9] and thus not necessarily *in this life*.

It may be asked what this approach to rationality achieves other than merely a rephrasing of a much used and abused concept, and the criticism is fair, even if not entirely justified. Referring to religious violence as a rational concept is not merely a political exercise like other similar attempts often are. Rather, more is achieved, or *could* be achieved, by accepting this theory. A deeper, ontological problem can be addressed by the acceptance of religious violence as a rational phenomenon, which will facilitate the concluding framework. As with the ontological discussion of 'terrorism', irrationality is a threat by definition, in that it is self-referential. There is no possible way in which one can have a *rational* dialogue with an irrational party. In response, the secular actor (the military strategist, government policy maker, etc.) assumes that the religious actor is completely irrational, and does not share the paradigm of the Rational Actor Model, and strategies, policies and actions are therefore not accommodating of the motives, intentions and thinking influencing the religious actor. There is, in short, no rational response to a perceived irrational action or actor. If the rationality of the actor is acknowledged, however, together with a qualification, if necessary, that it constitutes a different type of rationality and does not entail 'evil', for example, possibilities exist for a 'rational' exchange. That this works in practice has been more than researched in respect of the Cold War where rationality 'succeeded' in that it only brought the world to the brink of nuclear war once, and then only for thirteen days. With this, too, religion was pushed further from conventional (secular) rationality. To paraphrase Max Weber, the more rational and *political* order becomes, the worse *religious* tensions becomes,[10] as they are far removed from the rationality required by the international system. This is clear today as religionists, for whom violence is often as rational a choice as political activism, are quickly filling the 'void' left by the end of the Cold War.

In relation to the ontology of rationality, it is furthermore interesting to note that the self-referential nature of rationality means that every actor will necessarily assume the unrelenting rationality of him/herself. Tautologically one does not knowingly do irrational things. In addition, the rationality of actors functioning within the RAM, which is defined *in others* rather than in oneself, is always assuming the rationality in 'the other' person to be what one perceives it to be in oneself. As with the ontological difficulty of the 'Golden Rule', this proves to be a circular argument. Rationality, by this reasoning, is defined as the 'good' that one would like to see in others with whom one associates. Likewise, to be deemed rational these associates in turn need to find a similar 'good' in one's self. It may also entail an attempt at making the others 'good' in order for one's own peace and security in a RAM to be assured. Modern Western Liberal Democracies, referred to earlier as semi-secular liberal protestant states, have become very adept at this through the process of globalisation in the last decade. However, this is an old praxis in religious terms, where proselytising, missions and Crusades have existed in every tradition throughout history. It is completely rational, therefore, not only to ensure one's own security but also that of others, so that everyone conforms to the same rationality through an intersubjective understanding. Since there are usually only two alternatives (for or against), the choice is often perceivably easy;

either convert to the model in question (whether secular or religious) or have your person compromised (killed, incarcerated, persecuted or otherwise discriminated against). It is thus completely rational, even in secular international political terms, to wage war against an enemy because they do not subscribe to the same paradigm as 'us', and this is indeed a very common practice even among the most liberal and 'modern' states in the world today (whether it is against Iraq or its so-called 'Axis of Evil' accomplices). It is by qualifying this argument that war is rationalised within the secular RAM *and* for religious rationality. Indeed, both types of rational choice can even justify the death of the individual if it is for the greater good, although earlier this was somewhat refuted as incomprehensible for the secularist.

Earlier it was argued that secular observers usually find martyrdom incomprehensible as it does not conform to their view of rationality, which defines individual life as the most fundamental of human needs. This, however, must be qualified in light of the recent argument that war can be rationalised for the greater good of the community, or society, as a whole. According to the Westphalian tradition of an international system of sovereign states, the political entity known as the state has a complete monopoly of the use of (or threat of) political violence. It is the state that by its legislative and political processes decides when and how to go to war, after due rational calculation according to the RAM. As with religion, the state requires and expects its subjects to kill and die for its values and on its command. Soldiers who are killed in battle 'for their country', 'their flag' or 'their king' are received back home as heroes and are ultimately often awarded with posthumous commendations, honoured with ceremonies and war-memorials erected to their memory. On annual commemorative days, they are remembered and celebrated for decades, and sometimes centuries, after their death. The similarity with religious martyrology is striking and does not need much elaboration. Nationalism, patriotism and religion in this sense conform to the same type of rationality, according to which dying for someone or something else –an 'abstract' such as God, the flag or the forefathers – is seen as a 'beneficent act' (promoting the 'good' of another) and/or a 'benevolent action' (desire that the other should have this 'good'). Despite this, there are historical reasons why religion is seen as not conforming to the Rational Actor Model of international politics.

Before investigating this historical 'causation', there are a number of further factors that should be briefly highlighted in any discussion about religious rationality. All types of rationality, whether secular or religious, depend on informed choice after a calculation of interests and consequences. However, as John Rawls points out, 'the rationality of a person's choice does not depend upon how much he knows, but only upon how well he reasons from whatever information he has, however incomplete'.[11] This argument opens an interesting aspect of religious rationality. It is possible, even without qualifying Rawls' statement, to see that religious actors are in fact *more* rational than the secular actors who pride themselves on conducting international politics according to the RAM. Making an informed decision in the political sphere involves the use of political intelligence, gathered both openly and clandestinely from a variety of sources. The process of analysing such intelligence is an endeavour that employs thousands of individuals throughout the world to make informed decisions, or at least provides the intelligence necessary for a policy-maker to make the necessary choices. Incomplete, irrelevant or plainly wrong information can have disastrous consequences, even if the opponent is a 'Rational Actor'. In international relations, misunderstandings are likely due to a vast range of variables such as cultural differences or bad communication, and these can similarly ensure that the world is an unsafe place for many years to come, whether the threat is nuclear, biological, chemical, or – indeed – human. With hindsight, a decision may be deemed to have been lacking in rationality, but is usually justified as being outside one's sphere of influence, and by claiming that the decision was rational in that it was taken with the best available information and intelligence. Religious actors, however, do not generally face this difficulty. Although theologians or clerics are sometimes required to interpret a particular religious precept and thus adopt a position on various situations, there is often a wealth of already existing scripture, 'judgements' and precedents to employ. In the case of religious scriptures, of course, these are often considered by believers as law, or divinely revealed, and therefore cannot change. Although religion is never static *per se*, but incorporates a great deal of change, its scriptures, decrees and historical precedents often provide unchanging goals. The Islamic paradise, for example, which is a reward to anyone who dies for the faith, is the same for Hamas martyrs today as it was for the Nizari 'Assassins' a millennium ago. Similarly, the Jewish allegiance to Jerusalem or the Promised Land is not something that is reinterpreted for every generation, but is rather an essence that remains the same (or at least similar) throughout history, and stays true to the religion. Furthermore, most religions have a constant concept of the ultimate victory of Good over Evil, although the struggle itself is not predetermined, or known empirically. Religious rationality therefore arguably provides a *sounder* base for knowledge and intelligence than does its secular counterpart in that the precepts are predefined, and often revealed from a divine and thus infallible source.

Having established that both religion and international politics are rational, the question remains as to why these are perceived to be in direct competition at decisive points. It may be that despite the explicit wishes of the international system, individuals are nevertheless profoundly religious and where a choice is offered, or imposed, between secularism and religion many believers choose the latter. It is even possible to invoke John Rawls' claim of the 'Aristotelian Principle' here, in that intelligent beings (such as humans, but also including other primates, for example) prefer to act according to their highest abilities. Rawls illustrates this with the example of the preference to play chess rather than checkers if one knows both, or study algebra rather than arithmetic.[12] In short, if one is capable of both, one prefers to choose the more complex (and thus more rewarding) than the more facile (which will resemble a chore). Rational human beings, therefore, may actually have a choice between secular rationality (and to be a Rational Actor according to the RAM) or religious rationality (and be irrational according to the RAM), and indeed even choosing on a situation-to-situation basis between daily pragmatism and spiritual reward. Where these mixed loyalties conflict (at the decisive points), religion is often perceived as being higher than secular politics, and where the obligation to choose conflicts in the minds of the believers, the choice is therefore usually in favour of the spiritual. Despite man's inherent rationality, the spiritual or divine still plays an important part where outcomes are uncertain. This theme, of mixed loyalties, is also apparent in Hedley Bull's Rationalist writings, but in accordance with the English school of International

Relations (of which Rationalism is a branch), this is rather a case for the continued secularisation of the international arena where a return to religion as a meaningful entity of loyalties is 'fanciful' and where 'reason, not religion, remains the ultimate arbiter'.[13]

The above investigation of rationality in respect of religious violence on the international arena is necessarily brief and many arguments would need further exploration if a theory of rationality is to be proposed. However, arguments can be raised that the scientific approach to Rational Choice Theory is nothing more than 'curve-fitting' and that it denies the existence of any other 'non-rational' actor. It is clear that if that was the case very little could be gained in the furtherance of the understanding of religious violence supported here. In the same way as proponents of formal logic see no possibility of establishing a generally applicable logic of all religions, the theory of Rationalism claims that as yet 'no philosophical system has emerged which transcends the horizons of epoch and culture and resolves fundamental moral differences'.[14] Understanding that there is a rationality underlying every ontology, and hence the actions based on that ontology, may be the missing aspect that is necessary for conflict transformation where religion is an element. Violence can be rationalised in any system, whether religious or not, and rather than seeing the incompatibility of the goals, it is arguably necessary to see the phenomenological similarity of rationalisation within these systems. There may be genuine incompatibilities of doctrines, which cannot be accepted jointly without absurdity, but rationality may nevertheless depend on compromise. As opposed to a compromise of ideas, proving to be the main downfall of contemporary conflict resolution techniques, here this rather pertains to a compromise of the concept of rationality. Accepting that any activity, violent or not, can be made rational, and treating it as such, removes the tautological threat of something that is irrational, as seen above. Not only must it be assumed that the 'terrorist' is human, as Joseph Margolin suggests,[15] in addition it would also further the objectives of 'peace and security' to acknowledge that he or she is therefore also rational, although the rationality may be different from what would traditionally be referred to as rational. Understanding this difference, but also the phenomenological 'sameness' of rationality, will ultimately lead to successful conflict transformation. It is important to bear this in mind throughout the exploration in the next section of the historical background of the perception of religion as inherently irrational, and therefore a dangerous actor on the international arena.

Legacy of Westphalia

The Peace of Westphalia serves as the 'historical causality' not only of the perceived irrationality of religion, but also of the role of religion on the international arena in general. The Treaty of Westphalia, of 1648,[16] is commonly thought to have brought peace between Protestants and Catholics in Europe after a century of religious warfare, and officially marked the end of the Thirty Years War. This is not an investigation of the history of this war or the peace-process, nor is it an exploration of the chronological heritage of the war. Whereas there have always been a number of problems associated with the Treaty, its contemporary legacy now has a detrimental effect on the role of religion in international politics, and particularly in relation to armed conflict. Therefore new thinking may be necessary for future conflict transformation. I will also explore why the meetings in the German region of Westphalia in the 17th century are thought to have such momentous influence on contemporary international affairs, with the view of improving understanding, both clarifying concepts and redefining parameters of religious violence on the international arena.

To most political scientists, and many other scholars, the Peace of Westphalia has comforting connotations. Many theologians, however, dabbling with history or politics, are left feeling short-changed by a political instrument that had as an explicit purpose the removal of religion from all subsequent international politics. Politicians working within the international system of states, whether in 'Western' Liberal Democracies or any number of 'rogue' states (however defined), similarly have accepted some version of the so-called Westphalian system, however reluctantly. The main reason for this is that it is commonly recognised, although not exclusively agreed upon, that this peace that marked the end of religious wars in Europe, and thus in the rest of the world, marks the beginning of the modern system of states. Subsequent international relations were therefore not only inter-state, but by definition also secular. Of course, it has long been clear that the Peace did not end all religious wars as was anticipated at the time, and the notion of secular state-centric international politics may today be a misnomer. Although it can therefore be argued that the insistence upon the continuing relevance of the Westphalian Peace may be perceived as anachronistic, and of little value today, the two-fold issue of the *secular* international *state* system still has serious implications on the international arena. For the present discussion at least, the lasting legacy of Westphalia relates to this 'mission' of taking religion out of the political sphere and its creation of the (by definition, therefore) secular international system of states. Not only are the contemporary international consequences apparent due to the Judeo-Christian heritage of Westphalia, but paradoxically also due to its supposed secularity. To come to terms with the concepts of the previous chapters, and the first part of this chapter, the legacy of Westphalia must be understood.

It is not difficult to see why the international system, including international law, international economy and international politics, is rooted in Western Judeo-Christian notions of ethics and morality. There is nothing inherently wrong with this attempt, *per se*. Many such attempts have been made throughout history by virtually all (ancient and modern) civilisations. However, by assuming – as it must – that this system is the only valid one despite its very short life of 350 years, it is undermining itself. Whereas there is an immense literature on how 'other' cultures now 'revolt against the West', the international system and its academic counterparts must necessarily cling to its phenomenological background, namely the Westphalian system. Scant effort has been paid to attempting to overcome this inherent obstacle of the Western tradition. Other religious traditions than the Western (this term here excluding Islam) often find the legacy of Westphalia difficult to swallow, hence the many revolutions against the political, economic, social and legal ideals of 'the West'. In effect, as this is a cause of much conflict in the world, it may be suggested that a peaceful future world might not be ideally built on the Westphalian system of states, or at least not without fundamental changes.

As with most peace-treaties throughout history, the negotiations in Westphalia were intended not only to secure the immediate peace, but also ensure that there would be no cause of war in the future. Despite a few dissenting voices, it is generally agreed that the 'simple' motives of the Thirty Years War were based fundamentally on religious differences. Much has been written about the state of religion and belief in the decades prior to the outbreak of the war and whilst the underlying issue was more complex than the generally accepted tension between Catholics and Protestants (indeed, there were in actuality three warring factions, although two of these were nominally Protestant, namely the Calvinist and the Lutheran), religion was probably the most important source of conflict. No war exists in a vacuum, however, and even in this war allegiances changed, variables altered and the 'winner' ultimately wrote history. By removing the main cause of the war diplomats believed that they could avoid a repetition, or recurrence, of such conflict. In these new sovereign states, each political entity was established as a territorial entity where a governing body (though in those days mainly monarchies) would rule over its own affairs, as a sovereign state. Furthermore, religion was explicitly removed from their affairs with the view to it never again adversely influencing the peaceful relations between states. 1648 thus marks the beginning of the modern, *secular* international system of states, and the alleged termination of the significance of religion in the political sphere. The Treaty is thus regarded as the 'founding act' of modern international relations, despite it constituting a misnomer. The Peace of Westphalia neither ended religious warfare, nor removed religion from politics. Indeed, making such assumptions may be absurd as religion is still very much an element both in peaceful and violent international politics.

As religion is undeniably an actor on today's international arena, there is still unrelenting religious warfare, and as a range of trans-, multi-, and sub-national movements undermine state sovereignty, this may arguably indicate that as nothing has changed, 1648 is not such an important date. However, this would be to simplify international relations too much. Although religion was never removed from the political sphere as envisaged at the time, the Treaty nonetheless had a profound impact on subsequent international politics. The entire political system of today is based on the Westphalian peace on a variety of levels, including international law, diplomacy and to an extent even economics. As International Relations became more introspect, in ambition if not in genuine attempt, the Westphalian system has been criticised and a mass of 'new' political theories have appeared. By definition, however, they all adhere in some way to the Westphalian system, as that is the system which defines the parameters of scholarship. The most common position today is to recognise that religion never disappeared, as such, but that political society became secularised. This, however, is not satisfactory as it is still ignoring the social aspects of religion in statecraft. 'New' theories of international relations that incorporate this social aspect are nonetheless based in the ontology of the Westphalian system. This is mainly because of the Western philosophical heritage of most modern scholarship, because of the reluctance of the scholars to compromise their own field of inquiry, and ultimately because a completely new system is often regarded as a tautological threat to international peace and security (since it is by definition threatening to the *status quo*). Whilst various revolts against the Westphalian system became commonplace almost from its conception, few dare to completely renounce the idea of the state-system. This can be seen in those theories, which declare that politicised religion, and Islamism in particular, is the blueprint for a new international order based on religion. Although notionally innovative, it is nevertheless based on a 'religified' Westphalian system of states. Any such system, though conceptually religious, will be based on law and order, as is the 'anarchical society' of states today. Difficulties arise with this, in respect of religious Truths, in that these are often incompatible with any other system. Islamic theories of a new political order, for example, sometimes argue that 'all codes of law, ancient or modern, are deficient while the Islamic legislation alone is complete'[17] and necessarily so, as it was revealed by God. Where god is the ultimate source of right and wrong it is clear, however, that the previously highlighted choice between conversion and death is the only option.

The Treaty of Westphalia explicitly intended to remove this thorn in the side of peace. Never again was religion to be the ultimate arbiter over the minds of people, but sovereign governments were to have that privilege forever. At the time, it was recognised that religious issues were of sufficient influence to justify bloodshed, and thereafter war – where necessary – should be over more concrete issues, at intervals that are more regular and of a more interconnected character. Whilst not necessarily defended by religionists around the world, such statements are indicative of how the Peace of Westphalia came to be perceived as the foundation of the modern state system.

A major part of this system was its insistence on the legal foundations of the new international relations, as espoused in such traditions as Hugo Grotius' treatise on the laws of war and peace (*De Jure Belli ac Pacis*), and the later Emmerich de Vattel (*The Law of Nations*). With time, this law of the peoples came to be known as the 'laws of nations' and subsequently the term 'international law' was coined at the end of the 18th century. There is little – if any – doubt that the founding thinkers on matters of the international laws of states were not only Christian in their personal beliefs, but that they invoked Christian ideals of right and wrong, of ethics and morality and of good and evil in the formulation of the laws that were to influence the entire system. Both before and after the Treaty of Westphalia it would have been considered odd, if not outright impossible, to distance one's political and philosophical thinking from theological considerations. Indeed, religion was not only the dominant mode of thought, but also the only way both to be accepted as a serious scholar and to make valid statements. It comes as no surprise, therefore, that contemporary international law (and a variety of derivatives, such as international legal instruments, Human Rights discourses, the United Nations, and so forth) are based in Christianity. The conscientious scholar would furthermore have no difficulty in seeing how this has detrimental consequences for peaceful international politics today, as 'christian [sic] deep culture continues to shape Western politics'.[18]

The Christian foundation of international law, codified and solidified in the lasting legacy of the Westphalian system, is today one of the greatest challenges to international society. Academics, practitioners and laymen encounter difficulties in trying to consolidate the notion of a secular international system with its inherently religious foundations. Even common attempts to 'rectify' the mistakes of Westphalia have led some scholars to argue that Muslim politics, for example, although rooted in religion are none the less shaped by the Westphalian legacy. As the structure, nature and conceptual content of Westphalian international relations are Christian, though not all – or even the majority – of actors are, the 'resurgence' of religious violence on the world stage can be understood as a reaction to this traditional system. It is important, however, to remember in this context that the notion of a territorial and political entity – a 'state' – does exist in other cultural and religious traditions than the Christian. Western academics often 'forget' that in Islam, for example, the concept of the state exists, although it is not based in the same ontology as the West assumes and requires, but rather in the Qur'an. Indeed, by using a different ontology than the Western, Westphalian tradition, and one that does not shy away from religion and politics as being interlinked, it is possible to see how the solidarity and unity of purpose of any political system must be rooted in religion, as Ibn Khaldun suggested.[19] Rather than try to accommodate such views denied from the Western ontology of the international arena there may be an argument for a drastic modification of the nominally 'secular' Westphalian system. If it is clear that religion permeates the politics of all states, whether nominally 'secular' or explicitly religious, it may be necessary not so much to bring religion back into politics, but to acknowledge that it was never really removed, and that its continued influence cannot be ignored, but must be understood for any hope of peaceful future international relations. This, however, is an ambitious task, which I do not attempt here. It must suffice to indicate that religion serves as the main foundation for the morals and ethics of most traditions, although this argument is sometimes refuted by observers who claim that religion is more of an impediment to morality than its foundation, or – indeed – merely the 'outer clothing of inner moral truths, which the more instructed can hold without having any religion at all'.[20] Whilst such arguments are in a minority, it does indicate that the issue is not universally settled. Of course, I am not arguing that morality is dependant on religion, or that there is something inherently sacred about moral codes. Although it is perfectly possible to have morality without religion (and religion without morality), my point here is that when the morality of a particular religious system is codified in legal instruments that apply to individuals who do not necessarily belong to the same religious affiliation, there are irreconcilable obstacles. International relations, as founded on Christian ideals and perpetuated by the Westphalian treaties, today indicate how the difficulties of a historical heritage of a particular religious system endanger constructive and peaceful affairs.

If resigning ourselves, as Jean-Jacques Rousseau did, to the possibility that the Treaty of Westphalia is here to stay as the foundation of the political system,[21] the solution to the problem of religious influences on the international arena may be simple. Indeed, it may be *too* simple, as some scholars have suggested: '[it is] only necessary to suppress the religions from public life for a time of peace to dawn'.[22] Traditionally, from a Western philosophical perspective of International Relations, this has indeed been the express purpose of the discipline. Disregarding other cultures' ontologies, Western academics and practitioners have been striving to achieve complete secularisation of the international arena. Whilst some scholars suggest that this process was 'virtually completed by the conclusion of the War of the Spanish Succession',[23] it is clear that others are closer to the mark, suggesting that the Westphalian state-system has failed in its ambition of thorough-going secularisation.[24] Part of the 'problem' of political secularisation is that it never intended to remove religion *per se*, but only to remove it from politics, or the 'public sphere' of life. In the 'private sphere', the individual was still both encouraged and expected to be 'religious', or in any case had the freedom of choice, whilst the *state* was to be secular in its dealings with other states. This meant that religion always existed as an influencing factor for individuals and groups, and often also for state-leadership and legislature; there were few attempts to secularise the state *per se*; the sole concern was to make sure that religion was kept out of state affairs and relations with other states. The nominally 'secular' state is always 'in the right' and relies on aping religious ethics to provide moral backing for its values, and as religion remained a social element *within* the state a nation under threat still expects religious backing for its actions, as can blatantly be seen in the yearly 'poppy effect' and thousands of war-memorials around the world. Indeed, at times throughout history (and probably starting with Cato), the state's perception of itself through nationalism has indeed become a secular religion in itself. It would thus be absurd to argue continually for the confinement of religion to the 'private sphere' of life and politics to the collective. The two are interlinked, and are often not only inseparable, but – indeed – also indistinguishable. This dimension of religion is often missing from modern International Relations. Though religion should not be given more credit than it is worth, it should certainly not be ruled out completely from International Relations as the academy has continuously advocated. In order to know anything of the present, or future, it is necessary to have some understanding of the past, and of the historical causation of events as well as of ontologies, identities and beliefs.

Understanding the roots of the foundations of the contemporary international system entails acknowledging that the foundation of this system is the Peace of Westphalia. Recognising the Christian heritage of both international law and of the diplomatic system of states facilitates understanding the role religion is perceived to play on the international arena. By highlighting these historical causes of the discourse of religion as an unwanted phenomenon in international relations, as it was portrayed earlier, I hope that it is possible to employ a more open approach to violent conflicts in which religion is a factor. This, in turn, is necessary for successful conflict transformation, where knowledge of the underlying causes (including the basis of the ontology of the actors) is vital.

The legacy of Westphalia is in many ways obstructive to peace in the world, despite its noble aims. In conflict resolution research, a parallel may be drawn between the Treaty of Westphalia and a 'peace settlement', a process known for being able to bring short-term peace, but where tensions and discontent simmer and a 'new' conflict invariably erupts sooner or later. The Peace of Westphalia, being monumental in its role as formative for subsequent international politics, has on its 'conscience' not just one but hundreds of conflicts that have been made possible by the secular exclusiveness of the ontology of the Westphalian system. It is easy to see how the international system is incompatible with religion as a rational actor, and religion *should* therefore belong in the 'private sphere'. The issue is twofold, and both aspects make peaceful coexistence of religion and the state near impossible. On the one hand, the 'Westphalian' state claims monopoly for the legitimate use of force (and violence), and the international system in which it operates requires secularity. On the other hand, religious duty is invariably believed to be higher than any secular command in the mind of a believer. Secularity, or even indifference, may be seen as a threat in itself, against which violence is both legitimate and necessary. Whilst the state-system is ontologically secular and thus requires religion to be kept outside its foreign affairs, religion adopts a similar – though opposing – view of the state in that fighting against it may be a moral obligation and a neglected duty. With this, religious identity has become the main source of anti-Western sentiment, although such belief is neither anti-Western nor anti-Christian *per se*, but rather as a revolt against the essentially Western 'imperialism' of the Westphalian system. Where it is recognised that the entire international system is based on Western/Christian values, it is sometimes even argued that religious identity is a *prerequisite* for the struggle against this 'imperialism'.

Throughout the world there has been an academic 'revolt against the West' in that it has become generally accepted that the international system is based on the Western Judeo-Christian heritage I have described. Many religious traditions were not considered in the Westphalian negotiations and arguably rightly so since it was a peace settlement between warring Christian factions, in a Christian society by Christian negotiators. However, if this argument is accepted, the ensuing system (the international system of states, international law, human rights, etc.) should not be applicable to these other, so-called 'non-Christian' traditions. As it is, the Christian system of ethics and morals, which is codified in most international instruments, is applicable to billions of people who do not 'pledge allegiance' to the Christian religion, but who are bound to it by the international system of which they are necessarily a part. It should be clear that this will always constitute a potential for conflict as long as the Westphalian system is perpetuated in practice and in academia. Religion is not threatened with extinction, despite various theories propounded by political scientists, and as it provides a firm foundation for moral views and social behaviour it continues to exert its overwhelming influence on the international arena. In many instances, this is a violent influence, and sometimes perceived to be threatening to the very core of the international system of states. The solution to the problem does not, however, lie in the Westphalian-type 'peace-settlement' that aims to remove the 'obstacle to peace and security' (religion) by ignoring its influence, or hoping that it will disappear of its own accord. The ontological aversion and fear that political scientists, politicians, journalists and governments have of religion has meant that there have been few attempts made at trying to understand the rationale of religious actors on the international arena. 'Fundamentalists', 'terrorists' and 'fanatics' are instead generic terms applied to violent religious actors without any attempt to explore their ontology, on their own terms.

Understanding the bases of the historical legacy of the Westphalian system does not merely entail recognising its Judeo-Christian roots or the nominally 'secular' system of states, however. Whilst acknowledging that governments, media and academia all require the continuation of the Westphalian state-system for *their own* continued existence in their present form, it is also necessary to recognise that even secular structures, historical events and communal memories may take on religious significance and symbolism over time. Although Western politicians generally recognise the religious foundations of most civilisations they do not usually accept the idea that seemingly secular structures and institutions may become 'religified' even in their own 'secular' tradition. Indeed, the semi-secular Westerner is sometimes portrayed as an 'oddity' in his or her approach to the past and present without knowledge of its religious foundations. Due to this, in part, religion has often been portrayed in distorted or even hostile ways in the Western academy, at least. As with 'research' into the Nizaris, secular scholars often approach the subject of religion with the main concern 'to refute and condemn, not to understand and explain'.[25] Confined to the 'private sphere', as explored above, religion was thought to have lost significance, and academically the secularist discourses of chapter three were thus the inevitable result. This, however, does not mean that religion in actuality *had* lost its political significance. Although 'public expressions of religiosity are no index of popular beliefs and values",[26] opinion-polls seem to indicate that religion is neither in decline nor are the 'seculars' in the majority in any state. This, in turn, may mean that since state-security has long been thought to be paramount for successful international politics, strategies may require change to accommodate the shift away from a purely state-centric view of security.

The legacy of Westphalia requires secular relations between states, to ensure 'peace and security', whilst affirming the Christian bases of the international law that governs those relations. In academia, this apparent paradox has been perpetuated by International Relations scholars who, in their rush to embrace secularity, 'forget' to tell the religious stories that underlie the discourse. In political affairs, the paradox can similarly be recognised by the language employed by contemporary nation-states to justify their foreign policy; Western states tend to ignore (or even consciously hide) the religious ontology, or 'root paradigm' of their policies, due to the legacy of Westphalia, whereas 'non-Western' states often pursue overtly religious foreign policy goals. Apart from (political) academia and political affairs, lay opinion is influenced in a comparable way by the use of symbols (both consciously and unconsciously), plots and stereotypes throughout popular media. Novels and Hollywood films have, for example, replaced the Cold War Russians by portraying Muslims as 'east-of-the-Mediterranean Towelheads' wielding everything from AK-47s to scud-missiles. Documentaries and news-broadcasts similarly solidify stereotypes without due consideration to the underlying ontology, which is 'so taken for granted – so "obvious" to the members of that culture'[27] that it remains unquestioned.

To acknowledge that the Westphalian legacy is relevant in international relations today is not to say that it will remain unchanged. There have been a number of 'New World Order' theories in recent years trying to address this issue, although facing fears of being academically or politically excommunicated. Islam, argue certain scholars, provides the blueprint for the new 'non-secular' world order, based in the teachings of Islam. Similar views can be expounded from other religious quarters, like Buddhism which not only has a political role but may also form both the basis for modern political thought and a resource for contemporary power in the East, albeit that classical Buddhist philosophy *per se* distances itself from power and worldly affairs. Hinduism, with its characteristics as a 'sponge religion', could similarly be applied to modern international political theory, in an increasingly shrinking 'global village', where issues of multiculturalism and multi-religiosity are at the forefront of human concern, though with little consideration of the 'root paradigms' or ontology. By any reckoning, therefore, religion is still a powerful force on the international arena, but a force that has been suppressed due to the Peace of Westphalia. The 'resurgence' of religion that I explored earlier is thus not exerting real power by becoming politicised, but is rather retaining such power by resisting politicisation. It makes little sense to cling to the secular ideals of the privatisation of religion, claiming – as does Jürgen Habermas – that 'religion today is no longer even a personal matter'[28] when the very ontology of most systems prove to have both explicit and implicit religious meaning.

The main legacy of the Westphalian system of states, though often debated, thus lies in its inherent paradox of promoting and requiring secularity, on the one hand, with separation of Church and State, and the religious roots of the system, on the other. Religion *does* have a profound influence on people in the 'private sphere', but also in the 'public sphere', as is clear by the fact that religion is one of the few things rational human beings would fight for, until death if necessary. Indeed, as religion often sets the fundamental parameters for who can kill and who cannot, it is 'difficult to accommodate religion in an entirely state-centric model of international politics',[29] which confers use of force (violence) to the exclusive judgement of the state.

Notes

[1] L.A. Young (1997), see, e.g., p.75, etc.
[2] A.-M. Smith (2001), p.29.
[3] G.T. Allison (1971), p.13, emphasis original.
[4] J. Stern quoted in A.-M. Smith (2001), p.63.
[5] S. Radakrishnan (1961), p.19.
[6] S. Radakrishnan (1961), p.35.
[7] L.A. Young (1997), p.136.
[8] M. Ranstorp (1996), p.62.
[9] R. Collins (1975), p.373.
[10] M. Weber (1991), p.333.
[11] J. Rawls (1973), p.397.
[12] J. Rawls (1973), p.426. For a discussion of the Aristotelian Principle, see pp.424ff (§65) in Rawls (1973).
[13] D. Harbour (2001), p.136.
[14] A. Linklater (1996), p.101.
[15] J. Margolin (1977), p.271.
[16] Throughout the chapter, the various treaties signed in Münster and Osnabrück in the German region of Westphalia, are referred to collectively as the Treaty of Westphalia, the Peace of Westphalia, or a number of derivatives, as and when appropriate.
[17] S. Qutb (1977), p.69; Cf. B. Blanshard (1974), p.234; S. Radakrishnan (1961), pp.52, 57, 94.
[18] A. Osiander (2000), p.790 [NB: This scholar capitalises 'adjectives denoting geographical, ethnic or cultural affiliation ... but not adjectives denoting religious belief'].
[19] Ibn Khaldun, *The Muqadimmah* I, 284, see F. Rosenthal translation (1958), p.319 and C. Issawi translation (1950), p.131; K.J. Holsti (1991), p.355; A. Hussain (1988), p.10; A. Saad-Ghorayen (2002), pp.34-46.
[20] A.O.J. Cockshut (1964), p.49; D. Harbour (2001), p.78.
[21] J.-J. Rousseau (1964), p.572: '...le Traité de Westphalie sera peut-être à jamais parmi nous la base du systême politique'.
[22] R. Schwager in W. Beuken and K.-J. Kuschel (1997), p.119.
[23] K.J. Holsti (1991), p.149.
[24] J.R. Hall (2000), p.4.
[25] B. Lewis (1985), pp.19, 18.
[26] K.R. Dark (2000), pp.56-57; T. Breyfogle (2001), p.544.
[27] W.E. Biernatzki in C. Arthur (1993), p.127; Cf. G. Goethals in C. Arthur (1993), p.32.
[28] J. Habermas (1976), p.80.
[29] K.R. Dark (2000), p.ix; Cf. W.A. Brend (1944), p.96; J.W. Björkman (1988), p.17.

Chapter 6

Origins: Religious Origins of Contemporary Perspectives

Having now firmly progressed from 'explaining' the role of religion in the international system to trying to 'understand' it, here I will attempt to offer an understanding of the logic of religious violence. This is termed *origins*, as it refers to the roots of the arguments thus far presented by way of accepting that there is a specific set of genuine religious beliefs that not only makes stereotyping possible, but also makes violence, conflict and 'incompatibility' possible as well. In other words, the inherent logic of religious violence is not only permissive of actual, real-time violence, but it also constitutes the origin of the perceptions and misconceptions of chapter two. Understanding this logic serves as a means of overcoming the obstacles of conventional conflict resolution techniques, media misreporting and political decision-making.

To form the basis of such understanding, I will first offer a general overview of the logic of religious violence, and then highlight six violence-conducive elements that form a part of this logic. Two fundamental notions are explored first, followed by four briefer exposés. Each of the six sections highlights a specific religious belief, which although not necessarily pertaining to all religious systems at any one time is at least a tenet of abstract religion. These are elements that may be either conducive to violence within religions or that may allow violence to be perpetrated with the approval (tacit or otherwise) of the religious system in question. It is naturally acknowledged that these particular aspects of religious systems have often grown from a particular historical situation, as any comparison between the Meccan and Medinan revelations of the Qur'an would show, for example. Although this may perpetuate the imbalance of scholarship, the focus here is merely on the violent – and not the peaceful – aspects of religion. Whilst images of religious violence are not always or even necessarily re-enacted on the political arena as political violence, but are often in the minds of the believers, in the scriptures or in metaphysical imagery as in John Bunyan's holy war, it is important to have a sound knowledge of the *possibility* that these may indeed constitute real political violence rather than ignoring their existence.

The Logic of Religious Violence

Religious violence, and thus religious armed conflict, is neither illogical nor irrational. It is vital to explore this argument, if the recurrence and lethality of religious violence on the international arena is to be understood, and potentially ameliorated. By exploring the concepts that make the logic of religious violence possible, it is highlighted below why the simultaneous (in time and space) occurrences of religion and violence in the contemporary world, as well as in history and probably in the future, are not simply circumstantial, but in fact an essential dimension of religion. A caveat mentioned earlier must be kept in mind, however, which is that any formal logician would find the reasoning sadly lacking.

From a lay perspective, or even a misinformed professional perspective, the state of the contemporary world might indicate that religious violence is rife, and in the wake of its irrationality, there seems to be wanton death and destruction. Statistics of gruesome 'terrorist'-events are usually employed by scholars as an indication of the importance of their work. It is true, however, that not only do the majority of international 'terrorist' incidents today have religious influences, the intensity and lethality of this violence also far outweighs purely secular forms of political violence. However, agreeing that religious violence exists, and that statistically it generates a higher frequency of casualties and destruction, is not necessarily to say that it is irrational. On the contrary, religious violence is on many levels *more* logical and rational than purely secular forms of political violence, and its intensity further supports this argument. The main argument for the logic of religious violence consists in its inherent incompatibility with compromise.

This sense of religious violence being incompatible with compromise and conflict resolution is a notion that is prevalent within all religious traditions. Similarly, it is because of this incompatibility that instrumentalist religious violence (religion used as a tool for political violence) often becomes intractable. Where the conventional political scientist view is lacking is that its explanations of religious violence fail to see not only where the violence originates in terms of religious precepts, but also how peace could be a near impossibility when religion is a dimension of the conflict. This gap in understanding has had disastrous consequences following media-reports, political decrees and academic statements. Invoking religious rhetoric as a metaphor or literary liberty, without sufficient knowledge of the logic of religious violence can on occasion take even the author of such by surprise. Although no religious connotations are implied, the very use of religious terminology in relation to conflict, war and violence can open a Pandora's Box of genuine religious violence. Whether taken literally or as a metaphor, any religious claim is necessarily a premise for sacred warfare. Once a religious conflict has been entered into, there is no possibility either of compromise or of withdrawing from it. This would be to betray not only oneself, as a believer, but also the community of other believers, the precepts of one's faith and ultimately god. However, it must also be remembered that it is not merely instrumental religious violence that is affected by the incompatibility of religious rhetoric in terms of religion and violence. Where there are genuine precepts for violence within a religion, and a genuine religious conflict is thought to exist (at least in the minds of certain believers), conflict resolution is likewise near impossible. In many ways, religion makes unconditional demands on the believers on a level that is the envy of most other authoritative bodies, such as the state. Religion motivates and inspires followers to fight for a particular cause and it is furthermore capable of sustaining that motivation, until death for the believer and for generations to come, if necessary. Although nationalism and a number of other nominally 'secular universalisms' make similar claims on their followers these are, in fact, mere 'metamorphoses of religious logic' and thus similarly 'mutually irreconcilable'.[1]

Religious incompatibility often seems to be related to another major tenet of religious violence, namely its ultimate desire for peace. However, as religious logic is generally believed to be exclusive and absolutist, peace is generally not unconditional. If peace requires compromise, believers invariably see this as 'making concessions upon points of fundamental moral significance'.[2] Invariably, religious violence is employed for the ultimate good to triumph and for the world to be a peaceful place. Religious wars therefore are wars to end all wars. Where the logic of religious violence differs from secular violence is the belief that the end-result (peace) compensates for the means employed in the struggle to reach that goal. Comparisons can be drawn with fictional narratives, where a happy conclusion usually makes up for any number of gruesome details throughout the story.

A particular aspect of these 'gruesome details' that makes religious violence generally more lethal than secular political violence is the impossibility of 'innocents', 'non-combatants' or 'civilians' in a religious conflict. An act of political violence, or 'terrorism', motivated in whole or in part by religious precepts may be entirely legitimate in taking the lives of 'the enemy', although this may include 'ordinary people' 'whom most [outside] observers would regard as innocent victims'.[3] There are a number of reasons why the logic of religious violence is reluctant or unable to recognise anyone as a neutral or innocent bystander. The most potent of these is the religious precept that in a conflict involving religion it is necessary to choose sides. Ranging from the monotheistic religions to the semi-secular rhetoric of politics, 'you are either with me or against me', and – indeed – any possible sin will be forgiven apart from the choice of the latter. In a religious war, 'there will be no "Mr. In-betweens"'.[4] The very existence of an 'Other' guarantees one's own identity, as there is no possibility that the other is *not* an enemy. Although the very existence of an (eschatological) enemy is a threat, it is also a promise, as it defines the 'rightness' and 'goodness' of one's own cause. It may even be *necessary* that all those who are not 'with us' are considered as 'them', and thus the enemy, in order to know one's own true identity. Ultimately, all conflicts are derived from a perception of this dichotomy; '"we" fight "them" because they are different, and their difference is threatening in its challenge to the validity of the ideas we live by'.[5] In religious conflicts, this dichotomy between 'us' and 'them' invariably takes on cosmic dimensions, as I will explore further in relation to cosmic dualism below.

Preceding the issue of the insider/outsider-aspect of religious violence as a rationale for its intensity and lethality, questions must be raised as to why religion exerts such a hold on the minds of the believers in the first place. One reason, which is associated with the above dichotomy of 'us' versus 'them', is that once a religious war has been declared, or violence decreed, it is impossible to choose *not* to fight. Pacifism or conscientious objection to war may be seen as a fundamentally religious ideal, whether it is rooted in the Sermon of the Mount, Qur'anic verses revealed at Mecca, or Hindu/Buddhist *ahimsa*. However, this ideal requires qualification in these three examples, as in all religions. Pacifism may even be argued to be absurd for Christianity for 'until men become Christian indeed, junctures will arise in which, when everything has been done, nothing is left for it but war'[6] as compromise with evil is impossible.

The same precept is applicable to Islam, with little need for elaboration. Religions that are based on *ahimsa* similarly allow for violence since 'exceptional times require extreme measures'.[7] There is no possibility of a conscientious objector in a religious war, as the individual has no right to question the divine precept for violence or war. Used as an argument by radical atheists, this perceived incompatibility of pacifism and religion is sometimes made into a case for the secularism of international politics. Although the goal of all religious traditions ultimately is peace, pacificism ('eventually pacifism') may be a more apt term than pacifism in that no religion adheres to unconditional pacifism.

In this striving for peace, religion necessarily justifies (and legitimises) a certain degree of violence. In doing so, it perceives the cause to be right and good and therefore just. It therefore also perceives God to be on the side of the believers and the religion. In turn, the enemy is demonised or dehumanised, as being evil, along with Satan,[8] or as belonging to the dark side. This constitutes part of the logic of religious violence, and not only assures victory for the believers, but is also a determinant in the intensity and prolonged nature of religious conflicts. In most conflicts, whether 'secular' or overtly religious, each side believes itself to be on the side of god, against a demonic adversary. In such a war losing the battle, or being numerically inferior, does not entail losing the war. In addition to this, in a conflict against a 'less-than-human' opponent, the enemy does not have to be afforded the same protection according to international law as an entirely human opponent. Again, this pertains to the notion of there not being any 'innocents' in a religious war. Although different on certain levels, the rhetoric of the American Camp X-Ray on Guatanamo Bay in Cuba, which insists that its prisoners are not 'Prisoners of War' but 'unlawful combatants', illustrates this, as would examples from every religious tradition. In religious conflicts, as in any conflict, it is generally recognised that there are international laws of war. However, there are two types of situations when these may not apply; when the opponent is dehumanised or where the law is deemed false due to being in conflict with the precepts of god or the religion.

The perceived danger of allowing religious laws of war to take precedence over (nominally) secular laws of war has led scholars to exclaim that religious language is merely an analogous interpretation of the world, and that neither by faith nor by theology can people be made to fight. This, however, is to misunderstand religion as for many believers, religious violence is not 'a metaphor or a figure of speech but … a literal fact'.[9] Religion decrees that violence is not only *permitted* under certain circumstances, such as for self defence, to stop greater violence and to protect values and morals, for example, but that it may also be a *duty* or obligation for believers. Indeed, a necessary war may be perceived to be both just and holy, as Machiavelli's Prince learned.[10] Not only does violence and conflict seem to be endemic to human civilisation, it is also true that religion is a part of this paradigm. Theologians, clerics, academics and others must therefore respond to the violence in the world. Often, this is done either by condemnation or alternatively by providing moral justification for this 'necessary' violence. Again, religion tends to favour the latter, pacificistic stance, rather than the former, pacifist perspective. In a spiral of violence religious 'terrorism', for example, is primarily a response to such theological imperatives or decrees. Ever since the earliest laws of war made a distinction between righteous (or justified) violence and unrighteous, unlawful or illegitimate violence, religion has been forced to grapple with its ambivalent attitude towards issues of violence, war and peace. There are a great variety of reasons why one response to violence and conflict is chosen over another, such as why dialogue is chosen over violence, for example, or vice versa. Acknowledging this does not, however, resolve the difficulty pertaining to why certain approaches are deemed by 'outsiders' as being defensible on the international arena and others are not, such as why peace initiatives are 'understood' but 'terrorism' abhorred.

Every religion seems to show an equal propensity for violence and war. If disregarding the motives, justifications and legitimation – and thus the 'rightness' or 'wrongness' – of violence, it nonetheless seems to be a constant in all religions throughout history. This has caused scholars to coin truisms such as Peter Sherry's classic (referring to the relative truth-hood of religious statements): 'either statements of this type are compatible with each other, in which case there is no problem of conflict, or else they contradict each other in which case they cannot all be true'.[11] Such platitudes are of little value for understanding what underlies violence, however. Because religion appeals to the most fundamental moral imperatives in the majority of human beings, it is possible to see how religion is often consulted in times of crises. As most human crises throughout history have involved violence, the parallel has often been drawn between religion and violence. Although religion is not always, nor even necessarily, a source for violence and tension and 'can neither be attacked nor defended by arms',[12] history shows that the relationship between religion and violence is far more than merely circumstantial.

Apart from inherent violence-permissive elements in religion, a number of which I will highlight below, religion often guarantees courage in conflict and thus ensures victory. Whilst it may be difficult for the believer to *like* cruelty, religion makes violence permissible, where the cause is right, just and for the greater good of the community or faith, although sceptics, like Friedrich Nietzsche, take the opposite view that a good war sanctifies any cause. The varying levels of militarism apparent within every religious tradition and in different eras of human history hint at the wide range of responses religion has towards violence. Concentrating on the violent and conflictual elements of religion does not, however, mean that religion is in any way limited to these, although it is acknowledged that such a perspective does increase the imbalance of research to a degree. Apart from being the ultimate goal for religion, peace is also the norm in day-to-day life and war is the exception. The explorations of the origins of religious violence do not, therefore, serve to explain the recurrence of the phenomenon, but will aid understanding of the logic of violent religious actors on the international arena, which in turn may ameliorate the root-source of violence. Rather than focusing on 'obscure religious reasons'[13] for violence and terrorism, it is necessary to recognise and understand that the underlying logic of such actions provides clear and inexorable precepts and legitimation. Although such religious legitimation may be used for less noble means to *justify* violence, there is no apocalyptic threat to the West, religious terrorists do not act without motive or cause and no act of killing is wanton or indiscriminate. Violence can be understood as religiously legitimate, although it is essential to realise that faith, and therefore actions derived from it, is different from purely secular knowledge. Religious beliefs *are* complicated and the reasons why believers hold them even more so. A complete understanding of the logic of religious violence may be impossible for an outsider, since – as with Tolstoy's unhappy families – every interpretation of religion and every conflict is unique. It is, however, crucial that an understanding of the abstract nature of the logic is attempted.

Although literature relating to the logic of religious violence is largely nonexistent, it is possible to discern a number of violence-conducive elements within religion from the few comparative and nomothetical works that do exist. The most central beliefs in religion are also the ones that are permissive of – or conducive to – violence, either within religions or allowing violence to be perpetrated externally with the approval (tacit or otherwise) of the religious system in question. To understand the logic of religious violence it is important that the relationship between these beliefs and violence is recognised. First, therefore, the concept of religious truth will be highlighted, since ultimately all religions profess truth. Moreover, religious truth must assume superiority over every other 'claim of truth' of other belief-systems, whether these are secular or religious. Secondly, I explore the concept of cosmic dualism (Good vs. Evil, light vs. dark, God vs. Satan, etc.), prevalent in post-Zoroastrian religions, followed by the beliefs pertaining to the existence of evil and fear. The next religious belief to be highlighted is the non-monotheistic version of cosmic dualism, and pertains to the vices and virtues of both (anthropomorphic) gods and human beings. Finally, in a somewhat ironic parallel to Darwinian evolutionary theory, I explore the concept of 'survival of the fittest' and 'fight for survival'. For most believers, all six beliefs pertain to a spiritual or metaphysical struggle and are very rarely transposed onto the social arena as real, physical and political violence. However, although Mohandas Gandhi saw the battles of the Gita as purely allegorical, for example, others have seen them as real, or – in any case – that which can be re-enacted in real-time modernity. On the Indian subcontinent, as elsewhere throughout the world, therefore 'the political forces of the twentieth century were mobilized to fight the battles of an earlier age' and, continues John Stoessinger, 'the battle of God continues unabated, though with more awesome weapons and under bleaker skies'.[14]

The Concept of Religious Truth

One of the most central tenets of religion is its unconditional belief in truth, which is also one of the most fundamental violence-conducive elements of religion. To understand the underlying reason for this, it is important to remember that religions do not merely 'claim' to profess truth, as most secular observers argue; rather, it is for them an undeniable reality. Ultimately, all religions profess truth and where such truth differs from other 'types' of truth is both the sense of being superior to every other 'claim of truth', whether these are religious or secular, and the conviction that it must also actively strive to promote that truth. Truth pertains to a religion's *raison d'être*, and it is therefore often seen as the most important element of a religion in relation to conflict. For a religion, its truth is not only more valid than the claims of other systems of thought, but it must necessarily be the *only* valid belief. There can only be one way to reach paradise, according to the monotheistic faiths, for example, and – contrary to common belief – although a mystical religion (such as Hinduism or Buddhism) clearly accepts that there are many paths to the goal, the latter is not compatible with the former.

It is not entirely accurate to claim, as some scholars do, 'that there is no special kind of religious truth as such'.[15] Despite its philosophical and conceptual similarities to purely secular types of truth (such as the results of scientific experimentation or mathematical calculation), religious truth is based on the premise that it is exclusive. It is based on a source of knowledge only available to those who accept it and thus denied to those who do not. As such, religious truth assumes and requires superiority and therefore constitutes the primary tenet of religion, with all other beliefs secondary. The reason for this is that the exclusivity of religious truth is the basis upon which all other characteristics of the religion are based. Within the religion, it is impossible for the believer to question the validity of the religion. Indeed, such doubt is often seen as heretical or blasphemous. Furthermore, as allegiance to a religious truth is necessarily incapable of compromise, this also makes religion intolerant and exclusivist in relation to other 'truths'. From this, it is not difficult to draw the conclusion that the superiority and exclusivity of religious truths are one of the main causes of violence between and within religions.

It is often argued that religious truth is more exclusive, and thus more prone to violence, within the revealed traditions of the prophetic monotheistic religions than in other traditions. However, even the 'pagan' religions necessarily have a sense of having the ultimate truth that, for the believer, signifies the only way to salvation, knowledge, harmony and peace. It is a universal of all religions to lay claim to truth. Where the monotheistic religions may be more extreme (and thus violent) in relation to their truth is that such truth does not recognise the validity of any other truth, and when another truth is degraded as being a lie (or less-than-truth), conflict is inevitable. Mystical religions may claim that since the goal is the same for all religions, the varying traditions are merely different paths to this same goal, and each religion or religious truth may be true *for* someone. Whilst this has often been hailed as a solution to the problem of religious truth, it is nonetheless a perspective as incompatible as the absolutist religion it is attempting to include. Not only does such an inclusive view assume a similar superiority of truth as an exclusive view, it also negates the truth of the exclusivist belief, which may be firm in its conviction that there is only one truth. In this way, the mystical religions treat their truths as uniquely superior and it is thus impossible to acknowledge a claim that all religions are variants of the same truth.

This sense of superiority of religious truths is often seen as an obstacle on the international arena as it renders any genuine pluralism or conflict resolution near impossible. Making such a statement does not, however, further any understanding as to why violence is a response to this perceived superiority. One of the most fundamental reasons why religious truth is conducive to violence is rather simple and pertains to a desire to be faithful to god by protecting the truth against any corruption or perversion. Being a good believer, by this logic, entails protecting the faith at all costs because this also ensures a fundamental manifestation about the believer's own self. Although most believers at some stage in their religious journey experience doubt, the adherent of a religion ultimately believes in the truth of that religion. Belief, in the religious sense, is equal to truth, which is also its target. One would not believe something that one did not believe was true. Indeed, since 'the concept of belief can never be prised apart from that of truth'[16] this is what makes religious truth incompatible with its opposite, which is invariably and inevitably believed to be 'the worst and deadliest of errors ... [and] a diabolical testimony of falsehood and darkness'.[17] As with my earlier conceptualisation of religion, it is important to recognise that belief in this sense is not primarily reached through intellectual rationalisation. Instead, religious belief is *by definition* the truth and no amount of external arguing can change this, although this would be unthinkable to radical atheists or secularists. The belief remains true no matter how much 'evidence' or 'historical proof' to the contrary can be found by those who do not believe, by outside observers or by other disciplines (such as science).

To outsiders, including the vast majority of conflict management specialists around the world, it seems clear that the opposite of truth may not necessarily be a lie, but rather another, alternate truth, and religious conflict is thus manifested 'when right clashes with right'.[18] Realising this, it is sometimes (somewhat naïvely) argued, would be a huge step towards conflict resolution, and thus a more peaceful international society. From a religious point of view, however, the matter of truth is far too serious and significant to be shared with obvious lies. It is thus 'obvious' for the believer that the truth is exclusive, though outsiders may not share this view. In matters of religious truth, it is the belief that is important, not that the believer can produce evidence of his or her faith. The belief in a religious truth is thus not 'rational' in the strict sense. However, whilst it may seem theologically impossible to an outside scholar to invoke god in war, this may be a perfectly rational and religiously legitimate precept for the sake of defending, promoting or upholding a unique and fundamental truth. This truth, different from purely secular truths in that it refers to the absolute spiritual life, not only explains why and how something happens but also indicates to the believer 'how what they do and ought to do can be justified'.[19] If truth is perceived as a divine precept, violence in its defence is not only justified but a duty. To some believers, this undoubtedly entails killing as many enemies as possible, to establish the superior justice of the right cause, whereas to others it may be impossible to reconcile the belief of truth being god with the possibility of realising god by killing. In either case, the believers' perception of truth as exclusive and absolute may either be the root of the intrinsic intolerance and opposition that forms the basis for religious conflict or religion is contrary to truth, and should therefore not be pursued, as Tolstoy's Pierre Bezuhov would have it.[20]

On a philosophical level, of course, incompatibilities of religious truths are not necessarily violent nor must they be construed as a legitimate basis for religious violence and conflict. Religious truths, though exclusive and absolute, are rarely manifested in doctrinal conflicts with other truths. Indeed, it is sometimes argued that religious *doctrines* very rarely conflict since they are secondary to truth within religion, and the express opposition to another religious truth is often only found in the early stages of religious development when the religion is defining itself as *not* being an existing tradition. Where this is the case, or when the truth is perceived as a material, rather than a spiritual reality, there is a possibility – or even a likelihood – of violent clashes in this space-time. In this way, as for Chairman Mao, war becomes the highest form of struggle for resolving contradictions. There is a danger, of course, that this struggle, in turn, may rouse the passion of the believers, which – for Leo Tolstoy at least – stifles truth, though this is not necessarily the case for the believer who may take an opposite view.[21]

The difficulty in acquiring satisfactory knowledge of any religious truth from an external perspective lies in the fundamentals of religion. Religious truth cannot be grasped through intellectual or philosophical reasoning, and any such attempt would arguably be fundamentally misguided. Belief, by definition, is a phenomenon that can only be grasped by complete immersion into a religion. Marcel Proust's observation that 'the surest way of being convinced of the excellence of the cause of one party or the other is actually to be that party'[22] still holds true today. To many conflict resolution experts, academics, politicians and journalists this is not only an impractical practice but often also an unwanted one. For the secular observer (or the religious observer from a different confessional background) the need to completely accept a truth to understand it may indicate some kind of 'brain-washing' in favour of a particular truth, as with any exclusive ideology, and anyone who cares about truth according to radical secularists, must therefore be an atheist.

The need to combat the often violent exclusivity of religious truths plays into the hands of the academics and practitioners who want to see a continuation of the separation of religion into public and private 'spheres', at least on the international arena. Completely secular international relations would, according to these perspectives, remove the possibility of incompatible religious truths and therefore potential violence. An alternative view, proposed by the more fundamental religionists, is the opposite course for the future; namely the acceptance of the one true religion for all humankind. By its nature, every religious truth has some sort of belief in this possibility as the religion is for all (who accept it, or submit to the truth it proclaims). Both approaches to global peace seem rather naïve due to the nature of religious truth. In the same way as different religions are not necessarily divisive, 'a common religion or ideology does not guarantee peace'.[23] Indeed, the earlier exploration of the 'Other' affirms that it is necessary that an eschatological enemy exists in that it guarantees one's own religious identity. It may therefore even be inevitable that where there is no religious division, or where a common religion is shared, a division, another truth or even an entirely new (or 'other') religion must be *created*, as the story of Robinson Krotzmeir illustrates. In this Jewish joke, the protagonist is the only inhabitant on a desert island, and ends up building two synagogues – one Orthodox and one Reformist – and swearing never to go into the one, to show God how faithful and true he is as a believer.[24] Although this story is far from unique *per se* and exists in virtually every tradition, it does serve to illustrate not only the importance of the 'Other', but also the exclusivity of religious truths.

Cosmic Dualism

'The World', affirms John Esposito, 'is a battleground on which believers and unbelievers, the friends of God and the enemies of God or followers of Satan, wage war'.[25] This concept of cosmic dualism is another element of the logic of religious violence that is most prevalent (and thus most clearly seen) in the post-Zoroastrian religions. In short, cosmic dualism pertains to issues of Good versus Evil, light vs.

dark, God vs. Satan and so forth, and violence is often a consequence of this. Although the terminology is slightly different, the most common facet of contemporary cosmic dualism is the notion of 'us' and 'them'. Though not always used in an explicitly religious context, both the language and rhetoric derives from the logic of cosmic dualism, or divine warfare, and any conflict transformation approach would be wise to try to understand how this phenomenon may be permissive of real-time violence.

Cosmic dualism is not a separate religious tenet, *per se*. Indeed, one half of its inherent dichotomy is arguably the concept of religious truth explored previously, the other half being invariably error, evil, perversity, Satan, or any similar derivative. Where cosmic dualism takes on a violent manifestation, though by no means inevitable, believers are thus 'fighting for truth itself'.[26] Every religion has some concept of what it believes to be true, although truth, and religious truth no less, must philosophically be defined in relation to its perceived opposite, as it is not an objective concept. As with something that is 'tall' it can only be so in relation to something that is 'short'. The diametric opposite of truth thus becomes of utmost importance. Although religion does not subscribe entirely to the same logic, it would nevertheless be philosophically impossible to have something that is true without also acknowledging that something is false. On a religious plane, this becomes the opposite of the good, the truth and the religion and this 'something' is invariably referred to in terms of evil, unbelievers, darkness and infidels. This dualism is commonly thought to be derived from the Persian religion of Zoroastrianism, which serves as the foundation for the three large monotheistic religions of the contemporary world, and many other systems of belief. Though frequently misunderstood, the dualism of Zoroastrianism pertains to the eternal struggle between the great god Ahura Mazda (Ormuzd) and the evil spirit of Ahriman (Angro-Mainyus), the former being lightness and the latter darkness. Unfortunately, this is neither the time nor the place to expound the detailed precepts of Zoroastrianism and it must thus suffice to claim, as many scholars recognise, that much of the dualism of religion during the last three millennia has been greatly influenced by this ancient faith.

The post-Zoroastrian religions (that is, those derived from the last 3000 years) all have interpretations throughout their scriptures and traditions of how the struggle is to be approached. For most believers, the struggle is an internal and personal one, of goodness and righteousness against temptation, wrongdoing and evil, and ultimately 'between faith and lack of faith'.[27] However, as the structures exist within religion to deal with the struggle of the dualism, it is entirely possible – and frequently practised – that the struggle may be transferred onto the social plane, and religious violence, conflict and war are the inevitable result. Though it often takes a charismatic leader to sow the seed of violence or militarism within the minds of the believers, it is not up to them whether the religion permits or abhors violence. These are precepts that do not change with time, and will hold true for the present and future as they did in the past. Against the backdrop of contemporary international relations, apologetics, liberal theologians and academics are quick to emphasise and reaffirm the entirely metaphysical and spiritual meaning of the ancient struggle between Good and Evil. They argue at length that all scriptural passages concerning fighting or killing, or of violence for the faith, are metaphors for the internal struggle against sin and wickedness. Though the majority of believers may hold this to be true, it does not automatically mean that *all* believers do, or indeed that they should. This is not to condone violence, but rather to emphasise the importance of understanding that the cosmic dualism of the scriptures can be transposed onto the social plane of reality.

Monotheistic theologians have struggled with the concept of dualism for as long as there has been religion. The main difficulty is that the recognition of some kind of dualism (derived from Zoroastrianism) may compromise the singularity of the religion and of God. However, if there is no need to believe 'in a dreadful god called M'shimba M'shamba'[28] the monotheistic religion must be able to accommodate evil within itself. This theological difficulty has taken many different shapes. Within Christianity, for example, it surfaces most frequently as the 'dilemma' of theodicy. Theologians have grappled with the issues of theodicy in vast amounts of scholarship, but this is not an occasion to provide an overview of that research. Without attempting to answer any of the questions inevitably raised by theodicy I merely accept it here as existing as a theological consideration. Very briefly, theodicy pertains to the idea that either god is not fully benevolent, in that violence – for example – is 'permitted', or that God is not omni-potent, as violence exists in opposition to god's wish. Islam, similarly, is faced with the problem of reconciling Zoroastrian-type dualism with the singularity of God. Indeed, Islam cannot recognise such duality, but since 'it does allow for a struggle against duality itself',[29] it is nonetheless establishing and perpetuating a type of duality; of truth versus untruth.

It is because of this absoluteness of cosmic dualism that concepts such as 'holy war' (Christianity), '*herem*' (Judaism), '*jihad*' (Islam) have developed within every religion, though for most of history, and certainly for most believers, this struggle or strife has been fought within the pages of the scriptures and minds of the believers. It is a contentious issue as to how these concepts are to be interpreted. Though there exists an unfortunate connotation due to the often flippant use by most scholars, it is possible take 'fundamentalist' as not necessarily meaning fanatic or violent, and it is usually such groups that take concepts of cosmic war literally as a divine precept or decree. Such war becomes a duty for true believers whenever the war is in a decisive phase. Those fundamentalist groups that are militant, fanatical or violently extremist take the notion of the decisive phase of the struggle as being now, in this space-time. Though the terminology may differ, a cosmic war is thus for the furtherance of peace and harmony. Indeed, the very object of the war is victory for the 'Good' – namely peace – over the 'Evil' – war. It is also this belief in the ultimate victory of truth over error that sets most contemporary interpretations of cosmic dualism apart from pure Zoroastrian notions of dualism. Zoroaster proclaimed that the struggle between light and dark was eternal and that it was one of the constants in the world. Though it may seem like a lost cause, and an eternal battle, most religions today believe that in practice, a cosmic war is by definition never 'unwinnable' as god is on the side of the inevitable victor, that is, those in the right. However, this does not mean that a cosmic war is an affair to be taken lightly, and it does not mean that the duty for the true believers to struggle is not necessary. Indeed, as Gandhi proclaimed, 'though good is always victorious, evil does put up a brave show and baffles even the keenest conscience'.[30]

There are no redeeming features in one's opponent in cosmic dualism, and the enemy is furthermore often dehumanised or demonised. Where cosmic dualism is manifested as cosmic war on the reality of the social plane this invariably compromises adherence to secular (so-called 'universal') Laws of War or Human Rights. Such war is, and must be, fought by whatever means will achieve victory, and in the pursuit of victory every action will thus become legitimate. Even if purely secular laws are disregarded for the purpose of argument, this may also be applied to religious precepts. Every religion, for example, includes some notion of the illegality of killing, or at least the prohibition of the taking of life. This precept, like most concepts, cannot be accepted as entirely universal without qualification. It is possible to argue, as theologians indeed have, that there are many instances where the commandment of 'thou shalt not kill' (in whichever religion and language) may still be permissible of killing. First, of course, this precept is usually restricted in that what is prohibited is only the killing of human beings. Killing is thus legitimate if the adversary is less than human (dehumanised by the rhetoric used, or genuinely believed not to be entirely human) or not human altogether (demonised, for example, by his or her belief in falsity). Furthermore, it is possible to find arguments in support of the theory that by killing an adversary who does not (cannot or will not) accept the truth, the true believer is saving him or her. By this reckoning, killing an unbeliever is an act of good, a mercy killing. Salvation for the unbeliever comes as a result of being reunited with god, and as the believer is furthering the supreme good, he or she is also saved. Closely related to this is the idea that killing an unbeliever is a form of punishment (for unbelief), in the same way as capital punishment deprives the murderous criminal of life. Indeed, this is such an act of good that the believer will never meet his victim in hell. As the language of cosmic war is by definition of a highly religious nature, such notions indicate that it is indeed impossible for a human being to kill any other human being, as only god can give and take life, and that the killing of one's adversary in battle is thus also impossible. Similarly, of course, it is also the case according to this theory, that in the same way as it is impossible to kill it is also impossible to be killed in a cosmic war, as only god has the power over life and death.

Cosmic dualism is a concept of absolutes. It is not possible to be in the middle, undecided or a bit of each. As with religious truth, no half-measures satisfy god and the individual is either a believer (and thus right) or an unbeliever (and thus wrong). Manifested as violence, cosmic dualism thus becomes a total war with no respite until the war is won, which comes with the total destruction of the enemy, after which universal peace would reign in perpetuity. This victory will come at Armageddon, the final and ultimate war between the cosmic dualisms of Good and Evil. As the victory at Armageddon will forever remove cosmic dualism from the realm of religion, it could be argued that the concept is not a 'constant' in religion, but rather an 'interim dualism'. However, although the truths of religion must hold true for all time, it is important to remember that there are always at least two interpretations to every religious concept, one for the time it was written, with limited future relevance, and one that has eternal relevance and is valid for all time. As such, the concept of cosmic dualism may at any point in the history of a religion be a personal struggle of faith against unfaith, a societal struggle between believers and unbelievers, or an absolute total war between the forces of Evil and the forces of Good. This depends not only on how the precept is interpreted, and by whom, but also on other factors in the world that require a response from religion, such as perceived portents in nature or a decadent and immoral world.

Cosmic dualism thus pertains to a perceivably natural separatism between 'us' and 'them'. The all-important communal memories of any culture or society are made up of myths, at once true and unreal, concerning 'the Other' for there to be more order and cohesion within the 'in-group'. Although these communal memories are traditionally based in religion, science has relatively recently (within the last century, or so) offered similar interpretations of this dualism within disciplines as varied as zoology and psychology. The scientific disciplines would, however, be loathe to refer to this either as cosmic or indeed as dualistic. In any case, whether referring to the absolute dualism as proclaimed by Zoroaster, the archetypal example of cosmic war of Manichaeism, or the in-group/out-group dichotomy of chimpanzees as the basis for human conflict, it is nevertheless important to understand how dualistic rhetoric may be a source for perpetuating violence. Furthermore, violent conflicts may not only be perpetuated by the concept of cosmic dualism but such conflicts are also likely to be more intense and lethal than other types of conflict as their aim is the complete annihilation of one's enemies. In today's armed conflict, even the most secular causes are identified using religious language and rhetoric. As all states identify with good, righteousness or a just cause, all conflicts can be recognised as manifestations of cosmic war, though not necessarily with explicitly divine – or otherwise religious – decrees.

The Concept of Evil

In the same way as there could be no cosmic dualism without 'Good' or Truth, it could also not exist without Evil. Evil may be conducive of religious violence in a variety of ways. There are, however, three main beliefs that make the existence (whether real or imagined) of evil inseparable from violence. One such belief stems from the 'original sin' theories that exist in various religions, namely, that since humans are naturally evil and sinful, violence is an inevitable product. Another way in which evil and violence are usually combined is that humans are inherently good, and it is therefore the duty of good believers to employ violence to eradicate evil. Both these theories place the existence of evil firmly on humankind. A third perspective places the 'blame' on god, and violence therefore exists because god is evil, or – alternatively – that god is good but there are other evil deities that god is unable to stop. Although other conceptions of evil exist, these three perspectives are amongst the most common.

Because of the apparently permanent existence of evil in the world, every religion has an inevitable duty to offer a response to this perceived evil. As such, the subject has occupied scholars and theologians for almost as long as the other half of the dichotomy has interested them. In many respects, the concept of evil marks a failure of religion, as it has been unable satisfactorily to explain its existence. This is more apparent in the monotheistic religions, as highlighted earlier regarding the dilemma of theodicy, which questions how evil can exist if God is both omnipotent *and* good. Indeed, according to most religions, the existence of evil must be due to it being created by divine powers, though this in no way answers *why* there is evil. Two of the three Abrahamaic religions usually concede that it is a punishment for man's 'original sin', whereas for many polytheistic religions it is a fact of life that some gods are evil, in the same way as some are good.

The 'original sin' of Adam and Eve in the garden of paradise does not explain why there is evil. Indeed, it is clear that evil existed before this as it was the 'Evil One' (the Serpent, Iblis, Satan, Shaitan) who tempted these original humans to be 'immoral'. The concept of evil as being due to the 'original sin' does, nonetheless, explain to religionists that since humankind is naturally evil, violence is inevitable until all humanity becomes free of sin. This particular religious belief is in some ways compatible with scientific explanations of violence in that violence and aggression, for example, are natural tendencies in human beings, as they are in other primates and in animals in general. Though this 'biological explanation' of violence is not investigated here, it may be interesting to bear it in mind through the subsequent discussion. The human animal is different from other species in many ways, not least in that it brings religious passion and legitimation to violence and war. The religious response to evil, therefore, is vital in order to understand religious conflict on the contemporary international arena. If humans are inherently evil, and thus violent, there is little hope for successful conflict resolution. However, as human beings have witnessed in relation to chimpanzees, for example, there are nonetheless reasons for hope.

Even if the inherent sinfulness of humankind is acknowledged, it is nevertheless possible to believe that it is up to each believer to overcome this irreligious nature and thus – by complete submission to God – evil is eradicated. Such submission, or true belief, entails doing good and acting in a religious way at all times. This may entail using violence to protect the faith and defend it against evil, to struggle against evil, and ultimately to eradicate evil from the world. The second main perspective in relation to evil is thus that it is the duty of every true believer to wage war against evil. The concept of 'holy war' thus entails 'an armed confrontation with Evil [which is arguably] the first and foremost rudimentary ethical act'.[31] Such violence, to eradicate evil and promote good, becomes a righteous and legitimate duty and religion thus provides necessary precepts for how war can promote justice. War is always against the evil 'Other', if the parallel is drawn with the previously explored dichotomy. The other is necessarily and inevitably evil, if one's own forces are good. In the struggle against an evil adversary, all means of warfare are condoned lest evil gains an advantage. As highlighted earlier, in the international political arena, therefore, the limitations placed by international legal instruments seem futile. Despite the obvious 'loop-holes' of secular Laws of War and Human Rights such as the dehumanising of the enemy so that the laws do not apply to them, other more subtle compromises can be made if the adversary is evil. It is likely, for example, that an evil opponent will not follow Laws of War, and thus use unlawful methods of war against the true believers. In these instances, it is perfectly legitimate for the believers themselves to pre-empt the enemy by using otherwise unlawful methods. This can be illustrated by the concept of deceit. All religions prohibit deceit in some form. However, most also condone it, and actively ask for it, where it may benefit the believers in the struggle against an evil adversary. For some analysts, of course, the very use of 'less-than-noble' methods means that 'in defeating evil, the righteous have [themselves] become evil',[32] though this is not a religiously defensible statement as in the cause of Good and truth over Evil and darkness any means are condoned.

If the human combatants of a holy war have no right to change the way in which the war is fought, for example with less intensity or lethality than a total war, it raises further questions as to the goodness of god. If violence and warfare are permissible to eradicate evil, and to protect and promote the greater good, it raises the question of who defines this 'greater good'. Depending on whether it is by divine decree, in theological interpretation or through the statements of a charismatic and zealous leader, the responses will be markedly different. Some scholars would argue that the existence of evil is merely atomistic and as a whole, the world is entirely good. However, others argue that in the wake of events like those Hiroshima and Nagasaki are remembered for, such a view is impossible since god is not *only* good, but also intrinsically evil. If god did *not* make religion a fount of darkness and evil for humankind, a case may be made that believers have more power over the institution of god than omnipotence would allow. Indeed, god is sometimes perceived as what has made religion – throughout history – resemble a 'catalogue of human evil'.[33] Although apologetic theologians frequently claim that god neither created nor communicates with evil, and certainly does not allow it, this is probably due to a selective use of the scriptures or due to a sense of responsibility to defend religion. A more holistic reading of the scriptures may indicate, as does the Bible (Isaiah 45:7), that God indeed creates evil. It is, of course, impossible for mortal believers (and unbelievers) to comprehend the full scale of the concept of evil within religious systems of belief, and especially within monotheistic traditions.

Whilst I have focused on the problem of evil within the monotheistic religions, this is not to say that evil is restricted to these. However, it is due to the singularity of these traditions that the concept of evil has posed such problems, ranging from theodicy to an unforgivable 'original sin'. Evil deities and spirits exist in every religious tradition and culture. From Aipaloovik in the northwest to Kukalikimoku in the southeast, gods and goddesses personify evil, violence and war. The tribes that have no such deities, like the Anroguacos of Colombia, the Abron of the Ivory Coast, the Chatharm islanders, the Semai of Malaya and the Mru Chittagong Hill tribe, seem to be the exception rather than the rule. However, in most polytheistic traditions the existence of evil is seen not as a problem, but as a 'comforting' explanation for illness, disaster, death or anger, for example. Such traditions need not grapple with the complexities of the monotheistic creator-god that would either not be wholly good, or not be wholly omnipotent. Despite the fact that it does not constitute a theological problem *per se* it is important to recognise that the existence of evil may be as conducive to violence in the 'public sphere' as it may in the minds of the believers.

Whilst the duty to eradicate evil, the natural inevitability of evil and the existence of evil deities may all serve to highlight evil as a violence-conducive element of religion, these three elements fail, other than in passing, to address another important aspect of evil within religion; namely what evil is. Like several other terms in this book, evil is both a self-referential and a correlative term. The former indicates that by labelling something 'evil' it becomes evil, and the latter indicates that in order to have something 'evil' something 'good' is also required. The self-referential nature of the concept of evil makes it an ideal accomplice in political (and religious) rhetoric, ranging from George W. Bush's 'Axis of Evil' to Saddam Hussain's 'Evil West' and any number of other examples. In addition, whilst evil lends itself to various definitions pertaining to morally bad, harmful or sinful, the interpretations are inescapably religious. This, in turn, indicates that the term is correlative to 'good'. In the dichotomy of cosmic dualism, therefore, that which is not part of 'us' is thus evil. Individuals or groups rebelling against a conventional teaching may thus find 'evil' a suitable description for their new, opposing belief-system. The connotations of 'evil' are not necessarily the same for these groups as they are merely used as opposing correlatives to the 'good' that constitute the old tradition. Though not necessarily conducive to violence, this interpretation of evil indicates that the complexity of the issue is deeper than a superficial observation or use of religious rhetoric would recognise.

The connotations associated with the tacit, and implicit, definition of 'evil' within religion does not need elaboration. It is sufficient to state that the notion of evil and its existence – whether real or imagined – as the ultimate adversary for individual believer and communal religion alike, is a violence-conducive element of religion. This brief exploration of evil is not intended to add any new knowledge to the study of 'evilology', but rather to continue building the base for understanding religious violence. This understanding means questioning certain long-held beliefs, and may include a rejection of the concept that everything that is 'evil' is necessarily bad, and vice versa. For the present purpose, it may be important to understand the importance of evil as being based in absolute truths, of the type that were highlighted earlier.

The Concept of Fear

Evil is something to fear according to most religions. However, so is god. The God of Islam, Christianity and Judaism is quite adamant that the true believers shall fear God, whereas in many polytheistic religions it is not only wise to fear the gods, but also to keep on their good side with sacrifices and offerings. In all religious traditions the concept of fear is in some way prevalent, and will be briefly introduced here as the fourth religious belief that may help an understanding of the logic of religious violence. As with evil, there are many variants of how the notion of fear in religion may be conducive to violence. These include the fear of the wrath of a god, the fear of a powerful enemy, and – indeed – fear of death. Religion has not only struck fear in the hearts of human beings for as long as it has existed, it has also worked to eliminate fear and provide unchangeable certainties. Both types of fear are conducive to violence.

Of the two emotions people may hold that are potentially harmful, Machiavelli told his Prince, it is better to be feared than to be hated.[34] Although this type of fear may, in certain instances, be perceived as slavish, it is more a case of respect and reverential awe, and in many ways a 'good' form of fear. Usually, this type of fear translates as fearing god, or being god-fearing, in the language of religion. It indicates a type of 'affection' to the authority, making the fearful individual inclined to obey the commands, and – especially in the case of religion – abhor whatever may be sinful and evil. Religious fear is, however, not necessarily a case of submission to a powerful authority, but also the fear – or dread – of god's wrath and punishment, for sins committed. This fear usually arises from an inner sense of guilt. As this guilt may manifest itself due to not doing enough as a believer to protect and defend the faith, it is possible to argue that it is permissive of violence. Such violence is condoned to 'win back' the respect of the deity, and avoid punishment for not being a true believer, or in other words, violence would be used for fear of betraying the ideal of the deity. In many religions, the punishment for not striving in the cause of god, for example, or not living an entirely pure life comes after death. There is a real fear, for many believers, that their lot after death will be in a state of hell unless the commands of the religion are followed in this space-time.

One of the most fundamental sources of human fear is this fear of death. Rather, it is not death *per se* that is to be feared, but what happens afterwards. Arguably, the main duty for religion has been to provide answers to this question throughout human history, as it is believed that if one knows what happens after death, one does not fear it. Whereas the more 'rational' religions, like Buddhism, have offered answers relating to the importance of overcoming the fear of death for a better *life*, the more 'irrational' religions, such as Christianity, have adopted a more robust interpretation (heaven and hell), which in itself perpetuates the fear of death. This can even indicate that the source of all religion is fear in that belief seeks to remove fear. By recalling the qualification made earlier, it is possible to assume that if the human life is the most fundamental need for the individual, he or she would do anything and everything to prolong and preserve that life. As this may lead to immoral or outright 'wrong' behaviour, religion has been forced to remove much of the fear of death. This is not an unconditional removal, however, and only applies to the good believers. Though many religions claim that it is possible to repent before death for any sins to be forgiven, the point of the religious life may arguably be that repenting should not be necessary; there should be no sins to be forgiven. Religion provides the answers to what happens after death, but does not remove fear. Rather, it perpetuates fear for irreligious behaviour, false beliefs and sin, for example.

Religious notions of fear are complex. Rather like a Catch-22 situation, the believer fears betraying the ideal of the religion, on the one hand, and, on the other, religion is perceived to be a prerequisite for overcoming fear. Overcoming fear refers to overcoming not only the fear of death, but also other fears. Religion provides a necessary certainty in a world of chaos. It puts the primacy of order over confusion; salvation and redemption over damnation; the promise of love over the fear of hate. Of course, being guaranteed this order requires a commitment that is often stronger than any other. The adherent of the religion must *believe* that the security and safety are real and that the fear will be removed. It is not enough to claim that one believes in the credo of the religion, one actually *has to* believe. By making this 'ultimatum', religion secures its existence. The belief in religion, however, not only provides comforting answers to the problem of fear for the believers, it also perpetuates the in-group/out-group dichotomy highlighted earlier.

Dealing with fear through religion thus has two main manifestations, both of which have implications for violence on the international arena. It either makes the believer fear the punishment or retribution of religion for not living one's life as a true believer, or it makes the believer fear the outsider, that is those who do not believe in the religion. Religion has ensured that otherness is to be feared, and it is indicative of the definition and continuance of the group identity. For humans, as for other primates, this fear of 'them', argues Jane Goodall, an authority on chimpanzees, 'is far more sophisticated than mere xenophobia'.[35] The group identity is not a notion that is established and maintained within one generation. By the use of communal memories, imagined communities and myths, the identity of the group is perpetuated throughout history. Fear of the other, therefore, does not merely threaten oneself and the present constitution of the group, but the greatest fear lies in the potential betrayal of both past and future generations. As such, both fear and the resulting violence mark a profound dedication to the group, though not necessarily entirely voluntary. The believer may experience personal fear of having no other place to go than staying within the group structure, which may require violence for reasons of communal memories of identity.

The individual believer, then, is bound by fear. There is both implicit and explicit fear within the religion, which guarantees moral behaviour, and there is external fear threatening the in-group. There is also fear from the in-group should the believer not identify completely with its ideals, as there is no room for compromise. In addition, there may be other types of societal fear that the believer is faced with, and that may be permissive of violence. Cowardice, for example, is usually condemned, even when it is manifested as non-violence. The fear of being labelled as a coward, which in itself is a result of fear, may make even the most ardent pacifist turn to violence. Even Mohandas Gandhi believed 'that where there is only a choice between cowardice and violence, I would advise violence'.[36] This, however, indicates a creation based on very particular societal values and principles. The cultural origins of most contemporary notions of fear are, like other concepts explored throughout this book, based in a particular religious tradition that may not necessarily hold true for all time. Where the fear is divine, on the other hand, it becomes unavoidable. Deities are often the very objects of fear, and it thus *produces* gods. The all-merciful deities should not need to be feared, though the 'not-so-merciful' may need to be pampered and 'bribed'.

Violence may be the result of fear for many reasons, some of which have been briefly touched upon above. It is also important to acknowledge that in many instances, especially on the contemporary international arena, fear may not so much be conducive to violence as it is an obstacle to peace. It may be argued that there is some mileage in the current 'buzz-word' of inter-faith dialogue for the improvement of the world, and to make it a more peaceful place. However, an obstacle to dialogue was addressed earlier as it is subject to a sometimes inconceivable compromise; in order for dialogue to even be conceived, the existence of an 'equal' other must be acknowledged. In the present discussion, the success of dialogue may similarly be called into question. The Chief Rabbi of the United Hebrew Congregations of the Commonwealth, Rabbi Dr Jonathan Sacks, indicates that any dialogue starts with the fear of having certainties challenged.[37] Whenever a crisis is apparent, religion offers confidence and comfort, the very concepts that are called into doubt by the inherent fear of dialogue. As fear, in turn, is one of the most consistent factors in the mobilisation of popular opinion, the potential success of inter-faith (or, indeed, intra-faith) dialogue may need to be re-evaluated.

Fear, then, is a complex element in religion, but one that may have vital influence on the decision to use – or, indeed, not resort to – violence on the contemporary international arena. One of the greatest 'successes' of religion has been the answers it offers to the questions regarding death. The god-fearing, for example, need not fear death, on condition that the god-fearing attitude of the believer is sustained. This does not, however, explain why the inhabitants of Jericho 'built a circular wall, dug a moat and erected a tower to protect their little city as early as 8000BC'.[38] What did they fear? Certainly, their physical protection did not derive from fearing divine beings that are not generally deterred by moats, walls or towers. The fear that prompted such protection indicates a physical enemy, and it is likely that in the case of that enemy approaching the fortifications, the inhabitants of Jericho would have fought back, rather than flee. This is a fundamental of human nature, and is invariably referred to as 'fight or flight'. Fear, in this case at least, is permissive of violence against the adversary. Whilst this adversary may have similar perceptions towards the inhabitants of Jericho (in this case), the fear may be due to lack of understanding of the opponent. On a more fundamental level than mere xenophobia, as was highlighted, this lack of understanding as a source of fear may be equally true. Today, fear of that which is not understood, be it 'terrorism', war or violence, is characteristic of the contemporary world. That which is perceived to be irrational, for example, is immediately feared. Actions that are not understood perpetuate fear and thus the continuation of such actions. This is apparent in a wide range of human interactions, from media broadcasts to political speeches and from school curricula to legal instruments. Understanding the logic of religious violence may facilitate the reduction of fear, and thus lower the intensity or frequency of such violence. In any case, an understanding of fear as a religious belief conducive to – or permissible of – violence is likely to further the understanding of this violence as a whole.

The Concept of Anthropomorphism, Vices and Virtues

Whilst the monotheistic religions recognise some sort of cosmic dualism between Good and Evil, this does not necessarily mean that dualism, *per se*, is acknowledged, as it is in dualistic systems of religion (such as Zoroastrianism). A different type of religious experience is polytheism, where there are many deities with different characteristics, duties and 'responsibilities'; some that are 'good' and some that are 'evil'. Religions of this type are by the previous classification pre-Zoroastrian, though not necessarily chronologically so, and this section could thus be argued to be a non-Zoroastrian version of the earlier 'cosmic dualism' argument. In these religions, human vices and virtues are mirrored in the gods, and it is the war gods and goddesses that are often the most important. Such anthropomorphism is thus a constituent part of the logic of religious violence. However, anthropomorphism is also fundamental for the monotheistic religions and other post-Zoroastrian traditions, and this has a significant influence on matters of war and peace in the contemporary world.

Although anthropomorphism is often theologically contested, in that God created man in his own image rather than *vice versa*, it is a natural tendency to imagine God or gods in one's own image. Whilst this is invariably used for rhetorical purposes (see, for example, feminist-, liberation- or 'black' theology), it is as natural for human beings to imagine humanoid gods as it would be for horses to imagine 'the gods as similar to horses, and oxen as similar to oxen, and … make the bodies of the sort which each of them had'.[39] Although Xenophanes of Colophon was firmly opposed to anthropomorphism of this kind, it is undeniable that implicit anthropomorphism continues to shape perceptions, as shown by Michelangelo's Christian God as an elderly Caucasian man with a long white beard. It is clear how an implicit concept of anthropomorphism may be apt for exclusivist narratives, perpetuating the 'us' versus 'them' dichotomy. If the true believers are created in the image of God, it must mean that they are God's chosen people and this notion, along with the notion of land given by God, echoes true throughout the conflict-ridden world from Palestine via Northern Ireland to Sri Lanka. True believers imagine themselves not only as the people chosen to benefit from God's favour, but equally importantly that the unbelievers will be subjected to the wrath of God. This wrath may also be assisted by the true believers to please the God and prove one's belief. The tautological perception of the adversary ensures that they are firmly against the chosen people who have God on their side. As with cosmic dualism, anthropomorphism is another 'proof' that God is always on the side of the believer in an armed struggle, although this is ostensibly contended by (political) theology. Whilst 'God has no favourites among nations'[40] each nation – especially at the time of crisis – imagines itself as a nation of God and therefore unquestionably in the right.

Where the concept of anthropomorphism takes an implicit manifestation in the notions of a chosen people or a promised land is where it becomes the most lethal on the contemporary international arena. It becomes an uncompromisable religious truth of the kind investigated above. However, closely related to this is the polytheistic perception of human beings possessing vices and virtues similar, or the same, as those possessed by the divine. It is unclear whether the process is 'top down' (humans mirroring the characteristics of the deities) or 'bottom up' (humans perceiving the deities in their own image), and the allegiance to either theory has a certain impact on the conclusions. The latter to an extent raises graver theological issues, for example, whilst the former may be seen as apologetic and thus makes any violent action permissible due to it being unavoidable. In either case, polytheistic gods are both good and bad, and often every combination in-between. In many cultures gods/goddesses of war are also, for example, god/goddesses of happiness (as is Bishamon), fertility (as Indra) and sexuality (as is the Celtic goddess Medb). The nature of the deities greatly influences the human interaction with them. In many instances, an evil or violent god may be feared to the extent that its followers surpass the mere showing of respect and actually try to placate the deity. The Yezidis, for example, though they constitute an odd variant of monotheism, revere the devil. Whilst they believe in a supreme god who is kind and benevolent, this deity has not involved himself in worldly affairs since he created the world. The devil, on the other hand, is worshipped in order to be appeased, lest he do harm to the believers. Although this simplifies Yezidi belief, it is a valid illustration here.

As with the Yezidis' peacock-resembling Lucifer, other violent deities may require loyalty from believers, in order to avoid injury, disease, disaster and havoc. In this sense, religion is merely a manifestation of loyalty. Paying tribute to the violent or evil deities may involve sacrifice, which is a common theory of religious violence. In addition, tribute may involve behaving in a way that is pleasing to the deity: for example, by mirroring its characteristics. A violent deity may thus require believers to be violent, or suffer the consequences. This notion is easily translatable into what it is virtuous for the believer to do. For the *Kshatriya* warrior caste within Hinduism, for example, there is no higher virtue than war, and the ultimate evil and thus the greatest sin for the *Kshatriya* is to die peacefully in bed. However, violence as a virtue is not necessarily only due to such caste-obligation to violence, but it may also be manifested as a virtue in relation to the perceived 'vice' of non-violence in certain circumstances.

As was highlighted earlier, for many human beings, the worst vice is often perceived to be cowardice. Violence may therefore be required as an 'antidote' to cowardice, a virtue to remove the vice.

Violence may similarly be a virtue where it is perceived to be for the greater good of the religion or community of believers. It is not only a virtue for the believers to resort to violence for a religious precept, it would be a vice not to. Again, orthopraxy outweighs orthodoxy as it would seem impossible for the religionist to believe in a religious or moral precept without living it. Although this borders on a theological enquiry, it is possible to see how the protection of what are seen as noble or desirable characteristics may result in violence, and that such violence is therefore legitimate. This may be seen as defensive violence, as it is employed to protect the (anthropomorphic) characteristics that are believed to be important and possibly even vital for true belief. However, similar arguments can be conducive of offensive violence. In most instances of religious violence, the 'aggressor' poignantly creates guilt in the recipient of the violence. It is the unbelievers' fault that they are subjected to violence, whilst there is no blame on the innocent believers for employing violence. In the same way as cosmic dualism condones and requires violence, this sense of guilt versus innocence is a notion that inevitably leads to violence within religious systems.

The unbeliever has, according to most religious systems, the right to improve him/herself by accepting true belief, and thus avoids being subjected to violence by becoming virtuous. Indeed, it is sometimes argued that religion is a challenge for the improvement of human beings. This, of course, is applicable for believers and unbelievers alike, albeit on different levels. Though polytheism is often discarded as scenes of anachronistic myths by the self-professedly more 'advanced' religious systems, these 'ancient myths' and narratives of violent gods have come to saturate even the staunchest of contemporary monotheisms. As the Judeo-Christian myths became formalised in (political) theology and other disciplines it was the anthropomorphism, vices and virtues from these traditions that became the norm for politics, and later for international relations. Ancient polytheistic anthropomorphism permeates contemporary international politics, where certain religious virtues are deemed defensible by force, and vices similarly to be annihilated by force. It becomes a duty to kill or otherwise destroy destructive forces on the international (and domestic) political arena. Violence is condoned, as not only are the believers obeying god they are also – from a more pseudo-secular perspective – obeying their own conscience.

Most violence rooted in variants of anthropomorphism nonetheless place most of the blame in the human sphere of influence; wars are fought to please the gods, to eradicate vices, increase virtue or simply mirror the characteristics of certain deities. Violence and war are in these cases due to the notion of 'free will' and do, in a way, remove problems of theodicy and blame to be placed with the gods. Another variant on this theme takes a different, and somewhat more theologically controversial, approach. In certain polytheistic systems, like the Greek, the Pharaohic and the Viking traditions, the deities may be perceived to be amoral in that they create human wars for their own entertainment and amusement. Though such perceptions may again be a manifestation of anthropomorphism, satisfying the human urge to refashion the world in one's own image, the previous argument can be carried that if the gods are amoral and violent, so too are human beings.

It should be clear from the brief exposé above that although there are various theories using anthropomorphism for a variety of purposes, violence is often a central tenet in this notion, rather than a circumstantial phenomenon. Violence may be condoned and required as the most noble and least selfish act of a believer, or it may provide an explanation for the existence of evil, within polytheistic traditions, as a sacred entity worthy of at least as much respect (if not more) as the good deities. Alternatively, violence may be unavoidable as it is the duty of moral humans to destroy destructive forces in the same way as it is their duty to destroy rabid dogs. In addition, the notions of a 'chosen people' or a 'promised land' are potent reminders of how concepts of anthropomorphism may be amongst the most violent forces on the contemporary international arena. Conflict resolution (and – indeed – international relations in general) must recognise that anthropomorphism is a fundamental underlying tenet in most types of contemporary narratives and rhetoric. This is apparent ranging from mass media to politics and the academy. It is vital to understand this centrality in order to make the rhetoric of violence more transparent, and recognise that it is on this basis that God (or any number of deities) is always on the side of the believers in any physical manifestation of religious violence. As was noted earlier, this has invariably been the case in most religious, pseudo-secular and secular conflicts throughout history, and is no less so today.

The Concept of Survival

One of the most common expressions of religious violence is where notions of survival are invoked. In this context, this does not refer to individual survival but the survival of the religion as a system of belief. The last of the beliefs I use to illustrate and investigate the logic of religious violence is therefore an ironic parallel to Darwinian evolutionary theory. Violence is legitimate in religion due to several fundamental beliefs, as I have explored throughout this chapter. It can be argued, however, that the survival of religion is of utmost importance, as without it there would be no religious truth to defend and protect, no cosmic dualism to identify the true believers from the unbelievers and so forth. Despite this tautological argument for the importance of violence to the survival of religion, it nonetheless builds on the notion of religious truth, as do the previous beliefs. The two most common variants of this 'survivalist' theory of violence are usually expressed as the 'fight for survival' and the 'survival of the fittest'. It may be beneficial to reflect on Buddhism as an illustration of the latter concept, and Judaism as exemplifying the former.

Most religious systems justify violence for the survival of their beliefs. This may be manifested either as defensive or offensive violence. Defensive violence is usually more theologically acceptable, as it refers to protecting the religion from an external attack, which may prove lethal. In religious manifestations of violence, more so than purely secular manifestations, the very existence of the enemy is a threat. The enemy must be completely destroyed to guarantee the survival of the religious community of believers. In a religious war, there can only be one survivor, and compromise is thus, as noted earlier, impossible. Religious wars are 'total wars' since it is the complete destruction of the enemy that matters most. The ultimate goal of such violence is, as before, a more peaceful society, without an enemy that threatens the survival of the believers and their religion. That is, defensive violence is legitimate against those who threaten the peace and security of the world. In addition, the logic of apocalyptic, millenarian and messianic religions may even call for violence to create this idyllic world in the first place. Certainly, most extremist religious groups thus take a view of security as equalling the annihilation of the enemy. However, such rhetoric is in abundance throughout perceivably less extremist and thus more tolerant systems of belief, whether these are (pseudo-) secular or religious. President George W. Bush's rhetoric concerning the 'Axis of Evil' that threatens the survival of 'our way of life' – or 'us' – is an obvious example.

A theme that is apparent here is the complex commitment to 'us', which is a trend within all systems of belief. In the context of survival, the notion can be enlarged from the dualistic dichotomy of merely 'us' versus 'them', to include the survival of an idea, an ideal, a community or even humanity itself. It is a complex ethical problem that in order to ensure the survival of the many, it may be necessary to kill the few. However, as the continuing failure (with or without a 'roadmap') of the Middle East peace process shows, justifying violence according to this principle does not merely raise ethical considerations, it also invariably overrides the commitment to peace. 'Terrorists' and 'freedom fighters', along with liberal politicians, judicial courts, medical ethics committees and invariably journalists, all grapple with the issues of whether it can be justified to kill one child to save one hundred (by finding a cure for leukaemia, for example). Similarly executing one serial killer to save future potential victims, or rooting out one group of extremists to save a hundred other 'tolerant' groups, or whether it is justified to kill those who do not believe in the system of belief to save those that do. Religion provides clear answers to these issues, and religious violence is therefore often legitimised according to the principle of pre-emptive strikes, defensive response and ultimately the survival of the believers and their ideals.

What makes religious wars for survival more intense and lethal than, for example, capital punishment or medical research is that in such a war the means justify the ends. Not only does this mean that all means are justified, but that all means *should* be used to guarantee victory. If survival is at stake, exclaims the extremist militant religion WCOTC, 'is so-called "illegal" terrorism justified? … the answer overwhelmingly is – hell yes!'[41] As with the concept of fear, such hate towards the adversary is more than mere xenophobia, as the very existence of an enemy entails an existential threat. It is not possible to be tolerant towards such an enemy, or enter into a dialogue that by nature involves compromise. Where self-preservation is the highest law, the 'fight for survival' is more a matter of life or death than any other manifestation of violence. What seems like an unwarranted action or disproportionate retaliation may be perceived to be entirely legitimate if it is based on narratives of survival.

What is important to acknowledge in the exploration of the 'fight for survival' is that the combatants invariably perceive themselves as a defensive force. The believers see themselves as the victims of external attack, against which violence is justified as a defensive measure to ensure that the continuity provided by religion between past, present and future is upheld. Once referred to as victims, however, it is easy to identify the enemy, as Jewish narratives throughout history prove. If a communal religious identity is based on victimhood, as Judaism is, violence is easily justified. The outsider threatens the very unity and stability of the community, and is again perceived as an existential threat. Religions that take this view of survival are in general fundamentalist (again, without the connotations of militarism or fanaticism) and tolerate very little change. Fighting for survival, within such a faith, then comes to mean fighting against change, or for conservatism. Like a biological species, fundamentalist religions adopt perceivably aggressive or violent behaviour to protect their particular characteristics and lineage. The other side of the 'survivalist coin' is the logical continuation of such an 'evolutionary theory', and relates to the 'survival of the fittest'.

Whilst Judaism may fight to survive as a distinct religion, with unchanged characteristics throughout generations, this is not necessarily the most prudent path for a religion that *does* want to survive. As circumstances change, religion – and thus also theology – changes in response to new situations. A religion that remains static has little chance of survival, and the history of most religious traditions shows that change is virtually a universal trend. To survive, therefore, it may be necessary to adapt and change. One of the main reasons why Buddhism, for example, has not been annihilated although it has been subjected to almost incessant threat from external beliefs, has been its ability to adapt. One reason for the worldwide success of Buddhism from its origins in the philosophy of one man 2500 years ago is that it, like Hinduism, is a 'sponge' religion that soaks up influences from its environs. Christianity, similarly, embraced certain 'pagan' traditions and beliefs as it spread around the world, not least as it entered the Viking territories of northern Europe. Using the evolutionary analogy, again, it may be argued that the old mystical religions have survived for a comparatively long time, as they are 'the fittest' for such survival due to their ability to adapt. In a discussion about the implications of 'survival' for religious violence, however, it must be remembered that not even Buddhism is entirely non-violent.

Although (particularly) Western observers have identified Buddhism as a pacifist religion, it is not averse to violence. To guarantee survival, as was argued above, violence is justified in Buddhism in certain circumstances. Briefly, it may be interesting to note the two types of reasoning in Buddhism for when exceptions to the general rule of non-violence are permitted. Philosophical reasoning usually brings up the five-fold rationality for deciding whether an act of lethal violence has occurred: something living must have been killed (1), in addition, the killer must have known that it was alive (2), and must have intended to kill it (3). Furthermore, an actual act of killing must have taken place (4) and the creature (human or animal) must, in fact, have died (5). This refers to the illusionary nature of existence and, according to some scholars, it is even *impossible* to kill as there is no self or soul to kill.[42] The more practical approach relates back to the issue of survival, as violence is generally a legitimate course of action if the teaching is (existentially) threatened, in times of *mlecca* (savage), or against enemies of the true teaching. Indeed, violence is even allowed in situations highlighted earlier, where it is righteous to kill one to save two, or to stop a killer from killing. It must be acknowledged in this very brief outline of Buddhist ethics of violence that there are many more interpretations of violence within this religious tradition, as with every tradition, and the justifications furthermore change with time. As Buddhism, like Hinduism, lacks a canonical scripture, establishing under what circumstances violence may be justified has proved all the more difficult than in canonical religions. It is a curious tangent that the Theravada tradition, with its reluctance to recognise life, has overall been stronger in its prohibition of violence than the Mahayana tradition, which frequently has found means of justifying the killer. It is equally curious, perhaps, that Siddharta Gautama, the Buddha, belonged to the *Kshatriya* caste, and was thus a warrior by birth and heritage with a duty to fight.

Survival of the fittest, which is a fundamental tenet of contemporary thinking of both species and concepts, does not therefore rule out violence. Whilst the 'fight for survival' argument may build too much on the perceived superiority of the faith to the disadvantage of tolerance, complete tolerance or adaptation by being a 'sponge' religion may actually threaten the uniqueness – and thus the survival – of the religion in itself. For survival, it may actually be necessary for the believers to understand that dreaded word 'compromise' in light of violence. Arguably religions 'survive a long time by having within the reservoir of their resources a wide variety of responses to peace and violence'.[43] In the fight for survival, therefore, which is perceived to be necessary and inevitable lest the religion perish, there is nonetheless some form of natural selection in religion. The religion that is most adaptable, both in its own development and in its interpretation of violence, seems to be the fittest for survival according to this argument.

Understanding that though there may be many reasons for and causes of religious violence, most religions are capable of legitimising violence in order to protect the faith, the truth and the believers. Ultimately, the goal of such struggle is to end all war and build a more peaceful world without threat. The natural biological tendency to fight for one's survival on an individual level, or as a species, can also be applied to concepts, ideals and thus religions. Any framework for conflict transformation must acknowledge the protection of the uniqueness of such concepts, and the desire of believers to protect their faith at all costs, so that it will survive for future generations.

Notes

[1] D. Martin (1997), p.160.
[2] C.O. Lerche Jr., *et al.* (1995), p.123.
[3] M. Juergensmeyer (2000), p.175; Cf. B. Ehrenreich (1998), pp.136, 207, 212; M. Nicholson, (1992), p.114.
[4] B. Klassen (1992), p.402. Cf. the Bible: Matthew 12:30-32. See also the USA and UK's campaign against 'terrorism' in the latter part of 2001, where 'the greatest sin' was to criticise the campaign.
[5] R. Fox quoted in B. Ehrenreich (1998), p.135.
[6] P.T. Forsyth (1916), pp.23, 188.
[7] R.S. Appleby (2000), p.89.
[8] There seems little value in using this term with a definitive article, *the* Satan, as in Hebrew, indicating that it is a 'title' rather than a name (in accordance with Job 1:6-12 in the Hebrew Bible), although the existence of such theories is acknowledged. Cf. J. James (1960), p.25n1.
[9] A. Wallis (1973), p.7.
[10] N. Machiavelli (1961), p.135; Cf. P. Tournier (1978), p.143; R.S. Appleby (2000), pp.74, 117; Faraj in J.J.G. Jansen (1986).
[11] P. Sherry (1977), p.182. Cf. O.L.F. Richardson (1960), pp.231-246; M. Nicholson (1996), p.130.

[12] The Dalai Lama (1990), p.133. Cf. D.C. Rapoport in M. Juergensmeyer (1992), p.123; A. Riccardi in W. Beuken and K.-J.Kuschel (1997), p.77; M. Merleau-Ponty (1969), p.355; M. Bakunin quoted in B. Ehrenreich (1998), p.23.
[13] D.C. Rapoport (1984), p.662.
[14] J.G. Stoessinger (1985), pp.116 and 138 respectively.
[15] P. Sherry (1977), p.185.
[16] R. Trigg (1998), p.22.
[17] R. Eucken (1913), p.6.
[18] J.G. Stoessinger (1985), p.141.
[19] J. Habermas (1976), p.119.
[20] L.N. Tolstoy (1982), p.418.
[21] L.N. Tolstoy (1982), p.1443.
[22] M. Proust quoted in R. Hardin (1995), p.142; B. Blanshard (1974), p.232; P. Sherry (1977), p.88.
[23] H.J. Berman (1974), p.124.
[24] H.D. Spalding (1972), pp101-102. Cf. J.W. Richards (2000), p.30 for the same story regarding the Welsh.
[25] J.L. Esposito (1995), p.33.
[26] M. Juergensmeyer (1988). See also M. Juergensmeyer (2000), p.148; J.M. Allegro (1956), pp124, 128 and 158; M. Juergensmeyer (2002), pp.14-15.
[27] M. Juergensmeyer (2000), p.148.
[28] J.B. Wilson (1958), p.4.
[29] M. Juergensmeyer (1992), p.112.
[30] R.-S. Puri (1987), p.17.
[31] J.A. Aho (1981), p.218.
[32] J.A. Aho (1981), p.26.
[33] D. Harbour (2001).
[34] N. Machiavelli (1961), pp.61, 96.
[35] J. Goodall (2000), p.130.
[36] Quoted in J.V. Bondurant (1958), p.28; M. Juergensmeyer (2002), pp.ix, 13.
[37] J. Sacks in H.P. Fry (1996), p.xiii.
[38] J. Keegan (1999), p.28.
[39] Xenophanes of Colophon, *fragment 15*, pp.24-25, 89 in J.H. Lesher's commentary.
[40] J.C. Bennet and H. Seifert (1977), pp.19, 20.
[41] B. Klassen (1992), pp.424, 244 (WCOTC = World Church Of The Creator).
[42] Cf. M. Juergensmeyer (1996), p.8.
[43] M. Gopin (2000), p.168.

Chapter 7

Conclusions: A Framework for Conflict Transformation

By exploring various aspects that are generally either ignored or not acknowledged as having any influence, the previous chapters have all built towards an approach to religion and violence on the international arena. I highlighted that explanations of situations and events are often not sufficient for successful conflict management, conflict resolution and ultimately for conflict transformation. Rather, a better approach to these matters is to replace such explanations with sound understandings, using a number of prerequisites, causes and origins. From this, a framework of conflict transformation can be deduced, which I will introduce in this concluding chapter. Before doing so, however, it may be useful to reiterate the basic arguments– for clarification and as a basis for the framework.

We started the journey with a somewhat superficial exposition of the most common contemporary arguments pertaining to religion and violence (armed conflict) on the international arena. Most of these arguments are those of (secular) political scientists, politicians and – through popular mass media – the general ('lay') public. Using similar terms of reference as these approaches, I highlighted the often casual use of terms and concepts, dismissive approaches and ultimately rash conclusions, by the *absence* of any explicit definitions, clarifications or acknowledgement of 'problematic' argumentation. I justified this in order not only to draw attention to much of the obvious bias that underlies current academia but also to break with a convention that is unmistakably an unsuccessful approach to the practice and study of contemporary international relations. Chapter 3 explored some correlates of these perspectives by offering five empirical examples of various types of religious violence. This, I claimed, is the closest this book comes to reflecting the ideographic investigations so popular within the social sciences in particular. The cases were carefully discerned to provide clear illustrations of some basic tenets of 'terrorism' (The Nizaris), politically motivated religion in a state context (The Sudan), religiously influenced politics in a state context (Sri Lanka), how pre-existing religious narratives can be determinate of violence (India) and finally how an externally imposed religious identity may be conducive to violence (Myanmar).

Chapter 4 provided some basic prerequisites for understanding how the contemporary (mis-)perceptions of religion and violence have come to be formulated. First, of course, 'religion' was conceptualised and 'understanding' was distinguished from 'explanation'. Thereafter, generally unacknowledged factors, such as assumptions, bias and ontology were highlighted to provide a sound basis for a new framework of conflict transformation. Thereafter, I offered a causational theory of these contemporary perspectives in chapter 5. The first of the 'causations' pertained to the inherent rationality of religion and how it differs from the political (secular) rationality usually epitomised in the Rational Actor Model; and the second cause highlighted how the Peace of Westphalia in 1648 still has an unmistakable legacy on the international arena, not least in issues of religion and violence. Wondering what underlies the stereotypes, and how religion could possibly be construed, used and abused for violent purposes formulated chapter six into a brief overview of a number of elements in religion that may be conducive, permissive or indicative of violence. In short, the last few chapters pointed towards how religious violence may be inevitable rather than circumstantial on the contemporary international arena.

Relatively easily, this 'journey' can be translated into five principles of conflict transformation, though it should be remembered that these are not posited as a linear 'step' or logical progression from one to the other. Each of the five fundamental chapters provides a basic 'rule', though the approach is perturbative, and requires users to employ them with care, and not accept these principles unquestioningly:

- Refuse to accept explanations of 'facts' about religion and conflict on the international arena without questioning the validity of these notions. Any assumptions on the international arena must be based on a perturbative approach, which means that any assumptions may be changed as more details are known and not retained when contradicted (cf. ch.2);
- In order to understand why narratives take the shape they do it is vital to look at the situation in hand with as open a mind as possible. Strive to understand the situation. This includes highlighting sources of information, how information is presented and why (cf. ch.3);
- Realise that no concepts (or terms) are value-neutral, but rather saturated with assumptions and bias and must be subjected to a vast number of qualifying conditions. Therefore, concepts such as 'religion' and 'terrorism' that perpetuate conflict by being taken for granted need to be reconsidered (cf. ch.4);
- Acknowledge that even the most basic of 'truths' are derived from a particular historical tradition. Working with these truths implicitly affirms the particularism of that tradition. A new interpretation of rationality is thus needed and the international system of states may need altering (cf. ch.5);
- Know (understand) the underlying origins of religious narratives of violence in that these may (by some) be manifested as physical violence on the international arena. This means that a thorough understanding of how religions can be violent, and the logic this violence entails, is necessary (cf. ch.6).

Whilst these principles can be reformulated in many different ways, the fundamentals of the framework that they begin to constitute rests on a reformulation of traditional conflict *resolution* approaches to conflict *understanding*. This reformulation is partly needed due to the misuse of the concept of 'conflict resolution' (and associated concepts), as 'a trendy way for some NGOs to obtain money'[1] However, a framework using 'new' terms is not merely – or even mostly – linguistic. The conventional way of viewing the world, and thus of resolving any conflict that arises within such a paradigm, is not entirely satisfactory in the contemporary world as has been my implicit argument. The 'old' theories that have grappled with religion and violence (from a wide range of disciplines) have usually only been able to provide a limited answer to a limited query (such as the existence of a particular manifestation of religious violence). Whilst many of the approaches have thus been successful in ideographic and limited application, most fail as they are not applicable in other situations. The most common reason for the failure of the majority of theories of conflict resolution is that they fail to acknowledge the inherent assumptions, ontologies and paradigms that influence both the process and the result of conflict resolution. This is not, however, to claim that most approaches do not have limited relevance and may have successful application. The lack of a thorough introspective framework means that most approaches to conflict resolution fail to acknowledge their own historical (religious, cultural, social) background. The allegedly Jewish roots of so-called 'shuttle diplomacy' may serve as an apt illustration of this, as will the following examples from various perspectives, though not as explicitly as Aaron's shuttle diplomacy between conflicting parties.

As noted, virtually every discipline interested in the relationship between religion and violence (at some level) has developed theories of conflict resolution. The state of the world, with its vast number of armed tensions, may signify the fundamentally unsuccessful nature of the various approaches even where the ontology of each approach is understood. For example, the apparent failure of the international system of secular states to bring about a more peaceful and secure world seems to indicate that theories built on secularisation may be impossible in a world of religious identities and genuine religious belief. The separation of private religion and secular (public) politics is thus also not a viable approach. It is therefore possible to sustain an argument that the relatively short experiment of the state as removed from religion has been an unsuccessful practice in a world of genuine belief. Similarly, suggestions from other disciplines that offer in themselves useful theories – such as gender-explained roots of conflicts, conflict-theories based on class or economics, or the 'human nature' arguments from various biological disciplines – have consistently fallen short of a nomothetical understanding of religious conflict that is widely (and universally) applicable.

It is not difficult to find obstacles in other, less disciplinary bound approaches that, for example, include notions of dialogue, pluralism and 'cohabitation'. Problems of genuine dialogue were highlighted earlier, as the 'other' must be recognised to be on par – equal – with oneself, which is a theological impossibility for many religionists. Genuine pluralism is similarly problematic in that the recognition of the 'Other' may either constitute an impossible (or unwanted) compromise of one's own ideals or assume superiority ("as they don't know any better they may exist, but I am still right"), in which case it is not genuine pluralism. 'Cohabitational' theories, generally based on legal instruments of religious tolerance, easily become hypocritical as the ingrained value-ideals of even the most liberal society make a mockery of its own laws of tolerance. Liberal societies (for example, those in North/Western Europe) may cherish their reputation as being magnanimous in allowing 'every' religion to flourish within their borders. This, however, is where 'tolerance' becomes hypocritical, as it is not unconditional acceptance. Only those faiths that are deemed sound, fair and have some degree of truth are allowed. Whilst this generally includes the so-called 'great world religions' it excludes equally valid religions that are deemed to be cults, non-religious or 'dangerous'. These categories are, of course, self-referential and judged using the ideals of the society in question and not by examining the actual group in question.

Hezb'allah is thus a legitimate political organisation in Lebanon but a 'terrorist' group in most Western societies, and thus illegal in the same way as chanting by Hare Krishna is tolerated on European streets, but similar Satanist 'rituals' are forbidden.

Every approach to religious violence is thus deemed ultimately right and perhaps the 'only' possible approach by the 'adherents' of that particular approach. In a way, therefore, even the most secular approaches are theological in that they strive for an acceptance of a particular brand of 'universalism'. According to this argument, once all sides accept the 'right' approach there will be secure and lasting peace. It is hardly worthy of mention that this is a variant of the exclusivist religious language discussed at some length earlier. Conventionally, therefore, 'until all men become Christian indeed',[2] until religion is completely removed from international politics, or until women rule the world there will be violence, armed conflict and war (from religionist, secularist and feminist perspectives respectively).

If existing approaches can be said to be not entirely successful, the prospects for lasting and genuine peace may seem very distant. Indeed, an entirely new theory may be necessary to fully comprehend the complexities of religious violence. Using the understandings gained from using such a theory, then, a successful framework for conflict transformation could be built. Although ambitious, it is not an impossibility. Whilst this is not my intention, one could, for example, envisage that in order to incorporate all factors of religious violence a suitably outrageous theory may take its cue from the ancient archenemy of religion, namely science. One of the latest theories to emerge from the field of quantum physics has been tentatively called M-theory and is derived from what only recently was the predominant feature of the quest for a Theory of Everything (ToK), namely String Theory or Superstrings. According to M-theory, there are an infinite number of parallel universes (actually, a 'multiverse'), each of which may have different laws of physics. Without going into the mathematical physics of M-theory, and its 11-dimensional framework,[3] a non-physical 'corruption' can possibly be applied to the understanding of religious violence and conflict. An infinite number of parallel universes ('many-worlds') existing simultaneously may not only facilitate a new understanding of religious 'pluralism' without compromising the absoluteness or exclusivity of religious truths, but also – due to this – religious conflicts may prove to be impossible. Religious conflicts are only possible where incompatible and mutually exclusive truths compete for/in the same universe, but may be defunct in terms of parallel universes where complete monotheism exists in one universe, polytheism in another, secularity in a third and any variants in-between and beyond. These could never be in conflict as they function within different universes and thus do not follow the same laws. Similarly, an earlier dismissal of the impossibility of doctrinal opposition can thus be recalled now, if reformulated to derive from M-theory. In one universe Jesus did die on the cross and in another he did not, in a third he never existed and in a fourth he is still alive. Any possibility is not only equally plausible as any other, but also equally true and does – in fact – occur. All it takes, according to M-theory, is that someone somewhere observes the event. The event may, or may not, have taken place 2000 years ago. This application of M-theory to religious experience may explain apparitions, religious experiences and even divine inspiration as universes collide, overlap, merge and split apart. Although this is may be too literal an application of M-theory and quantum physics, there may be some mileage in further research into this field. This is not 'Quantum Theology'. In fact, the quantum leap Diarmud O'Murchu claims to make[4] is barely a shuffle forward compared to this theory.

However, this book is not a proposal of M-theory as applied to religious conflict, as interesting and novel as that may be, though it is acknowledged that such a theory could be built on the framework of understanding as proposed here. The five principles suggested above are based on the importance of *understanding* religious violence in order for a framework of conflict transformation to be explicated. In light of the need to reformulate understandings of conflict transformation, a four-fold model can be established, upon which the above five-fold framework (the principles) is based:

- Understanding contemporary perspectives and approaches to the relationship between religion and violence, and realising the failures thereof;
- Understanding the logic of religious violence, which includes a grasp of the prerequisites, origins and causes both of language and manifestation of violence and conflict;
- Understanding the limits and applicability of conventional conflict resolution techniques that are often attempting to pour new wine into old wineskins;
- Understanding that another paradigm may be needed for a more peaceful world, that is built on a new ontology, rather than reiterating old problems.

In the first principle, analysts of conflict are urged not to accept conventional approaches and perspectives that purport to *explain* the phenomena associated with religion and armed conflict without questioning the validity of such perspectives. Such questioning may include an investigation of the underlying ontology and paradigms of who is using the approach, how, why and for what purpose. Instead, the second principle highlights the importance of understanding the fundamentals of religious violence. A large part of this is constituted by a grasp of the violence-conducive/permitting tenets of religion (cf. ch.6) but also other ways in which religion can be genuinely violent on the international arena are important. This includes having a grasp of religion as one of the most fundamental elements of individual and societal identity that thus often serves as the basic differentiation between 'us' and 'them'. In turn, a number of correlates (cf. ch.3) can be identified where religion may play a violent (or – alternatively – a peaceful, since this too is a reaction to violence) role on the international arena. The third principle invites a rethinking of so-called 'conflict resolution' into 'conflict understanding', as seen above. Various 'Gandhian' approaches to conflict resolution show, for example, that these may be far more fruitful than the traditional approaches of 'shuttle diplomacy', negotiation and dialogue, all of which are based on some kind of compromise that may be demeaning to all parties concerned. The 10 'rules' of one such Gandhian approach are in reality conflict transformation, rather than conflict resolution, though for lay-understanding of conflict the latter may be virtually indistinguishable from the former. The difference lies in the importance not to shirk conflict, but to transform it into something constructive *and non-violent*. Gandhian frameworks highlight this, and as they provide a basis for conflict resolution of all varieties, they are also applicable to an extent in the present investigation though not without slight modification:[5]

- *Do not shirk confrontation.* Avoiding conflict, or ignoring an aspect of it (as religion is avoided in the Westphalian system), will not remove the conflict, and it cannot thus be said to be resolved. Also, making one party illegal (for example) does not remove its cause, but rather removes any hope of peaceful resolution;
- *Stay open to communication and self-criticism.* Whereas dialogue is undoubtedly a factor in this, it should also not exclude 'terrorists' from being heard, though this may call for a change both in terminology and perception so that they may be treated on their own terms. Similarly, criticism should not be taken as a form of attack;
- *Find an acceptable resolution and pursue it.* Whilst this tenet on one level resembles ultimate religious peace ("the solution is easy, if everyone accepts my view"), many religious actors may find it difficult to agree with this aspect of Gandhian conflict resolution, as it may call for impossible compromise. The key word, however, is 'acceptable' and a resolution that is not acceptable to all parties is thus not a possibility;
- *Regard opponent as a potential ally.* To avoid future conflict it is vital that the opponent is at no point demeaned, or left feeling inferior. Twentieth century European politics have blatantly shown how this tenet was not followed, and what the consequences may be. In a religious context, it may include finding common ground, which all parties agree on, such as Jesus or respect for human life;
- *Make tactics consistent with goal.* If the goal is peace and harmony (as it is for all religions and most 'terrorist' groups) the way both the conflict is handled (conflict management) and resolved (conflict transformation) should be consistent with the goal; namely to be peaceful and harmonious. Similarly, if security of human life is valued (i.e. if the goal is the security of 'our people'), the tactics of the conflict should reflect this and killing would therefore be inconsistent with the goal;
- *Flexibility.* A liberal approach not only to one's opponent but also to one's self may be vital. Where actors are religious, this may have an application in not interpreting the scriptures of one's faith literally, but through a lens of historical relativism, for example, or in a metaphorical sense;
- *Temperate approach.* Although it is very easy to be passionate about one's position when religion is involved, the Gandhian approach advocates a temperate stance in order that inconsistencies can be resolved and that the process of conflict transformation can proceed;
- *Proportionality.* As above, criticism should not be seen as an attack on the religion as a whole. The reaction to a statement during the process of conflict resolution must be seen in its proper context and not as heresy, blasphemy or an attack on all believers;
- *Discipline.* To mix metaphors for a moment, it is important to remember that in any basket of red apples, there may be one or two green ones. Whilst this is not to say that they are any worse just because they are in the minority, one cannot judge the other apples by the same yardstick. Geopolitically, this may be translated as not equalling fanaticism with mainstream religion, for example. On the other hand, if negotiating conflict transformation, the followers must have enough discipline to follow their leader if a 'deal is brokered';
- *Know when to quit.* On one level, this principle is virtually never applicable in religious conflicts as it is not only a theological impossibility to quit a religious

conflict, but this would also eliminate any future claims based on religion. However, as a principle of knowing when to quit the peace process it is applicable, though by definition not favourable to peace. Where compromises of an impossible level are required, religious actors not only have the right (and duty) to decline, but other actors must accept this right. If peace depends on denying the existence of god, for example, most religionists would be outraged and not be in a position to accept the peace.

In the process of conflict resolution, these principles are applicable to all sides. In addition, each side should ideally grasp the other's application of them, and use them in his or her own actions but also apply them introspectively. An introspective application may force the actor to question his/her own motives and actions. Am I being temperate? Disciplined? Proportionate? Do I accept criticism? Am I shirking confrontation? An approach like this is not foolproof, however, and religious tenets can easily be found that are both consistent and contradictory to all of these principles. See, for example, the principle relating to the tactics being consistent with the goal. As with any killing, there are religious caveats, for example, and particular interpretations of divine (or scriptural) decrees may be deemed inconsistent with the above principles and religion does generally assume superiority over any other decree.

Returning to the last principle in the four-fold framework proposed here, the success of conflict understanding (such as the Gandhian model, above), as opposed to the conventional approaches to conflict resolution, *may* require an entirely new paradigm of intersubjective understandings on which the approach can be posited. It is plausible that the quest for the unification of physics may one day show that M-theory, for example, is the most probable basis for answering most questions, even including the possibilities for transforming religious conflicts. This, of course, is impossible to say as there has been no research conducted into its application in matters either of religion or of international relations, apart from a small number of theologians that have dabbled in quantum physics or the even rarer occasions where 'an abstract equation from theoretical physics has inspired a following among a religious group!'[6]

The importance of understanding the relationship between religion and violence (armed conflict, war, 'terrorism', etc.) cannot be over-emphasised. A lack of understanding leads to intractable conflict, solidifying of stereotypes and a failure to reach a successful transformation of the most lethal conflicts in human history. Whilst understanding is neither the first nor the last step in conflict transformation, it is arguably the most important and possibly the most difficult to achieve. It is impossible to make another individual *understand* something. One can explain, and one can facilitate understanding, but the ultimate understanding is up to the individual in question. Whilst a genuine *will* to understand must be present before the process can begin, this becomes all the more difficult where the situation or concept to be understood is distasteful or disagreeable. To understand violence from a pacifist perspective, for example, or a fundamentalist religious view from a liberal/conservative view, may hamper the *will* to understand and thus also its successful achievement. In any conflict transformation process, and not least where considerations of religious identity are involved, it may be necessary to understand one's own characteristics in order to understand those of the 'terrorist'. In any case, even if one does not agree it is none the less possible to partly comprehend, if not fully understand.

Whilst the possibility of genuine understanding is a largely philosophical one and based on the ideals of a very particular tradition, it is nonetheless possible to explicitly test the above framework of conflict transformation on a more practical – intellectual – level. This is a necessary step as any theory is only useful once it can be applied in practice; by itself theory alone is somewhat futile. There are as many ways of testing whether the model proposed here is valid as there are critics. However, in order to make satisfactory criticisms, it must be remembered what the background of the model is and what it purports to do, as any general theory, and its criticism, will show a bias towards concepts and terminology with which the theorist – and critic – is most knowledgeable. The aim is to understand religious violence on the international arena with a view to making peaceful conflict transformation more possible. Although it has drawn on a wide range of disciplines, this has been largely to highlight downfalls of conventional and traditional theories due to their lack of understanding. To this extent, it is a narrative approach in that it pays attention to stories, context and highlights the inherent relativism of any narrative. Any test of the framework must thus originate within – or explicitly deal with – narratives, as this model will not necessarily fit criteria applicable in other fields or disciplines. Whilst narratives are, however, notoriously difficult to evaluate, methods for evaluating and testing what may be called such 'analytic narratives' do exist. One possible way of testing the current model, therefore, could be to apply Robert Bates's (*et. al.*, 1998) five criteria to the four-fold framework outlined above. This would enable a basic evaluation of the viability of the model. Such an evaluation may resemble the following, though it is important to stress that this is not an actual evaluation of the model:

Do the assumptions fit the facts, as they are known?

Although it may be argued that contemporary perspectives and approaches to the relationship between religion and violence have partially succeeded in their aims, the state of the world seems to indicate that most conventional approaches have failed to understand this relationship. Furthermore, the logic of religious violence is rarely attempted to be understood, but is rather brushed away by instrumentalist arguments of religion on the international arena. The logical progression of this is that conflict resolution techniques are similarly tainted by the ontology upon which they are based. In the contemporary world, the catalogue of failed peace-processes and unrelenting conflict stand as proof of this. By Occam's Razor,[7] the last principle highlights an apparent deficiency in contemporary paradigms and suggests that a new ontology may be needed. The 'facts' seem to back up the assumptions made in this book, though in matters of religion it is often exceedingly difficult to discern the facts from the narratives.

Do conclusions follow from premises?

In contrast to scientific disciplines, it may be difficult to follow the line of reasoning in issues concerning narratives. To overcome this, the analogy of a journey from explanation to understanding, rather than using formal logic, has been employed to minimise any rash conclusions. By highlighting how most contemporary perspectives deal with the issues at hand and investigating the prerequisites, origins and causes of these, the conclusions have been drawn that whilst merely explaining religious violence is problematic, understanding it is vital for successful international relations and conflict transformation.

Do its implications find confirmation in the data?
There are a number of implications both of accepting the conventional perspectives and acknowledging the necessity of another approach. In short, an approach such as the one advocated here aims to reduce the phenomenon of religious violence (and the logic thereof) to the 'known' and the 'knowable'. That is, when 'de-mystified' it is possible to understand violence, and thus overcome it. Implications of accepting such a new framework are wide-ranging and applicable in most sectors of society. In media (fictional and factional), politics (professional and lay) and academia the most important implication would be a change in narratives. This would alter reporting, discourse, terminology, perception and ontology and thus increase the 'known'. It would also reduce stereotyping, which is often associated with 'irrationality' and illogical violence and is thus to be feared or hated. Accepting the model would mean rejecting old theories that are only partially successful, and formulating another epistemology and ontology that may form the basis for a more peaceful world.

How well does the theory stand up by comparison with other explanations?
As highlighted above, most other approaches are only partially successful in that their emphasis is on explaining rather than understanding. A number of contemporary approaches were highlighted at the beginning of this chapter and their weaknesses pointed out. The present theory may be less applicable to extremely ideographic situations, where a more 'situational' theory may be applicable.

How general is the explanation? Does it apply to other cases?
The main strength of this model is that it is nomothetical and as its approach uses conceptual forms of religion and associated concepts, it is equally applicable to all religions. Although most scholars agree on the importance of knowledge and understanding of conflict, few accept this unconditionally when the conflict is 'too close to home'. Using a non-judgemental framework such as the present one may overcome this difficulty, but only if approached with genuine epoché and eidetic vision.

Evaluating the framework may be built on such criteria as these five, although if used as a conflict transformation technique, the framework is likely to need testing for practicality 'in the field'. Its wider implications, pertaining to changing the intersubjective paradigms that underlie all perspectives and relations on the international arena, is a gradual process and can probably not be tested in the 'laboratory conditions' required by the evaluating methodology above. By actively changing education curricula, for example, the rewards may not be reaped for another generation or two. However, as a model for more peaceful relations on the contemporary international arena, the framework proposed here has a three-fold application in conflict management:

- *Before a conflict breaks out*, the knowledge and understandings gained from using this approach could be developed into an 'early warning' system. As such it would answer questions pertaining to what makes religious violence imminent or inevitable in particular situations. This is not merely *conflict prevention*, but the process of building a lasting (perpetual) peace that ameliorates instances where violent conflict may be inevitable;
- *During conflict*, the framework can be used as a guide for *conflict transformation*, by changing the way conflict is fought. For example, using a Gandhian-type approach such as the one that was highlighted above, conflict could be transformed from being violent and destructive to being non-violent and constructive. Similarly, by acquiring a deeper knowledge and understanding, negotiation techniques and other conflict management approaches could be successfully reformed to reflect these new insights. Such alterations could include the importance of face-saving measures, truth-claims and so forth. In other words, during conflict the framework answers questions as to what protracts religious violence;
- *After conflict*, the understandings relating to the conflict and the underlying considerations are vital for various approaches to post-conflict 'therapy' and counselling. This has potential to deal with issues of hate and fear of the 'Other' and would help groups and individuals come to terms with why what happened did happen. It would thus offer answers to why religious violence was manifested as it was and under what circumstances it could recur, for example. An important aspect of an approach like this to conflict resolution may be an entirely new ontology, as was the last principle highlighted above. In this context, that could be illustrated by the need not to accept *wrongdoing* following a conflict, but accepting having caused *injury*. Such an approach would remove the need to compromise the expression of genuine truths, whilst nevertheless accepting that there might have been a better way to deal with the conflict.

To be fully aware of the possibilities of this book it might serve a useful purpose at this point to establish where the resulting framework is perceived to be located. Without putting restrictive labels on knowledge, it may be possible to establish four 'ages' of humankind. This is not a theory that would stand up to any in-depth scrutiny or sceptical appraisal, but it is nevertheless helpful to an extent in clarifying the framework. As will be recalled, the fourth principle of understanding that constitutes the basis of this framework of conflict transformation advocates that a new ontology may be needed for more peaceful relations. This, however, may not be readily understood, as it is a rather complex notion. Most – if not all – disciplines can identify three distinct ontologies in their development, and often acknowledge that they are on the verge of a fourth 'ontological revolution' (although the fourth category is largely speculative). An example from astronomy will serve to illustrate this: The ancient view of the 'universe' (sky above) was that it was a supernatural firmament, variously a curtain, sheet, vault, dome and so forth. The Ptolemaic revolution established that the universe was geo-centric, with the sun and the planets orbiting the earth. The Copernican revolution similarly made the previous view redundant with its heliocentric claims that the earth, along with all other planets, orbited the sun. With (Super)String theories and subsequently by M-theory, this comfortable ontology may become replaced with the fourth ontology, that of Hyperspace, with its infinite number of universes. In each era, everyone – with negligible exceptions – not only *believed* that they knew, but they actually *did know* the truth. If anyone contested the ontology, they were naturally liars or heretics (or both). Ontology is invariably stronger than a mere understanding of the world to be a particular way. Experts from every discipline and field of knowledge can provide a similar lineage within their own disciplines, and lay-people – similarly – are usually able to discern certain trends in various fields, such as within industry, politics, religion, linguistics, health-science, and so forth.

In light of the above framework, its evaluation and its position on the 'ontological grid' above, it might be time, with Tennyson, to 'ring out the old, [and] ring in the new'[8] and accept that the traditional perspectives of religion and violence may not simply need considerable alteration, but that an entirely new approach may be necessary. Whilst I have argued that such an approach must necessarily be built on understanding rather than explanation, this is not to say that the process is straightforward. There are many problems with understanding, and it is important to realise that understanding is neither the first nor the last step in a process of conflict transformation. Such a process is ongoing and is not aligned with the Western philosophical tradition that calls for a beginning *and* an end to every story. Although this 'story' has neither, this does not mean it is timeless. Indeed, one of the main obstacles to the understanding of religion is the fact that religious language is not timeless. No interpretation can be removed from the time in which it arose, and it is therefore extremely difficult to make new interpretations using old standards and guidelines. Usually, this prevents any theory from becoming universally applicable, or a meta-theory. Physics, as mentioned above, is still striving to find a unified Theory of Everything (ToE), whilst most political scientists, for example, have given up on meta-narratives as 'no single nomothetic narrative is ever likely to be crowned as the master narrative'.[9] Such a claim is only partially true, and must be qualified in light of the present narrative.

Rather than merely offering a vast number of ideographic explanations of why particular situations occur, it *is* possible to establish a nomothetical narrative considering how and why religious violence recurs. This has been the aim here, but with one important caveat; the aim has not been to explain the existence of war, but to understand it, in line with the proclaimed starting-point of the research: 'If you wish for peace, understand war'.[10] Although the intention is good this does not mean that its application (by others) is necessarily so. Two points must be raised in connection with this; the one pertains to the seemingly implicit belief in the inevitability of religious violence and the secondly to the way of overcoming this obstacle.

As with the apparently incessant media-reports of religious conflict, this book seems to highlight the violent aspects of religion and thus over-emphasise these fringes of belief. The media tend to report the most extreme examples of religious violence, and the disparities of religion. This usually gives distorted and false images of certain aspects of religion, such as fundamentalism or decrees. Whilst 'media' in this case mainly pertains to Western media, it is important to remember that all media are culturally relative and their ontological perspectives may thus be limiting of reality. By focusing on these disparities, media and academia create a false balance that in turn may perpetuate conflicts and stereotypes. I may be criticised for a similar failure, although this is not the case: rather than perpetuating conflict, it is argued here (as throughout) that religious violence must be understood as a way to peace, rather than ignoring this important aspect of religion. A naïveté about religion or a lack of knowledge of the logic of religious violence, of the problems created by contemporary perspectives and of conventional conflict management techniques, will invariably lead to disaster. This is not to say that the violent aspects of religious belief should be over-emphasised, but rather that knowledge and genuine understanding are paramount.

The approach advocated here is therefore inclusive of groups and individuals that are invariably excluded by contemporary perspectives and conflict resolution techniques because they are not understood or because knowledge of their motives, intentions and beliefs is lacking. Where groups are excluded, usually by being referred to as 'terrorists', as being 'irrational' or 'illogical' and thus not open to negotiation, for example, leads to a feeling of betrayal and being let down and retaliation is imminent. Such retaliation is usually carried out by the only method that these excluded groups know is effective and will be listened to, and usually includes violence, such as suicide-attacks or 'wanton destruction'. Again, rather than ignoring violence or being under the misapprehension that it will automatically vanish, it is necessary to understand it if one wishes for a more peaceful world. In light of the conclusions drawn from the present research, and in particular the fourth point above, it should not need elaborating that even a seemingly 'neutral' approach to religious violence, built on understanding, is not removed from the particular tradition in which it arose. Discussing a possible application of parallel truths as an approach to religious consideration, for example, is entrenched in liberal non-confessional philosophy and would seem equally inapplicable for any religious believer. However, although the will to understand is an ideal, the 'understanding'-approach is probably applicable in every belief-system, if genuine conflict transformation is desired. This, in turn, may take the shape of various Gandhian approaches, which – similarly – are applicable in all systems.

In taking this rather unconventional and multi-disciplinary approach to one of the most controversial subjects in human history, and one in which everyone – at least since 11 September 2001 – is an expert, this book is similarly vulnerable to criticism from a wide range of fields, from the academy and beyond. If a debate can be stimulated, much of the battle has been won, and if the research helps to shed light on the relationship between religion and violence so that it can be understood, considerably more than half the battle will have been won. On the other hand, criticism may be similar to that received by Edward de Bono in response to an anecdote in a recent book. De Bono related the little-known fact that the Inuit language has a word that is roughly translated as 'I like you very much, but I would not go seal-hunting with you' to which William Hartston of the *Independent* newspaper retorted:

> Well, the English language has a word that means: 'I have listened to what you have to say and I understand the points you are trying to make, but I find your argument utterly unconvincing'. That word is 'bullshit', and this book is full of it.[11]

Notes

[1] J.A. Mertus (1999), p.265 n.21 [NGO = Non-Governmental Organisation].
[2] P.T. Forsyth (1916), p.32.
[3] Although it is impossible for human beings to visualise space in more than 3 dimensions, for example, it is possible to calculate mathematically the precise existence of more dimensions using a multidimensional version of the Pythagorean Theorem (2-dimensions: $a^2+b^2=c^2$; 3-dimensions: $a^2+b^2+c^2=d^2$; *N*-dimensions: $a^2+b^2+c^2+d^2+\ldots=z^2$). Cf. M. Kaku (1999), pp.37-38.
[4] D. O'Murchu (1997), p.42.
[5] The following exposition of a Gandhian approach to conflict resolution is adapted and modified from M. Juergensmeyer (2002), esp. pp.63-64.
[6] M. Kaku (1999), p.148.
[7] The principle attributed to the English philosopher William of Occam (d. c.1350) that one must use every contrivance to rid logic of unnecessary assumptions, and that as few assumptions – therefore – be used in explaining a thing. Cf. F.A. Wolf (1988), pp.66-67.
[8] From '*In Memoriam*' by Lord Tennyson.
[9] H. Suganami (2000), p.10.
[10] B.H. Liddell-Hart (1960), p.247; B.H. Liddell-Hart (1944), p.19.
[11] Reproduced in *Six Hats: Edward de Bono's Strange Lesson*, BBC News, 4th Dec. 1998 (www.bbc.co.uk/hi/english/special_report/1998/11/98/e-cyclopedia/newsid_226000/226700.stm).

Bibliography

Abdelmoula, A.M. (1998), *An Ideology of Domination and the Domination of an Ideology; Islamism, Politics and the Constitution in the Sudan*, United States Institute of Peace: Washington DC.

Abdul-Raof, H. (2003), *Exploring the Qur'an*, Al-Maktoum Institute Academic Press: Dundee.

Ackerman, P. & Duval, J. (2000), *A Force More Powerful; A Century of Nonviolent Conflict*, St. Martin's Press: New York NY.

Agrell, W. (2000), *Morgondagens Krig; Tekniken, Politiken och Människan*, Ordfront: Stockholm.

Aho, J.A. (1981), *Religious Mythology and the Art of War; Comparative Religious Symbolisms of Military Violence*, Aldwych Press: London.

Ali, T. (1970) in K. Gough & Sharma, H.P. (eds), *Imperialism and Revolution in South Asia*, Monthly Review Press: New York NY.

Allegro, J.M. (1956), *The Dead Sea Scrolls*, Penguin Books: Harmondsworth.

Allison, G.T. (1971), *Essence of Decision; Explaining the Cuban Missile Crisis*, Little, Brown & Company: Boston MA.

Al-Tel, O.I. (2003), *The First Islamic Conquest of Aelia (Islamic Jerusalem); A Critical Analytical Study of the Early Islamic Historical Narratives and Sources*, Al-Maktoum Institute Academic Press, Dundee.

Amunugama, S. (1991), 'Buddhaputra and Bhumiputra? Dilemmas of Modern Sinhala Buddhist Monks in Relation to Ethnic and Political Conflict', *Religion*, vol.21, April.

Anderson, B. (1991), *Imagined Communities; Reflections on the Origins and Spread of Nationalism*, 2nd ed., Verso: London.

Ankersmit, F.R. (1986), 'The Dilemmas of Contemporary Anglo-Saxon Philosophy of History', *History and Theory*, vol. 25.

Antoun, R.T. (2001), *Understanding Fundamentalism; Christian, Islamic and Jewish Movements*, Alta Mira (Rowan & Littlefield): Walnut Creek CA.

Appleby, R.S. (2000), *The Ambivalence of the Sacred; Religion, Violence, and Reconciliation*, Carnegie Corporation of New York, Rowman & Littlefield Publishers, Inc.: Lanham MD.

Arthur, C. (1993) (ed.), *Religion and the Media; an Introductory Reader*, University of Wales Press: Cardiff.

Asprey, R.B. (1975), *War in the Shadows; The Guerrilla in History*, Macdonald & Jane's: London.

Atwood, M. (1997), *Alias Grace*, Virago Press: London.

Ayer, A.J. (1990), *Language, Truth and Logic*, Penguin: Harmondsworth.

Bach, R. (1988), *One*, Dell Publishing: New York NY.

Bacon, W.A. (1979), *The Art of Interpretation*, 3rd ed., Holt, Rinehart & Winston: New York NY.

Bainton, R. (1979), *Christian Attitudes Towards War and Peace*, Abingdon: Nashville TN.

Banks, D.J. (1976) (ed.), *Changing Identities in Modern Southeast Asia*, Mouton Publishers: The Hague.

Barendt, E. (1985), *Freedom of Speech*, Oxford University (Clarendon) Press: Oxford.

Barkun, M. (ed.), *Millenium and Violence*, Frank Cass, London, 1996.

Bassols, M., & Garcia G.L. (1994) with Berenguer, E., Calvet, R.M, Romani, I., Guilana, E., Palmonera, V. & Paskvan, E., 'On Blasphemy: Religion and Psychological Structure' in

Bracher, M., Alcorn Jr., M.W., Corthell, R.J. & Massardier-Kenney, F., *Lacanian Theory of Discourse; Subject, Structure, and Society*, New York University Press: New York NY.

Bates, R.H, Greif, A., Levi, M., Rosenthal, J.-L. & Weingast, B.R. (1998), *Analytic Narratives*, Princeton University Press: Princeton NJ.

Bauman, R. (1971), *For the Reputation of Truth; Politics, Religion, and Conflict among the Pennsylvania Quakers 1750-1800*, The Johns Hopkins Press: Baltimore MD.

Bennett, C. (2001), *In Search of Jesus; Insider and Outsider Images*, Continuum: London.

Bennett, J.C. & Seifert, H. (1977), *US Foreign Policy and Christian Ethics*, The Westminster Press: Philadelphia PA.

Berger, A., Badham, P. (1989), *et al.* (eds), *Perspectives on Death and Dying; Cross-Cultural and Multi-Cultural Views*, The Charles Press: Philadelphia PA.

Berger, P.L. & Luckmann, T. (1967) (eds), *The Social Construction of Reality; a Treatise in [on] the Sociology of Language*, Penguin: Harmondsworth.

Berkhofer, R.F. (1978), *The White Man's Indian*, Alfred A. Knopf: New York NY.

Berman, H.J. (1974), *The Interaction of Law and Religion*, SCM Press Ltd: London.

Berman, R.A. (1999), 'From Brecht to Schleiermacher: Religion and Critical Theory', *Telos* No.115, spring.

Beuken, W. & Kuschel, K.-J. (1997) (eds), *Religion as a Source of Violence?* (Concilium 4, 1997), SCM Press: London.

Bicknell, E.J. (1946), *A Theological Introduction to the Thirty-Nine Articles of the Church of England*, Longmans, Green & Co.: London.

Biedermann, H. (1989), *Knaurs Lexikon der Symbole*, Droemersche Verlagsanstalt Th. Knaur Nachfolger: München.

Bierce, A. (1979), 'Religions of Error' (from 'Fantastic Fables') reproduced in Bacon, W.A., *The Art of Interpretation*, 3rd ed., Holt, Rinehart & Winston: New York NY.

Björkman, J.W. (1988) (ed.), *Fundamentalism, Revivalists and Violence in South Asia*, Manohar: New Delhi.

Black, J. (1987) (ed.), *The Origins of War in War in Early Modern Europe*, John Donald Publishers Ltd: Edinburgh.

Black, M., (1962) (ed.) *The Importance of Language*, Prentice Hall, Inc. (Cornell University Press): Englewood Cliffs NJ.

Blainey, G. (1988), *The Causes of War*, 3rd ed., Macmillan: London.

Blanshard, B. (1974), *Reason and Belief*, George Allen & Unwin: London.

Bloch, M. (1992), *Prey into Hunter; The Politics of Religious Experience*, Cambridge University Press: Cambridge.

Bochenski, J.M. (1965), *The Logic of Religion*, New York University Press: New York NY.

Bond, B. (1996), *The Pursuit of Victory; From Napoleon to Saddam Hussein*, Oxford University Press: Oxford.

Bondurant, J.V. (1958), *Conquest of Violence; The Gandhian Philosophy of Conflict*, Princeton University Press: Princeton NJ.

Bono, E. de (2001), *The De Bono Code Book; Going Beyond the Limits of Language*, Penguin Group: Harmondsworth.

Booth, K. (1998) (ed.), *Statecraft and Security; The Cold War and Beyond*, Cambridge University Press: Cambridge.

Bowker, J. (1970) (ed.), *Problems of Suffering in Religions of the World*, Cambridge University Press: Cambridge.

Boyle, K. & Sheen, J. (1997) (eds), *Freedom of Religion and Belief; a World Report*, Routledge: London.

Bradney, A. (1993), *Religions, Rights and Laws*, Leicester University Press: Leicester.

Brend, W.A. (1944), *Foundations of Human Conflict*, Chapman & Hall Ltd.: London.

Breyfogle, T. (2000), 'Some Paradoxes of Religion in the 2000 Presidential Election', *Reviews in Religion and Theology*, vol. 8, no. 5, November.

Brogan, P. (1998), *World Conflicts*, Bloomsbury: London.

Brothers, C. (1997), *War and Photography; A Cultural History*, Routledge: London.

Brown, C. (1993), *Understanding International Relations*, Macmillan: London.

Brown, M. E. (1993), *Ethnic Conflict and International Security*, Princeton University Press: Princeton NJ.

Brown, R.H. (1987), *Religion and Violence*, 2nd ed., Westminster Press: Philadelphia PA.

Browning, G., Halcli, A. & Webster, F. (2000) (eds), *Understanding Contemporary Society; Theories of the Present*, Sage Publications: London.

Bull, H. (1995), *The Anarchical Society; A Study of Order in World Politics*, 2nd ed., Macmillan: Basingstoke.

Bull, H. (1992) (ed.), *Hugo Grotius and International Relations*, Oxford (Clarendon) University Press: Oxford.

Bull, H. (1983), *The Revolt Against Western Dominance* (2nd of the Hagey Lectures), University of Waterloo: Waterloo, Ont.

Bull, H. & Watson, A. (1984) (eds), *Expansion of International Society*, Oxford University Press: Oxford.

Bunyan, J.(n.d. c1682), *The Holy War; Made by Shaddai upon Diabolus; for the Regaining of the Metropolis of the World or the Losing and Taking again of the town of Mansoul*, The Religious Tract Society: London.

Burchill, S. & Linklater, A. (1996) (with R. Devetak, M. Paterson & J. True), *Theories of International Relations*, Macmillan: London.

Buzan, B. & Herring, E. (1998), *The Arms Dynamic in World Politics*, Lynne Rienner Publ. Inc.: Boulder CO.

Cady, J.F. (1958), *A History of Modern Burma*, Cornell University: Ithaca NY.

Calvet, L.-J. (1998), *Language Wars; and Linguistic Politics*, trans. M. Petheram, Oxford University Press: Oxford.

Camara, H. (1971), *Spiral of Violence*, Sheed & Ward: London.

Camus, A. (1953), *The Rebel*, trans. A. Bower, Penguin Books: Harmondsworth.

Cantwell-Smith, W. (1962), *The Meaning and End of Religion; A New Approach to the Religious Traditions of Mankind*, Macmillan: New York NY.

Capps, W.H. (1974), 'Evaluation of Previous Methods: Commentary' in Honko, L. (ed.), *Science of Religion: Studies in Methodology*, Mouton Publ.: The Hague.

Carlton, E. (1990), *War and Ideology*, Routledge: London.

Carlyon, R. (1981), *A Guide to the Gods*, William Heinemann Ltd.: London.

Carruthers, S.L. (2000), *The Media at War; Communication and Conflict in the Twentieth Century*, Macmillan: Basingstoke.

Castells, M. (1997/98), *The Power of Identity*; *The Information Age – Economy, Society and Culture vol 2*, Blackwell Publishers: Malden, Marsa.

Cenkner, W. (1997) (ed.), *Evil and the Response of World Religion*, Paragon House: St. Paul MN.

Certeau, M. de (1993), *Heterologies; Discourse on the Other*, trans. B. Massumi, University of Minnesota Press: Minneapolis MN.

Chan, S. (2000), 'Writing Sacral IR; An Excavation Involving Küng, Eliade, and Illiterate Buddhism', *Millennium; Journal of International Studies*, Vol 29, no 3.

Chayes, A. & Chayes, A.H. (1996) (eds), *Preventing Conflict in the Post-Communist World; Mobilizing International and Regional Organizations*, The Brookings Institution: Washington DC.

Cheragh Ali, M. (1977), *A Critical Exposition of the Popular "Jihad"; showing that all the wars of Mohammad were defensive; and that aggressive war, or compulsory conversion, is not allowed in the Koran*, Karimsons: Karachi.

Chesterton, G.K. (1927), *Orthodoxy*, Dodd, Mead & Company: New York NY.

Chesterton, G.K. (n.d.), *Heretics*, John Lane: London.

Chomsky, N. (1986), *Knowledge of Language; its Nature, Origin, and Use*, Praeger Publishers: New York NY.

Christian, W.A. (1972), *Opposition of Religious Doctrines; A Study in the Logic of Dialogue among Religions*, Macmillan: London.

Christie, C.J. (1996), *A Modern History of Southeast Asia; Decolonization, Nationalism and Separatism*, I.B. Tauris Publishers: London.

Clark, I. (1988), *Waging War; a Philosophical Introduction*, Oxford (Clarendon) University Press: Oxford.

Clarke, M. (1993) (ed.), *New Perspectives on Security*, The Centre for Defence Studies / Brassey's: London.

Claude, I.L. (1955), *National Minorities; an International Problem*, Greenwood Press: New York NY.

Clausewitz, C. von (1976), *On War*, ed. & trans. Howard, M. & Paret, P., Princeton University Press: Princeton NJ.

Cockshut, A.O.J. (1964), *The Unbelievers*, Collins: London.

Cohn-Sherbok, D. & El-Alami, D.S. (2001), *The Israeli-Palestine Conflict; A Beginner's Guide*, Oneworld: Oxford.

Coleman, J. & Tomka, M. (1995) (eds), *Religion and Nationalism*, (Concilium Theological Journal), SCM Press Ltd.: London.

Coliver, S., (1992) (ed.), *Striking a Balance; Hate Speech, Freedom of Expression and Non-Discrimination*, Article 19 / University of Essex: London.

Collingwood, R.G. (1994), *The Idea of History*, ed. J. van der Dussen, Oxford University Press: Oxford.

Collins, R. (1975), *Conflict Sociology*, Academic Press: New York NY.

Coser, L.A. (1967), *Continuities in the Study of Social Conflict*, Collier-Macmillan: London.

Cottrell, J. (1978), *The Authority of the Bible*, Baker Book House: Grand Rapids MI.

Coward, H. & Kawamura, L. (1978) (eds), *Religion and Ethnicity*, Wilfrid Laurier University Press: Waterloo Ont.

Cragg K. (1992) (ed.), *Troubled by Truth; Lite-Studies in Inter-Faith Concern*, The Pentland Press: Durham.

Crevald, M. van (1991), *The Transformation of War*, The Free Press: New York NY.

Crosse, G. (1914), *Church and State; in Theory and Practice*, A.R. Mowbray & Co.: London.

Croxton, D. (1999), *Peacemaking in Early Modern Europe; Cardinal Mazarin and the Congress of Westphalia 1643-1648*, (Susquehanna University Press, Selinsgrove), Associated University Presses: Cranbury NJ.

Crystal, D. (1965), *Linguistics, Language and Religion*, Burns & Oates: London.

Cutler, D.R. (1969), *The World Year Book of Religion; The Religious Situation*, vol. I, Evans Brothers Ltd.: London.

Daftary, F. (1990), *The Ismailis; Their History and Doctrines*, Cambridge University Press: Cambridge.

Dalacovra, K. (2000), 'Unexceptional Politics? The Impact of Islam on International Relations', *Millennium; Journal of International Studies*, vol. 29, no.3.

Dalai Lama (Tenzin Gyatso, the XIV Dalai Lama of Tibet) (1990), *Freedom in Exile; The Autobiography of His Holiness the Dalai Lama of Tibet*, Abacus: London.

Dante (1994), *The Divine Comedy*, Trans. H. Cary, Everyman / J.M. Dent: London.

Dark, K.R. (2000) (ed.), *Religion and International Relations*, Macmillan: Basingstoke.

David, S.R. (1997), 'Internal War, Causes and Cures', *World Politics*, vol 49.

Davies, D.P. (1988), *Who Does Theology?* An Inaugural Lecture Delivered at St. David's University College, Lampeter, 17th May, 1988.

Davis, J. (1999), *Death, Burial and Rebirth in the Religions of Antiquity*, Routledge: London.

Dawkins, R. (1976), *The Selfish Gene*, Oxford University Press: Oxford.

Decosse, D.E. (1992) (ed.), *But Was It Just? Reflections on the Moralist of the Persian Gulf War*, Doubleday: New York NY.

Delillo, D. (1991), *Mao II*, Viking: New York NY.

de Silva, K.M. (1988), 'Buddhist Revivalism in Modern Sri Lanka' in Björkman, J.W. (ed.), *Fundamentalism, Revivalists and Violence in South Asia*, Manohar: New Delhi.

de Silva, K.M. (1998), *Reaping the Whirlwind; Ethnic Conflict, Ethnic Politics in Sri Lanka*, Penguin Group: New Delhi.

Dentan, R.K. (1976), 'Ethnics and Ethics in Southeast Asia' in D.J. Banks (ed.), *Changing Identities in Modern Southeast Asia*, Mouton Publishers: The Hague.

Devitt, M., & Sterelny, K. (1987), *Language and Reality; an Introduction to the Philosophy of Language*, Basil Blackwell: Oxford.

Dixit, J.N. (1998), *Assignment Colombo*, Vijitha Yapa Bookshop: Colombo.

Donnison, F.S.V. (1970), *Burma*, Ernest Benn Ltd.: London.

Doran, C.F. (1971), *The Politics of Assimilation; Hegemony and its Aftermath*, The Johns Hopkins University Press: Baltimore MD.

Dower, J.W. (1986), *War Without Mercy; Race and Power in the Pacific War*, Faber & Faber: London.

Doyle, M.W. (1983), 'Kant, Liberal Legacies, and Foreign Affairs', *Philosophy and Public Affairs*, vol. 12, no. 1 & 2.

Draper, G.I.A.D. (1958), *The Red Cross Conventions*, Stevens and Sons: London.

Dumézil, G. (n.d.), *The Destiny of the Warrior*, trans. A. Hiltebeitel, University of Chicago Press: Chicago IL.

Dymond, J. (1823), *War; its Causes, Consequences, Lawfulness, &c.*, Newman & Co.: London.

Economist, The, 24th November 2001, ('Special Report: Fighting Terrorism').

Ehrenreich, B. (1998), *Blood Rites; Origins and History of the Passions of War*, Virago Press: London.

Eisenstadt, S.N. (2000), 'The Reconstruction of Religious Arenas in the Framework of 'Multiple Modernities'', *Millennium; Journal of International Studies*, Vol. 29, no.3.

El-Awaisi, A.F.M. (1998), *The Muslim Brothers and the Palestine Question 1928-1947*, IB Tauris: London.

Ellul, J. (1969), *The Theological Foundation of Law*, Seabury Press: New York NY.

Elster, J. (1986) (ed.), *Rational Choice*, Basil Blackwell: Oxford.

Empson, R.H.W. (1928), *The Cult of the Peacock Angel; A Short Account of the Yezidi Tribes of Kurdistan*, H.F. & G. Witherby: London.

Enloe, C. (1983), *Does Khaki Become You? The Militarism of Women's Lives*, Pluto Press: London.

Eppstein, J. (1972), *Does God Say Kill? An Investigation of the Justice of Current Fighting in Africa*, Tom Stacey: London.

Eriksen, T.H. (1993), *Ethnicity and Nationalism; Anthropological Perspectives*, Pluto Press: London.

Esposito, J.L. & Voll, J.O. (2000), 'Islam and the West; Muslim Voices of Dialogue', *Millennium; Journal of International Studies*, Vol. 29, no.3.

Esposito, J.L. & Watson, M. (2000) (eds), *Religion and Global Order*, University of Wales Press: Cardiff.

Esposito, J.L. (1995), *The Islamic Threat; Myth or Reality?*, 2nd ed., Oxford University Press: Oxford.
Eucken, R. (1913), *The Truth of Religion*, 2nd ed., trans. W. Tudor Jones, Williams & Norgate: London.
Fain, H. (1970), *Between Philosophy and History; the Resurrection of Speculative Philosophy of History within the Analytic Tradition*, Princeton University Press: Princeton NJ.
Farrell, J.G. (1973), *The Siege of Krishnapur*, Penguin Group: Harmondsworth.
Ferguson, J. (1977), *War and Peace in the World's Religions*, Sheldon Press: London.
Fierro, A. (1977), *The Militant Gospel; An Analysis of Contemporary Political Theologies*, SCM Press: London.
Finucane, R.C. (1983), *Soldiers of the Faith; Crusaders and Muslims at War*, J.M. Dent & Sons: London.
Fischer, D.H. (1971), *Historian's Fallacies; Toward a Logic of Historical Thought*, Routledge & Kegan Paul: London.
Fischer, L. (1997), *The Life of Mahatma Gandhi*, HarperCollins: London.
Fischer, L. (1941), *Men and Politics; An Autobiography*, Jonathon Cape: London.
The Fletcher Forum of World Affairs (1996), vol. 20, no.1, winter/spring.
Forsyth, P.T. (1948a), *The Christian Ethic of War*, Longmans, Green & Co.: London.
Forsyth, P.T. (1948b), *The Justification of God; Lectures for War-Time on a Christian Theodicy*, Latimer House: London.
Fowler, R. (1991), *Language in the News; Discourse and Ideology in the Press*, Routledge: London.
Fox, J. (1999), 'The Influence of Religious Legitimacy on Grievance Formation by Ethno-Religious Minorities', *Journal of Peace Research*, vol. 36, no. 3.
Fox, J. (1998), 'The Effects of Religion on Domestic Conflicts', *Terrorism and Political Violence*, vol. 10, no. 4, winter.
Foy, W. (1985), *Man's Religious Quest*, Open University: Buckingham.
Fredén, J. (1998), 'Etniska konflikter – Finns de egentligen?', *Omvärlden*, no. 3.
Friedkin, W. (2000), 'Cinema: 80 Muslims in the line of US fire', *Financial Times*, August 10.
Fry, H.P. (1996) (ed.), *Christian-Jewish Dialogue*, University of Exeter Press: Exeter.
Fulbrook, M. (1983), *Piety and Politics; Religion and the Rise of Absolutism in England, Württemberg and Prussia*, Cambridge University Press: Cambridge.
Gardiner, S.R. (1898), *The Thirty Years War; 1618-1648*, Longmans, Green, & Co.: London.
Garfinkel, H. (1967), *Studies in Ethnomethodology*, Prentice-Hall: London.
Garnham, D. & Tessler, M. (1995) (eds), *Democracy, War and Peace in the Middle East*, Indiana University Press: Bloomington IN.
Garrison, J. (1982), *The Darkness of God; Theology after Hiroshima*, SCM Press Ltd: London.
Gat, A. (1991), *The Origins of Military Thought; From the Enlightenment to Clausewitz*, Oxford (Clarendon) University Press: Oxford.
Gay, P. (1985), *Freud for Historians*, Oxford University Press: Oxford.
Geertz, C. (1973), *The Interpretation of Cultures*, Basic Books: New York NY.
Gellner, E. (1992), *Postmodernism, Reason and Religion*, Routledge: London.
Genovés, S. (1970), *Is Peace Inevitable?*, Allen & Unwin: London.
Geyer, A., and Green, B.G. (1992), *Lines in the Sand: Justice in the Gulf War*, Westminster John Knox Press: Louisville KY.
Gibbs, N. (2000), 'Fire and Brimstone; How McCain and Bush waged a holy war over the power of the religious right and turned God into an election issue', *TIME*, March 3.
Girard, R. (1977), *Violence and the Sacred*, trans. P. Gregory, The Johns Hopkins University Press: Baltimore MD.
Goldman, R.B. & Wilson, A.J. (1984), *From Independence to Statehood*, Pinter: London.

Goodall, J. & Berman, P. (2000), *Reason For Hope; An Extraordinary Life*, Thorsons (HarperCollins): London.

Gopin, M. (2000), *Between Eden and Armageddon; The Future of World Religions, Violence, and Peacemaking*, Oxford University Press: Oxford.

Gough, H. (1897), *Old Memories*, Edinburgh.

Gough, K. & Sharma, H.P. (1973) (eds), *Imperialism and Revolution in South Asia*, Monthly Review Press: New York NY.

Govier, T. (2002), *A Delicate Balance; What Philosophy Can Tell Us About Terrorism*, Westview Press: Boulder CO.

Granot, H. & Levinson, J. (2002), *Terror Bombing; The New Urban Threat*, Dekel Publishing House: Tel Aviv.

Gray, C.S. (1999), *Modern Strategy*, Oxford University (Clarendon) Press: Oxford.

Gray, J.G. (1970), *On Understanding Violence Philosophically; and Other Essays*, Harper Torchbooks (Harper & Row): New York.

Green, D.P. & Shapiro, I. (1994), *Pathologies of Rational Choice Theory; A Critique of Applications in Political Science*, Yale University Press, New Haven CT.

Greenawalt, K (1989), *Speech, Crime, and the Uses of Language*, Oxford University Press: New York NY.

Greene, B. (1999), *The Elegant Universe; Superstrings, Hidden Dimensions, and the Quest for the Ultimate Theory*, Jonathan Cape: London.

Griffith, L. (2002), *The War on Terrorism and the Terror of God*, William B. Eerdman: Cambridge.

Guest, J.S. (1987), *The Yezidis; A Study in Survival*, KPI: London.

Gurr, T.R., & Harff, B. (1994), *Ethnic Conflict in World Politics*, Westview Press: Boulder CO.

Habermas, J. (1976), *Legitimation Crisis*, trans. T. McCarthy, Heinemann: London.

Hadham, J. (n.d. c1942), *God in a World at War*, Penguin: Harmondsworth.

Haggith, D. (2001), *Prophets of the Apocalypse; The Bible's Ultimate Revelations for the End of Time*, HarperCollins: London.

Haldane, J. (2003), *An Intelligent Person's Guide to Religion*, Duckworth: London.

Hall, D.G.E. (1968), *A History of Southeast Asia*, 3rd ed., Macmillan: New York NY.

Hall, J.R. (2000), *Apocalypse Observed; Religious Movements and Violence in North America, Europe, and Japan*, Routledge: London.

Hallam, E. (1991), 'Monasteries as War Memorials' in W.J. Shiels (ed.), *The Church and War*, Oxford.

Hallet, B. (1992) (ed.), *Engulfed in War; Just War and the Persian Gulf*, Spark M. Matunaga Institute for Peace, University of Hawaii: Honolulu HI.

Halm, H. (1991), *Shiism*, Trans. J. Watson, Edinburgh University Press: Edinburgh.

Hamilton, J.W. (1976), 'Structure, Function, and Ideology of a Karen Funeral in Northern Thailand' in Banks, D.J. (ed.), *Changing Identities in Modern Southeast Asia*, Mouton Publishers: The Hague.

Hansen, H.B. & Twaddle, M. (1995), *Religion and Politics in East Africa*, James Currey Ltd.: London.

Harbour, D. (2001), *An Intelligent Person's Guide to Atheism*, Duckworth: London.

Hardin, R. (1995), *One For All; The Logic of Group Conflict*, Princeton University Press: Princeton NJ.

Hare, W.L. (1925) (ed.), *Religions of the Empire; a Conference on Some Living Religions Within the Empire*, Duckworth: London.

Hartley, J. (1985), *Understanding News*, Routledge: London.

Hasenclever, A. & Rittberger, V. (2000), 'Does Religion Make a Difference? Theoretical Approaches to the Impact of Faith on Political Conflict', *Millennium; Journal of International Studies*, Vol 29, no 3.

Hashmi, S.H. (1996), 'International Society and its Islamic Malcontents', *The Fletcher Forum of World Affairs*, vol. 20, no.1, winter/spring.

Haught, J.A. (1995), *Holy Hatred; Religious Conflicts of the 90s*, Prometheus: London.

Haught, J.A. (1990), *Holy Horrors; An Illustrated History of Religious Murder and Madness*, Prometheus: London.

Hawkes, T. (1977), *Structuralism and Semiotics*, Methuen: London.

Hayes, C.J.H. (1960), *Nationalism; a Religion*, Macmillan: New York NY.

Haynes, J. (1993), *Religion in Third World Politics*, Open University Press: Buckingham.

Heath, A. (1976), *Rational Choice and Social Exchange; A Critique of Exchange Theory*, Cambridge University Press: London.

Hehir, J.B. (1996), interview by *The Fletcher Forum of World Affairs*, vol. 20, no. 1, winter/spring.

Heidegger, M. (1971), *On the Way to Language*, trans. P.D. Hertz, Harper & Row: New York NY.

Hellman, D.C. (1976) (ed.), *Southern Asia; The Politics of Poverty and Peace*, vol. XIII, Lexington Books: Lexington MA.

Hibbert, C. (1973), *The Great Mutiny; India 1857*, Allen Lane: Harmondsworth.

Hick, J. (1985a), *Death and Eternal Life*, Macmillan: London.

Hick, J. (1985b), *Problems of Religious Pluralism*, Macmillan: London.

Hick, J. (1977), *God and the Universe of Faiths*, Fount Paperbacks: London.

Hick, J. (1974) (ed.), *Truth and Dialogue; The Relationship Between World Religions*, Sheldon Press: London.

Hick, J. (1970), *Evil and the God of Love*, Fontana Library: London.

Hinde, R.A. & Watson, H.E. (1995), *War; A Cruel Necessity? The Bases of Institutionalized Violence*, I.B. Tauris & Co.: London.

Hjelmslev, L. (1970), *Language; an Introduction*, trans. F.J. Whitfield, University of Wisconsin Press: Madison WI.

Hjelmslev, L. (1961), *Prolegomena to a Theory of Language*, trans. F.J. Whitfield, University of Wisconsin Press: Madison WI.

Hoffman, B. (1999), *Inside Terrorism*, Indigo: London.

Hoffman, B. & Claridge, D. (1998), 'The RAND-St. Andrews Chronology of International and Noteworthy Domestic Incidents 1996', *Terrorism and Political Violence*, vol. 10, no. 2, summer.

Hoffman, B. (1993), *Holy Terror; The Implications of Terrorism Motivated by a Religious Imperative*, RAND Corp.: Santa Monica CA.

Hoffman, S. (1998), *World Disorders; Troubled Peace in the Post-Cold War Era*, Rownan & Littlefield Publishers, Inc.: Lanham MD.

Hollis, M. & Smith, S. (1990), *Explaining and Understanding International Relations*, Oxford (Clarendon) University Press: Oxford.

Holloway, R. (1999), *Godless Morality; Keeping Religion out of Ethics*, Canongate: Edinburgh.

Holsti, K.J. (1991), *Peace and War: Armed Conflicts and International Order 1648-1989*, Cambridge University Press: Cambridge.

Honey, J. (1997), *Language is Power; the Story of Standard English and its Enemies*, Faber & Faber: London.

Honko, L. (1974) (ed.), *Science of Religion: Studies in Methodology*, Mouton Publishers: The Hague.

Horowitz, D.L. (1985), *Ethnic Groups in Conflict*, University of California Press: Berkeley CA.

Horsley, R.A. (1993), *Jesus and the Spiral of Violence; Popular Jewish Resistance in Roman Palestine*, Fortress Press: Minneapolis MN.

Howard, M. (1984), *The Causes of Wars*, Harvard University Press: Cambridge MA.

Huband, M. (1999), *Warriors of the Prophet; The Struggle for Islam*, Westview Press: Boulder CO.

Hudson, G.F. & Rajchman, M. (1938), *An Atlas of Far Eastern Politics*, Faber & Faber Ltd.: London.

Hunter, B. (1997), *The Statesman's Yearbook 1997-98*, Macmillan: London.

Huntington, S.P. (1993), 'The Clash of Civilizations?', *Foreign Affairs*, vol. 72(1), no 3, summer.

Hussain, A. (1988), *Political Terrorism and the State in the Middle East,* Mansell Publishing: London.

Huxley, A. (1962), 'Words and Their Meanings' in Black, M., *The Importance of Language*, Prentice Hall, Inc. (Cornell University Press): Englewood Cliffs NJ.

Hyakawa, S.I. (1941), *Language in Action*, Harcourt, Brace & Co.: New York NY.

James, J. (1960), *Why Evil? A Biblical Approach*, Penguin Books: Harmondsworth.

James, S. (1999), *The Atlantic Celts; Ancient Peoples or Modern Invention*, British Museum Press: London.

James, W. (1985), *The Varieties of Religious Experience*, Harvard University Press: Cambridge MA.

Janke, P. (1994) (ed.), *Ethnic and Religious Conflicts; Europe and Asia*, Dartmouth Publishing Co. Ltd for RISCT: Research Institute for the Study of Conflict and Terrorism: Aldershot.

Jansen, G.H. (1979), *Militant Islam; An Informed and Incisive Analysis of Islam's Confrontation with the Western World Today*, Pan Books: London.

Jansen, J.J.G. (1986), *The Neglected Duty; The Creed of Sadat's Assassins and Islamic Resurgence in the Middle East*, (inc. trans. of Faraj's text), Macmillan: New York NY.

Jayatilleke, K.N. (1953), *Early Buddhist Theory of Knowledge*, Motilal Banarsidass: Delhi.

Jenkins, D.E. (1988), *God, Politics and the Future*, SCM Press Ltd.: London.

Jenkins, K. (1991), *Re-thinking History*, Routledge: London.

Jettner, A. (1972), *The Study of Religious Language*, SCM Press Ltd: London.

Joad, C.E.M. (n.d. c1942), *Journey Through the War Mind*, Faber & Faber: London.

Johnson, G.A. & M.B. Smith (1990) (eds), *Ontology and Alterity in Merleau-Ponty*, Northwestern University Press: Evanston IL.

Johnson, J.T. (1981), *Just War Traditions and the Restraint of War; A Moral and Historical Inquiry*, Princeton University Press: Princeton NJ.

Johnson, J.T. and Kelsay J. (1990) (eds), *Cross, Crescent and Sword; The Justification and Limitation of War in Western and Islamic Tradition*, Greenwood Press: New York NY.

Johnson, J.T. and Weigel, G. (1991), *Just War and the Gulf War*, Ethics and Public Policy Center: Washington DC.

Johnston, D.M. (1996), 'Religion and Conflict Resolution', *The Fletcher Forum of World Affairs*, vol. 20, no. 1, winter/spring.

Johnston, D.M. & Sampson, C. (1994) (eds), *Religion, the Missing Dimension of Statecraft*, Centre for Strategic and International Studies, Oxford University Press: Oxford.

Jomini, Baron de A. (1838), *Précis de l'Art de la Guerre*, Anselin libraire: Paris.

Joseph, S. & Pillsbury, B.C.K. (1978), *Muslim – Christian Conflicts; Economic, Political and Social Origins*, Westview Press: Boulder CO.

Joshi, L.M. (1983), *Discerning the Buddha*, Munshiram Nanoharlal Publishers, New Delhi.

Juergensmeyer, M. (2002), *Gandhi's Way; A Handbook of Conflict Resolution*, University of California Press: Berkeley CA.

Juergensmeyer, M. (2000), *Terror in the Mind of God; The Global Rise of Religious Terrorism*, University of California Press: Berkeley, CA.

Juergensmeyer, M. (1996), 'The Terrorists Who Long For Peace', *The Fletcher Forum of World Affairs*, vol. 20, no. 1, winter/spring.

Juergensmeyer, M. (1993), *The New Cold War; Religious Nationalism Confronts the Secular State*, University of California Press: Oxford.

Juergensmeyer, M. (1992) (ed.), *Violence and the Sacred in the Modern World*, Frank Cass & Co.: London.

Juergensmeyer, M. (1990), 'What the Bhikku Said', *Religion*, vol. 20, January.

Juergensmeyer, M. (1988), 'The Logic of Religious Violence' in Rapoport, D.C., *Inside Terrorist Organizations*, Frank Cass: London.

Kaku, M. (1999), *Hyperspace; A Scientific Odyssey Through Parallel Universes, Time Warps and the Tenth Dimension*, Oxford University Press: Oxford.

Kaldor, M. (1999), *New and Old Wars; Organized Violence in a Global Era*, Polity Press: Cambridge.

Kaldor, M. & Vashee, B. (1999) (eds), *New Wars; Restructuring the Global Military Sector*, Vol. 1, United Nations University: London.

Kamenka, E. (1970), *The Philosophy of Ludwig Feuerbach*, Routledge & Keegan Paul: London.

Kant, I. (1934), *Religion; Within the Limits of Reason Alone*, trans. T.M. Greene & H.H. Hudson, The Open Court Company: Chicago IL.

Kaplan, J. (1997), *Radical Religion in America; Millenarian Movements from the Far Right to the Children of Noah*, Syracuse University Press: Syracuse NY.

Kaplan, R.D. (1993), 'A Reader's Guide to the Balkans', *The New York Times Book Review*, April 18.

Karlsson, I. (1994), *Islam och Europa; Samlevnad eller Konfrontation?*, Wahlström & Widstrand: Stockholm.

Kaye, J.W. (1878), *A History of the Sepoy War in India*, W.H. Allen & Co.: London.

Keegan, J. (1999), *War and Our World*, (The Reith Lectures 1998), Pimlico: London.

Kelsay, J. (1993), *Islam and War; The Gulf War and Beyond*, Westminster / John Knox Press: Louisville KY.

Kelsay, J. & Johnston, J.T. (1991), *Just War and Jihad; Historical and Theoretical Perspectives on War and Peace in Western and Islamic Traditions*, Greenwood Press: New York NY.

Kepel, G. (1994), *The Revenge of God; The Resurgence of Islam, Christianity and Judaism in the Modern World*, trans. A. Braley, Polity Press: Cambridge.

Kesey, K. (1973), *One Flew Over the Cuckoo's Nest*, Picador: London.

Khadduri, M. (1955), *War and Peace in the Law of Islam*, The Johns Hopkins University Press: Baltimore MD.

Khaldun, Ibn (1958), *The Muqaddimah; An Introduction to History*, Trans. F. Rosenthal, Routledge & Kegan Paul: London.

Khaldun, Ibn (1950), *An Arab Philosophy of History: Selections from the Prolegomena of Ibn Khaldun of Tunis*, Trans. C. Issawi, John Murray: London.

Kick, R. (2001), *You Are Being Lied To; The Disinformation Guide to Media Distortion, Whitewashes and Cultural Myths*, Disinformation Co. Ltd.: New York NY.

Kippenberg, H.G. (1984) (ed.), *Struggles of Gods; Papers of the Groningen Work Group for the Study of the History of Religions*, Mouton / Walter de Gruyter & Co.: Berlin.

Klare, M.T. & Chandrani, Y. (1998), *World Security Challenges for a New Century*, 3rd ed., St. Martin's Press: New York NY.

Klassen, B. (1992), *The White Man's Bible*, Church of the Creator: Milwaukee WI.

Kreyenbroek, P.G. (1995), *Yezidism; Its Background, Observances and Textual Tradition*, Edwin Mellen: New York NY.

Kubálková, V. (2000), 'Towards an International Political Theology', *Millennium; Journal of International Studies*, Vol. 29, no. 3.

Küng, H. (1991), *Global Responsibility; In Search of a New World Ethic*, trans. J. Bowden, SCM: London.

Laqueur, W. (1999), *The New Terrorism and the Arms of Mass Destruction*, Phoenix Press: London.

Lasker, B. (1944), *Peoples of South-East Asia*, Victor Gollancz Ltd.: London.

Lautsen, C.B. & Wæver, O. (2000), 'In Defence of Religion; Sacred Referent Objects for Secularization', *Millennium; Journal of International Studies*, Vol. 29, no. 3.

LaVey, A.S. (1976), *The Satanic Bible*, Avon Books: New York NY.

Lawton, D. (1993), *Blasphemy*, University of Pennsylvania Press: Philadelphia PA.

Leach, E.R. (1977), *Political Systems of Highland Burma*, The Athlone Press: London.

Lee, R. & Marty, M.E. (1964), *Religion and Social Conflict*, Oxford University Press: New York NY.

Lerche Jr., C.O. & Said, A.A. & Lerche III, C.O. (1995), *Concepts of International Politics; in Global Perspective*, Prentice-Hall: Englewood Cliffs NJ.

Lewis, B. (2003), *The Crisis of Islam; Holy War and Unholy Terror*, Weidenfeld & Nicholson: London.

Lewis, B. (1987) (ed., trans.), *Islam; from the Prophet Muhammad to the Capture of Constantinople* (2 vols: I: 'Politics and War'; II: 'Religion and Society'), Oxford University Press: Oxford.

Lewis, B. (1985), *The Assassins; A Radical Sect in Islam*, Al Saqi Books: London.

Lewis, B. (1940), *The Origins of Ismailism; A Study of the Historical Background of the Fatimid Caliphate*, W. Heffer & Sons: Cambridge.

Liddell-Hart, B.H. (1960), *Deterrence or Defence; A Fresh Look at the West's Military Politics*, Stevens & Sons: London.

Liddell-Hart, B.H. (1944), *Thoughts on War*, Faber & Faber: London.

Linder, J. (1977), *On the Nature of War*, (Swedish Institute of International Affairs), Saxon House: Farnborough.

Ling, T. (1979), *Buddhism, Imperialism and War; Burma and Thailand in Modern History*, George Allen & Unwin: London.

Llobera J.R. (1994), The *God of Modernity; The Development of Nationalism in Western Europe*, Berg Publishers: Oxford.

Lloyd-Jones, D.M. (1986), *Why Does God Allow War; A General Justification of the Ways of God*, 2nd ed., Evangelical Press of Wales: Bridgend.

London, K. (1968), *The Permanent Crisis; Communism in World Politics*, Blaisdell Publishing Co.: Waltham MA.

Löwy, M. (1996), *The War of Gods; Religion and Politics in Latin America*, Verso: London.

Luard, E. (1988), *The Blunted Sword; The Erosion of Military Power in Modern World Politics*, I.B. Tauris & Co.: London.

Luckmann, T. (1967), *The Invisible Religion; The Problem of Religion in Modern Society*, Macmillan: New York NY.

Ludden, D. (1996) (ed.), *Contesting the Nation; Religion, Community, and the Politics of Democracy in India*, University of Pennsylvania Press: Philadelphia PA.

Lunt, J. (1970) (ed.), *Edited Version of Subedar Sita Ram's From Sepoy to Subedar*, Routledge & Kegan Paul: London.

Lynch, C. (2000), 'Dogma, Praxis, and Religious Perspectives on Mulitculturalism', *Millennium; Journal of International Studies*, Vol. 29, no. 3.

Macdonald, A. [W. Pierce] (1996), *The Turner Diaries*, 2nd Ed., Barricade Books, Inc.: New York NY.

Machiavelli, N. (1961), *The Prince*, trans. G. Bull, Penguin: Harmondsworth.
Macquarrie, J. (1973), *The Concept of Peace*, (The Firth Lectures 1972), SCM Press: London.
Mahmoud, M. (1996), 'The Discourse of the Ikhwan of Sudan and Secularism' in D. Westerlund (ed.) *Questioning the Secular Sate; The Worldwide Resurgence of Religion in Politics*, Hurst & Co.: London.
Makkreel, R.A. (1975), *Dilthey: Philosopher of the Human Studies*, Princeton University Press: Princeton NJ.
Malleson, G.B. (1891), *The Indian Mutiny of 1857*, Scribner & Sons: New York NY.
Manninen, J. & Tuomela, R. (1976) (eds), *Essays on Explanation and Understanding; Studies in the Foundations of Humanities and Social Scientists*, D. Reidel Publishers: Dordrecht.
Mansfield, S. (1991), *The Rites of War; An Analysis of Institutionalized Warfare*, Belleus Publishing: London.
Margolin, J. (1977), 'Psychological Perspectives in Terrorism', in Alexander, Y. & Finger, S.M. (eds), *Terrorism; Interdisciplinary Perspectives*, The John Jay Press: New York NY.
Marighela, L. (1971), *Handbook of Urban Guerilla Warfare*, reproduced as chapter 7 in *For the Liberation of Brazil*, trans. J. Butt and R. Sheed, Penguin Books: Harmondsworth.
Martin, A.W. (1975), *Seven Great Bibles*, Cooper Square Publishing: New York NY.
Martin, D. (1997), *Does Christianity Cause War?*, Oxford (Clarendon) University Press: Oxford.
Martin, D. (1978), *The Dilemmas of Contemporary Religion*, Basil Blackwell: Oxford.
Martin, E.L. (2000), *The Temples that Jerusalem Forgot*, ASK Publications: Portland OR.
Marty, M.E. & Appleby, R.S. (1993), *Fundamentalisms and the State*, [Fundamentalism Project], University of Chicago Press: Chicago IL.
Marty, M.E. & Appleby, R.S. (1991), *Fundamentalisms Observed*, [Fundamentalism Project], University of Chicago Press: Chicago IL.
Marvin, C. & Ingle, D.W. (1996), 'Blood Sacrifice and the Nation: Revisiting Civil Religion', *Journal of the American Academy of Religion*, vol. 64, no. 4, winter.
Marx, K. & Engels, F. (1959), *The First Indian War of Independence 1857-1859*, Foreign Languages Publishing House: Moscow.
Matthews, B. (1996), 'Buddhist Activism in Sri Lanka' in Westerlund, D. (ed.), *Questioning the Secular State; The Worldwide Resurgence of Religion in Politics*, Hurts & Co.: London.
McDermott, A. (1988), *Egypt from Nasser to Mubarak; a flawed revolution*, Croom Helm Ltd.: New York.
McLeod Innes (1897), *The Sepoy Revolt; a Critical Narrative*, 2nd ed., A.D. Innes & Co.: London.
McNamara, P.H. (1974) (ed.), *Religion American Style*, Harper & Row: New York NY.
Mead, G.H. (1938), *Philosophy of the Act*, University of Chicago Press: Chicago IL.
Mearsheimer, J. (1990), 'Back to the Future', *International Security* vol. 15, no. 1.
Melton, J.G. & Lewis, J.R. (2000), *Religious Requirements and Practices of Certain Selected Groups: A Handbook for Chaplains*, US Department of Defense (MDA903-90-C-0062) (with the Institute for the Study of American Religion and the Department of the Army, Office of the Chief Chaplains): Washington DC, 2000.
Mensching, G. (1971), *Tolerance and Truth in Religion*, trans. H.-J. Klimkeit, The University of Alabama Press: Montgomery AL.
Mensching, G. (1959), *Die Religion*, C.E. Schwab: Stuttgart.
Merleau-Ponty, M. (1974), *Phenomenology, Language & Sociology*, selected essays ed. by J. O'Neill, Heinemann: London.
Merleau-Ponty, M. (1969), *The Essential Writings of Merleau-Ponty*, ed. A.L. Fisher, Harcourt, Bracc & World, Inc.: New York NY.
Merleau-Ponty, M. (1964), *Sense and Non-Sense*, trans. & ed. H.L. Dreyfus & P.A. Dreyfus, Northwestern University Press: Evanston IL.

Merkl, P. H. & Smart, S. (1985) (eds), *Religion and Politics in the Modern World*, New York University Press: New York NY.
Merton, T. (1963), *Faith and Violence; Christian Teaching and Christian Practice*, University of Notre Dame Press: Notre Dame IN.
Mertus, J.A. (1999), *Kosovo; How Myths and Truths Started a War*, University of California Press: Berkeley CA.
Míguez Bonino, J. (1983), *Toward a Christian Political Ethics*, SCM Press: London.
Miles, W.F.S. (1996), 'Political Para-Theology: Rethinking Religion, Politics and Democracy', *Third World Quarterly*, vol. 17, no. 3.
Miller, R.E. & Mwakabana, H.A.O. (1998) (eds), *Christian-Muslim Dialogue; Theological and Practical Issues*, Department of Theology and Studies/The Lutheran World Federation.
Minority Right Group (1997), *World Directory of Minorities*, MRG: London.
Mistree, K.P. (1982), *Zoroastrianism; An Ethnic Perspective*, Zoroastrian Studies: Bombay.
Moyser, G. (1991) (ed.), *Politics and Religion in the Modern World*, Routledge: London.
Mugglestone, L. (1995), *'Talking Proper'; the Rise of Accent as a Social Symbol*, Oxford University (Clarendon) Press: Oxford.
Murray, G. (1946), *Five Stages of Greek Religion*, Watts & Co.: London.
Murray, G. (1912), *Four Stages of Greek Religion*, Oxford University Press for Columbia University Press: New York NY.
Neiminathan, M. (1998), *Destruction of Hindu Temples in Tamil Eelam and Sri Lanka*, Federation of Saiva (Hindu) temples UK: London.
Nicholson, M. (1996), *Causes and Consequences in International Relations*, Pinter: London.
Nicholson, M. (1992), *Rationality and the Analysis of International Conflict*, Cambridge University Press: Cambridge.
Nicolai, G.F. (1919), *The Biology of War*, J.M. Dent & Sons Ltd.: London.
Nielsen, N. (1996), 'Religion and the Global Media: Improving a Strained Relationship', *The Fletcher Forum of World Affairs*, vol. 20, no. 1, winter/spring.
Nielsson, G.P. (1985), 'States and Nation-Groups: A Global Taxonomy' in Tiryakian, E. & Rogowski, R., *New Nationalisms of the Developed West; Toward Explanation*, Allen & Unwin: Boston MA.
Norman, R. (1995), *Ethics, Killing and War*, Cambridge University Press: Cambridge.
Nostradamus, (1974) *The Prophecies (of Nostradamus)*, trans., ed. & intro. By E. Cheetham, Spearman: London.
Obeyesekere, G. (1981), *Medusa's Hair; An Essay on Personal Symbols and Religious Experience*, University of Chicago Press: Chicago IL.
O'Brien, C.C. (1988), *Godland; Reflections on Religion and Nationalism*, Harvard University Press: Cambridge MA.
O'Brien, J. & Palmer, M. (1993), *The State of Religion Atlas*, Touchstone / Simon & Schuster: New York NY.
O'Brien, W.V. (1981), *The Conduct of Just and Limited War*, Greenwood Press: New York NY.
O'Fahey, R.S. (1995), 'The Past in the Present? The Issue of the Sharia in Sudan' in Hansen, H.B. & Twaddle, M., *Religion and Politics in East Africa*, James Currey Ltd.: London.
O'Flaherty, W.D. (1988), *Other Peoples' Myths; The Cave of Echoes*, Macmillan Publishing Co.: New York NY.
Oosten, J.G. (1985), *The War of the Gods; The Social Code in Indo-European Mythology*, Routledge & Keegan Paul: London.
Olson, R.N. (1982), *The Ba'th and Syria 1947 to 1982; The Evolution of Ideology, Party and State, from the French Mandate to the Era of Hafiz-al-Asad*, The Kingdom Press Inc.: Princeton NJ.

O'Murchu, D. (1997), *Quantum Theology; Spiritual Implications of the New Physics*, Crossroad Publishing Co.: New York NY.

Osiander, A. (2000), 'Religion and Politics in Western Civilisation; the Ancient World as Matrix and Mirror of the Modern', *Millennium; Journal of International Studies*, Vol. 29, no. 3.

Otto, R. (1973), *The Idea of the Holy; An Enquiry Into the Non-Fictional Factor in the Idea of the Divine and its Relation to the Rational*, trans. J.W. Harvey, Oxford University Press: Oxford.

Palmer, J.A.B. (1966), *The Mutiny Outbreak at Meerut in 1857*, Cambridge University Press: Cambridge.

Parfit, J.T. (n.d. c1920), *Marvellous Mesopotamia; The World's Wonderland*, S.W. Partridge & Co.: London.

Parker, G. (1984) (ed.), *The Thirty Years War*, Routledge & Kegan Paul: London.

Parkin, D. (1985) (ed.), *The Anthropology of Evil*, Basil Blackwell: Oxford.

Parrinder, G. (1962), *Upanishads, Gita and Bible; a Comparative Study of Hindu and Christian Scriptures*, Faber & Faber: London.

Partner, P. (1998), *God of Battles; Holy Wars of Christianity and Islam*, Harper Collins Publishers: London.

Paskins, B. (1993), 'Security in a New Age' in Clarke, M. (ed.) *New Perspectives on Security*, The Centre for Defence Studies / Brassey's: London.

Pelton, R.Y. (1998), *The World's Most Dangerous Places*, Fielding Worldwide: Redondo Beach CA.

Peters, R. (1977) (trans. & annotation), *Jihad in Mediaeval and Modern Islam; The Chapter on Jihad from Averroes' Legal Handbook* 'Bidayat al-Mudjtahid' *and The Treatise* 'Koran and Fighting' *by the Late Shaykh al-Azhar, Mahmud Shaltut*, E.J. Brill: Leiden.

Pfaltzgraff Jr., R.L. & Schultz Jr., R.H. (n.d.) (eds), *Ethnic Conflict and Regional Instability; Implications for US Policy and Army Roles and Missions*, SSI – Strategic Studies Institute (with US Army War College).

Phillips, D.Z. (1967) (ed.), *Religion and Understanding*, Basil Blackwell: Oxford.

Piscatori, J.P. (1986), *Islam in a World of Nation-States*, Royal Institute of International Affairs / Cambridge University Press: Cambridge.

Platinga, A. (1975), *God, Freedom and Evil*, George Allen & Unwin: London.

Polo, M. (1997), *The Travels*, Wordsworth Editions Ltd.: Ware.

Priestland, G. (1974), *The Future of Violence*, Hamish Hamilton: London.

Punchihena, G. de S.G. (1989), *Souvenirs of a Forgotten Heritage*, Desethiya for Department of Information: Colombo.

Puri, R.-S. (1987), *Gandhi on War and Peace*, Praeger Publishing: New York NY.

Pye, L.W. (1968), *Politics, Personality, and Nation Building*; *Burma's Search for Identity*, Yale University Press: New Haven CT.

Quinn, P.L. (1978), *Divine Commands and Moral Requirements*, Oxford (Clarendon) University Press: Oxford.

Qutb, S. (1977), *Islam and Universal Peace*, American Trust Publications: Indianapolis IN.

Radakrishnan, S. (1961), *An Idealist View of Life*, George Allen & Unwin: London.

Ranstorp, M. (1996), 'Terrorism in the Name of Religion', *Journal of International Affairs*, vol. 50, no. 1.

Rapoport, A. (1995), *The Origins of Violence*, Transaction Publications: London.

Rapoport, D.C. (1988), *Inside Terrorist Organizations*, Frank Cass: London.

Rapoport, D.C. (1984), 'Fear and Trembling: Terrorism in Three Religious Traditions', *The American Political Science Review*, vol. 78, no. 3.

Rauch, I., & Scott, C.T. (1967) (eds), *Approaches in Linguistic Methodology*, The University of Wisconsin Press: Madison WI.

Raven, C.E. (1935), *Is War Obsolete? A Study of Conflicting Claims of Religion and Citizenship*, George Allen & Unwin: London.

Rawls, J. (1973), *A Theory of Justice*, Oxford University Press: Oxford.

Reade, W. (1872), *The Martyrdom of Man*, Watts & Co.: London.

Reardon, B.A. (1985), *Sexism and the War System*, Teachers College Press: New York NY.

Reeve, S. (1999), *The New Jackals; Ramzi Yousef, Osama bin Laden and the Future of Terrorism*, André Deutsch: London.

Reich, W. (1998) (ed.), *Origins of Terrorism; Psychologies, Ideologies, Theologies, States of Mind*, Woodrow Wilson Centre Press: Washington DC.

Reynolds, P.A.(1994), *An Introduction to International Relations*, 3rd ed., Longman: London.

Rhodes, D. (2001) (ed.), *Peace Scroll; World Prayer for Peace and Healing*, The Seed of Life Peace Foundation: Machynlleth.

Richards, J.W. (2000), *The Xenophobe's Guide to the Welsh*, Oval Books: London.

Richardson, O.L.F. (1960), *Statistics of Deadly Quarrels*, Boxwood Press: Pittsburgh PA.

Rickman, H.P. (1979), *Wilhelm Dilthey; Pioneer of the Human Studies*, Paul Elek: London.

Ringmar, E. (1996), *Identity, Interest & Action; a Cultural Explanation of Sweden's Involvement in the Thirty Years War*, Cambridge University Press: Cambridge.

Rinpoche, S. (1998), *The Tibetan Book of Living and Dying*, Rider: London.

Roberts, A. & Guelff, R. (2000) (eds), *Documents on the Laws of War*, 2nd ed., Oxford University Press: Oxford.

Robinson, J.A.T. (1963), *Honest to God*, SCM Press / Westminster Press: Philadelphia PA.

Robinson, N. (2001), *The Fascination of Islam*, An Inaugural Lecture Delivered at the University of Wales Lampeter, 20 February 2001.

Rosenau, J.N. (1964) (ed.), *International Aspects of Civil Strife*, Princeton University Press: Princeton NJ.

Rousseau, J.-J. (1973), *The Social Contract and Discourses*, trans. G.D.H. Cole, J.M. Dent & Sons: London.

Rousseau, J.-J. (1964), *Ouvres Complètes*, III (Du Contrat Social et Écrits Politiques), Bibliothèque de la Pléiade / Éditions Gallimard: Geneva.

Rudolph, S.H. & Piscatori, J.P. (1997) (eds), *Transnational Religion and Fading States*, Westview Press: Boulder CO.

Rupesinghe, K. & Mumtaz, K. (1996), *International Conflicts in South Asia* (PRIO – International Peace Research Institute, Oslo) Sage Publications: London.

Rushdie, S. (1992), *The Satanic Verses*, The Consortium: New York NY.

Russel, F.H. (1975), *The Just War in the Middle Ages*, Cambridge University Press: Cambridge.

Russell, B. (1966), *Sceptical Essays*, Unwin Books: London.

Ryan, S. (1988), 'Explaining Ethnic Conflict; the Neglected International Dimension', *Review of International Studies*, vol. 14 no. 3.

Saad-Ghorayeb, A. (2002), *Hizbu'llah; Politics and Religion*, Pluto Press: London.

Said, A.A. & Simmons, L.R. (1976), *Ethnicity in an International Context*, Transaction Books: New Brunswick NJ.

Saler, B. (1993), *Conceptualizing Religion; Immanent Anthropologists, Transcendent Natives, and Unbounded Categories*, E.J. Brill: Leiden.

Samartha, S.J. (1974), *Living Faiths and Ultimate Goals: A Continuing Dialogue*, World Council of Churches: Geneva.

Sayers, D.L. (1946), *Unpopular Opinions*, Victor Gollancz: London.

Schecter, J. (1967), *The New Face of Buddha*, Victor Gollancz: London.

Schmidt, J. (1985), *Maurice Merleau-Ponty; Between Phenomenology and Structuralism*, Macmillan: Basingstoke.

Schram, S.R. (1967) (ed.), *Quotations from Chairman Mao Tse-Tung*, Bantam Books: New York NY.

Scott, J.G. (1886), *Burma; as it was, as it is, and as it will be*, George Redway: London.

Scupoli, L. (1978), *Unseen Warfare (ed. by Nicodemus of the Holy Mountain...)*, Mowbrays: Oxford.

Scruton, R. (2002), *The West and the Rest: Globalization and the Terrorist Threat*, Continuum: London.

Segel, P.N. (1986), *The Meek and the Militant; Religion and Power Across the World*, Zed Books Ltd.: London.

Sengupta, S.C. (1978), *Logic of Religious Language*, Prajna: Calcutta.

Seul, J.R., (1999), '"Ours is the Way of God": Religion, Identity, and Intergroup Conflict', *Journal of Peace Research*, vol. 36, no. 5.

Shannon, T.A. (1980) (ed.), *War or Peace? The Search for New Answers*, Orbis Books: Maryknoll NY.

Sharpe, E.J. (1983), *Understanding Religion*, Gerald Duckworth & Co.: London.

Sherry, P. (1977), *Religion, Truth and Language-Games*, Macmillan: Basingstoke.

Shibutani, T. & Kwan, K.M. (1975), *Ethnic Stratification; a Comparative Approach*, Macmillan: New York NY.

Shlaim, A. (1995), *War and Peace in the Middle East; A Concise History*, Penguin Books: Harmondsworth.

Shotter, J. (1993), *Conversational Realities; Constructing Life Through Language*, Sage Publishers: London.

Sicard, S. von, 'The Role and Abuse of Religion in Situations of Conflict' in R.E. Miller and Mwakabana, H.A.O. (eds), *Christian-Muslim Dialogue; Theological and Practical Issues*, Department of Theology and Studies / The Lutheran World Federation.

Sigler, J.A. (1983), *Minority Rights*, Greenwood Press: Westport.

Simpson, J. (2000), *Religion: Sword or Dove; An Overview of the Historical and Contemporary Role of Religion in Violence and Nonviolence*, Unpublished paper presented on 8/8-2000 at the Religion and Peace Commission of the 18th General IPRA Conference, Tampere, Finland.

Sinclair, A. (2003), *An Anatomy of Terror; A History of Terrorism*, Macmillan: London.

SIPRI Yearbook 1998; Stockholm International Peace Research Institute, Oxford University Press: Oxford.

Skorupski, J. (1976), *Symbol and Theory; a Philosophical Study of Theories of Religion in Social Anthropology*, Cambridge University Press: Cambridge.

Smart, N. (1986), *The Religious Experience of Mankind*, Collins (Fount): Glasgow.

Smart, N. (1969), *Philosophers and Religious Truth*, SCM Press Ltd.: London.

Smart, N. (1960), *A Dialogue of Religions*, SCM Press: London.

Smart, N. (1958), *Reasons and Faiths; An Investigation of Religious Discourse, Christian and Non-Christian*, Routledge & Kegan Paul: London.

Smilden, J.E. (2001), 'Middelalderens Osama bin Laden', *Dagbladet*, 6/11-2001.

Smith, A.D. (2000), 'The 'Sacred' Dimension of Nationalism', *Millennium; Journal of International Studies*, Vol. 29, no. 3.

Smith, A.D. (1989), *The Ethnic Origins of Nations*, Basil Blackwell: Oxford.

Smith, A.-M. (2001), *Advances in International Peacemaking*, vol.II (1996-2000), United States Institute of Peace: Washington DC.

Smith, D. (1997), *The State of War and Peace Atlas*, Penguin Group: London.

Smith, F.L. (1990), *Blasphemy; and the Battle for Faith*, Hodder & Stoughton: London.

Smith, M.J. (1998), *Social Science in Question*, Open University / Sage Publishing: London.

Smith, P. (1991), *Ethnic Groups in International Conflict*, Dartmouth Publ: Aldershot.

Smock, D.R. (1992), *Religious Perspectives on War; Christian, Muslim, and Jewish Attitudes Towards Force After the Gulf War*, United States Institute of Peace: Washington DC.

Snow, D.L. (1996), *Uncivil Wars; International Security and the New Internal Conflicts*, Lynne Rienner Publishers Inc.: Boulder CO.

Sollenberg, M. (1998), 'Major Armed Conflicts' in *SIPRI Yearbook 1998*; Stockholm International Peace Research Institute / Oxford University Press: Oxford.

Spalding, H.D. (1972) (ed.), *The Encyclopedia of Jewish Humor; From Biblical Times to the Modern Age*, W.H. Allen: London.

Sproxton, J. (1995), *Violence and Religion; Attitudes Towards Militancy in the French Civil Wars and the English Revolution*, Routledge: London.

Stanage, S.M. (1974) (ed.), *Reason and Violence; Philosophical Investigations*, Basil Blackwell: Oxford.

Staub, E. (1989), *The Roots of Evil; The Origins of Genocide and Other Group Violence*, Cambridge University Press: Cambridge.

Stavenhagen, R. (1990), *The Ethnic Question; Conflicts, Development and Human Rights*, United Nations University: Tokyo.

Stein, G. (1980) (ed.), *An Anthology of Atheism and Rationalism*, Prometheus Books: Buffalo NY.

Steinberg, P. & Oliver, A.M. (forthcoming), *Rehearsals for a Happy Death; the Testimonials of Hamas Suicide Bombers*, Oxford University Press: New York NY.

Steiner, H.J. & Alston, P. (1996), *International Human Rights in Context*, Oxford (Clarendon) University Press: Oxford.

Stern, S.M. (1983), *Studies in Early Ismailism*, the Magmes Press/The Hebrew University: Jerusalem.

Stoessinger, J.G. (1985), *Why Nations Go To War*, Macmillan: London.

Strange, P. (1983), *It'll Make a Man of You; A Feminist View of the Arms Race*, Mushroom Books: Nottingham.

Stuart, J. (1910), *Burma; Through the Centuries*, 2nd ed., Kegan Paul, Trench, Trübner & Co. Ltd.: London.

Suganami, H. (2000), *Narrative Understanding/Explanation Revisited*, Unpublished paper, April.

Suganami, H. (1997), 'Stories of War Origins: A Narrativist Theory of the Causes of War', *Millennium; Journal of International Studies.*

Suganami, H. (1996), *On the Causes of War*, Oxford (Clarendon) University Press: Oxford.

Suhrke, A. & Noble, L.G. (1977) (eds), *Ethnic Conflict in International Relations*, Praeger Publishers: New York NY.

Suksamra, S. (1977), *Political Buddhism in Southeast Asia, The Role of the Sangha in the Modernization of Thailand*, C. Hurst & Co.: London.

Sun Tzu (1991), *The Art of War*, trans. T. Cleary, Shambala: Boston MA.

Sutherland, C.W. (1987), *Disciples of Destruction*, Prometheus Books: Buffalo NY.

Sweeney, F.S.J. (1970), *The Vatican and World Peace*, Colin Smythe Ltd.: Gerrards Cross.

Taleqani Ayatullah, M., Mutahhari Ayatullah, M., & Shari'ati, A. (1986), *Jihad and Shahadat: Struggle and Martyrdom in Islam*, ed. M. Abedi & G. Legenhausen, The Institute for Research and Islamic Studies (IRIS): Houston TX.

Tambiah, S.J. (1992), *Buddhism Betrayed? Religion, Politics, and Violence in Sri Lanka*, University of Chicago Press: Chicago IL.

Tambiah, S.J. (1976), *World Conqueror and World Renouncer; A Study of Buddhism and Polity in Thailand Against a Historical Background*, Cambridge University Press: Cambridge.

Tarling, N. (1992), *The Cambridge History of Southeast Asia*, Cambridge University Press: Cambridge.

Tarling, N. (1966), *A Concise History of Southeast Asia*; Praeger: New York NY, 1966.
Tate, D.J.M. (1971), *The Making of Modern South-East Asia*, vol.1, Oxford University Press: Kuala Lumpur.
The Article 19 Freedom of Expression Manual; International and Comparative Law, Standards and Procedures, Article 19: London.
The Chicago Manual of Style, (1993) 14th ed., University of Chicago Press: Chicago IL.
The International Committee for the Defence of Salman Rushdie and his Publishers (1989), *The Crime of Blasphemy; Why It Should Be Abolished*, Article 19: London.
Thomas, S.M. (2000), 'Taking Religious and Cultural Pluralism Seriously; the Global Resurgence of Religion and the Transformation of International Society', *Millennium; Journal of International Studies*, Vol. 29, no. 3.
Thomas, S.M. (1995), 'The Global Resurgence of Religion and the Study of World Politics', *Millennium: Journal of International Studies*, vol. 24, no. 2.
Thomas, T.N. (n.d.), 'Global Assessment of Current and Future Trends in Ethnic and Religious Conflict' in R.L. Pfaltzgraff Jr. and R.H. Schultz Jr. (eds), *Ethnic Conflict and Regional Instability; Implications for US Policy and Army Roles and Missions*, SSI – Strategic Studies Institute (with US Army War College).
Thorogood, B. (1988), *The Flag and The Cross; National Limits and Church Universal*, SCM Press Ltd: London.
Thum, C. (1996), *Religion in Contemporary World Affairs with Particular Reference to Islam*, MScEcon Dissertation, University of Wales: Aberystwyth.
Tibi, B. (2000), 'Post-Bipolar Order in Crisis; the Challenge of Politicised Islam', *Millennium; Journal of International Studies*, Vol. 29, no. 3.
Tillich, P. (1974), *Dynamics of Faith*, Harper & Row: New York NY.
Tinker, H. (1957), *The Union of Burma*, Oxford University Press: London.
Tiryakian, E. & Rogowski, R. (1985), *New Nationalisms of the Developed West; Toward Explanation*, Allen & Unwin: Boston MA.
Toloyan, K. (1987), 'Cultural Narrative and the Motivation of the Terrorist', *The Journal of Strategic Studies*, vol. 10, no. 4, December.
Tolstoy, L.N. (1982), *War and Peace*, trans. R. Edmonds, Penguin Books: Harmondsworth.
Topel, L.J. (1979), *The Way to Peace; Liberation Through the Bible*, Orbis Books: Maryknoll NY.
Tournier, P. (1978), *The Violence Inside*, trans. E. Hudson, SCM Press Ltd: London.
Townshend, C. (2002), *Terrorism; A Very Short Introduction*, Oxford University Press: Oxford.
Toynbee, A.J. (1970) 'The Holy See and the Work of Peace; An Historian's View' in F.S.J. Sweeney, *The Vatican and World Peace*, Colin Smythe Ltd.: Gerrards Cross.
Trimingham, J.S. (1965), *Islam in the Sudan*, Frank Cass & Co. Ltd.: London.
Trigg, R. (1998), *Rationality and Religion; Does Faith Need Reason?*, Blackwell: Oxford.
[Unknown] (2001), *Dangerous Concepts; to Attack Islam and Consolidate the Western Culture*, Al-Khilafah Publications: London.
Vajpeyi, D. & Malik, Y.K. (1989), *Religious and Ethnic Minority Politics in South Asia*, Jaya Books: London.
Vasquez, J.A. (1993), *The War Puzzle*, Cambridge University Press: Cambridge.
Vaux, K.L. (1992), *Ethics and the Gulf War; Religion, Rhetoric and Righteousness*, Westview Press: Boulder CO.
Väyrynen, T. (1998) 'Ethnic Communality and Conflict Resolution', *Co-operation and Conflict - Nordic Journal of International Studies*, vol. 33, no.1.
Volf, M. (2000), 'Forgiveness, Reconciliation, and Justice; a Theological Contribution to a More Peaceful Social Environment', *Millennium; Journal of International Studies*, vol. 29, no.3.

Waal, F.B.M. de (1982), *Chimpanzee Politics; Power and Sex among Apes*, Jonathon Cape: London.
Wagner, R. (1986), *Symbols that Stand for Themselves*, University of Chicago Press: Chicago IL.
Wallis, A. (1973), *Into Battle; A Manual of the Christian Life*, Victory Press: Eastbourne.
Walsh, J. (1992), 'The Sword of Islam', *TIME*, vol.139, no.24, June 15, 1992.
Walters, L. (1971), *Five Classic Just War Theories*, PhD Dissertation, Yale University.
Waltz, K. (1959), *Man, the State and War*, Columbia University Press: New York NY.
Waltzer, M. (1979), *Just and Unjust Wars*, Basic Books: New York NY.
Watson, H.E. (1995) 'War and Religion: An Unholy Alliance?' in Hinde, R.A. & Watson H.E. (eds) *War: A Cruel Necessity; The Bases of Institutionalized Violence*, I.B. Tauris & Co.: London.
Weatherford, R. (1993), *World Peace; and the Human Family*, Routledge: London.
Weber, M. (1991), *From Max Weber: Essays in Sociology*, ed. H.H. Gerth & C.W. Millo, Routledge: London.
Weber, M. (1969), *The Methodology of the Social Sciences*, trans. E.A. Shils & H.A. Finch, Free Press: New York NY.
Webster, R. (1990) *Blasphemy; Liberalism, Censorship and 'The Satanic Verses'*, The Orwell Press: Southwold.
Wehr, H. (1994), *Dictionary of Modern Written Arabic*, 4th ed., ed. J.M. Cowan, Spoken Language Services Inc.: Ithaca NY.
Westerlund, D. (1996) (ed.), *Questioning the Secular State; The Worldwide Resurgence of Religion in Politics*, Hurts & Co.: London.
White, H. (1973), *Metahistory; the Historical Imagination in Nineteenth Century Europe*, The Johns Hopkins University Press: Baltimore MD.
Whittaker, D.J. (2002), *Terrorism; Understanding the Global Threat*, Longman: London.
Wiebe, D. (1981), *Religion and Truth; Towards an Alternative Paradigm for the Study of Religion*, Mouton Publishers: The Hague.
Wigram, W.A. & Wigram, E.T.A. (1914), *The Cradle of Mankind; Life in Eastern Kurdistan*, Alan & Charles Black: London.
Wilkinson, D. (1980), *Deadly Quarrels; O.L.F. Richardson and the Statistical Study of War*, University of California Press: Berkeley CA.
Wilson, B.R. (1970) (ed.), *Rationality*, Basil Blackwell: Oxford.
Wilson, H.T. (1984), *Tradition and Innovation; The Idea of Civilization as Culture and its Significance*, Routledge & Kegan Paul: London.
Wilson, J.B. (1958), *The Truth of Religion*, SPCK: London.
Winch, P. (1990), *The Idea of a Social Science; and its Relation to Philosophy*, 2nd ed., Routledge & Kegan Paul: London.
Wittgenstein, L. (1989), *Culture and Value*, ed. G.H. von Wright, Blackwell: Oxford.
Wittgenstein, L. (1953), *Philosophical Investigations* (also 1968 & 1995 eds), trans. G.E.M. Anscombe, Basil Blackwell: Oxford.
Wodak, R., (1989) (ed) *Language, Power and Ideology; Studies in Political Discourse*, John Benjamins Publishing Co.: Amsterdam.
Wolf, F.A. (1988), *Parallel Universes; The Search for Other Worlds*, Touchstone Books (Simon & Schuster): New York NY.
Wright, R. (1985), *Sacred Rage; The Crusade of Modern Islam*, André Deutsch: London.
Wyschogrod, E. (1998), *An Ethics of Remembering; History, Heterology, and the Nameless Others*, University of Chicago Press: Chicago IL.
Xenophanes of Colophon (1992), *Fragments*, Text and Translation with a Commentary by J.H. Lesher, University of Toronto Press: Toronto Ont.

Yinger, J.M. (1970), *The Scientific Study of Religion*, Macmillan: New York NY.

Young, L.A. (1997) (ed.), *Rational Choice Theory and Religion; Summary and Assessment*, Routledge: New York NY.

Zaehner, R.C. (1974), 'Religious Truth' in J. Hick, (ed.), *Truth and Dialogue; The Relationship Between World Religions*, Sheldon Press: London.

Zulaika, J. & Douglass, W.A. (1996), *Terror and Taboo; The Follies, Fables, and Faces of Terrorism*, Routledge: London.

A Note on Scriptures

Several versions of the religious scriptures have been used, mainly to avoid misinterpretation. In the list, below, a star [*] indicates the version used for quotes where no other qualification is made.

Buddhism

Mya Tin, D. (1990) *The Dhammapada; Verses and Stories*, Myanmar Pitaka Association: Yangon, Myanmar.

* Eknath Easwaran (1987) *The Dhammapada* Arkana (Penuin Books): Harmondsworth.

Ohlmarks, Å. (1983) *Dhammapada; Lärans Ord* in *Buddha Talade och Sade* Forum: Stockholm.

Austin, J. (1945) *The Dhammapada*, The Buddhist Society: London.

Christianity

* *The Bible*; Authorized Version (King James Version) (1994), The Bible Societies: Swindon.

Holy Bible; New Revised Standard Version with Apocrypha (1989) NRSV Bible Translation Committee: New York NY.

Bibeln; eller Den Heliga Skrift (Authorised 1917 version) (1970), Svenska Kyrkans Diakonistyrelsens Bokförlag: Stockholm.

Hinduism

* Radakrishnan, S. (1989) *The Bhagavadgita*, Mandala (Unwin): London.

Bhaktivedana Swami Prabhupada, A.C (1983), *Bhagavad-Gita; As it is*, The Bhaktivedanta Book Trust: Los Angeles.

Islam

* Ashraf, A.Y.A. (1995), *An English Interpretation of the Holy Qur'an with full Arabic Text*, Sh. Muhammad: Lahore.

Pickthall, M.M. (1930) *The Meaning of the Glorious Qur'an*, Ta-Ha Publishers: London.

Arberry, A.J. (1983) *The Koran Interpreted*, Oxford University Press: Oxford.

Zetterstéen, K.V. (1992) *Koranen*, Trans. K.V., Whalström & Widstrand: Stockholm.

Index